P9-ASB-809

Adobe® Photoshop Elements® 3:
50 Ways to Create Cool Pictures

Dave Huss

WITHDRAWN
No longer the property of the
Boston Public Library.
Sale of this material benefits the Library

ADOBE
PRESS

Adobe Photoshop Elements 3:
50 Ways to Create Cool Pictures

Copyright © 2005 Peachpit Press

This Adobe Press book is published by Peachpit Press.
For information on Adobe Press books, contact:
Peachpit Press
1249 Eighth Street
Berkeley, California 94710
510-524-2178 (tel), 510-524-2221 (fax)
www.adobepress.com

To report errors, please send a note to errata@peachpit.com. Peachpit Press is a division of Pearson Education. For the latest on Adobe Press books, go to www.adobepress.com.

Editor: Karyn Johnson
Production Editor: Myrna Vladic
Cover Designer: Aren Howell
Cover Images: Dave Huss
Copyeditor: Emilia Thiuri
Proofreader: Haig MacGregor
Compositor: happenstance type-o-rama
Indexer: Julie Bess

Notice of Rights

All rights reserved. No part of this book may be reproduced or transmitted in any form by any means, electronic, mechanical, photocopying, recording, or otherwise, without the prior written permission of the publisher. For information on getting permission for reprints and excerpts, contact permissions@peachpit.com.

Notice of Liability

The information in this book is distributed on an "As Is" basis, without warranty. While every precaution has been taken in the preparation of the book, neither the authors nor Peachpit Press shall have any liability to any person or entity with respect to any loss or damage caused or alleged to have been caused directly or indirectly by the instructions contained in this book or by the computer software and hardware products described in it.

Trademarks

Throughout this book trademarked names are used. Rather than put a trademark symbol in every occurrence of a trademarked name, we state we are using the names only in an editorial fashion and to the benefit of the trademark owner with no intention of infringement of the trademark. All trademarks or service marks are the property of their respective owners.

ISBN 0-7357-1415-0

9 8 7 6 5 4 3 2 1

Printed and bound in the United States of America

This book is dedicated to Jim Patterson—
a fellow writer, photographer and a good friend.
He will be missed.

Contents

Contents

Introduction

This book is all about the many cool ways (there are actually a lot more than 50) of making your photos look better and sharing your masterpieces with others. Let's face it: If you want to make a photo that is too dark a little lighter, you don't want a five-page explanation about light theory. You just want to know what steps are necessary to do it. That's what this book is all about: how to do cool (and necessary) stuff using Elements 3.

Who Should Read This Book

Before digital photography became so popular, photography was all about taking rolls of film to a photo processor and hoping for the best. The digital camera has changed all of that. While you can still take your digital image to the same photo processor and accept what they give you, there is a better way. Using the power of Adobe Photoshop Elements 3.0, you can bring light into a darkened photo, make a flat, lifeless photo into one with vivid colors, and even perform photo magic—removing physical distractions like warts, blemishes and even a few extra pounds.

If you are new to Photoshop Elements or you have just dabbled with previous versions of the program but realize there is more you can do if you only knew how, this is the book for you. As an experienced photographer and graphics designer myself, I designed this book for those readers whose time is a precious commodity. The content from the previous edition has been completely rewritten and the material distilled into the topics that are most important to folks who want to make their photos look better, fix old or damaged photos, share them on the web, or just print them out.

Who This Book Is Not For

If you recently won a Nobel Prize, this book isn't for you. This book does not teach you the theory of color, light, or the secrets of alchemy. Also, if you need a book that explains how each tool in Photoshop Elements 3.0 works in minute detail, I can offer a recommendation…it's called the User's Manual. I have a copy myself and it comes with Photoshop Element 3.0. Although my book shows you how to do cool stuff with Elements, it is not a 1,000-plus-page reference manual for the product that resembles the Manhattan-style phone directories that were so popular a few years ago.

Overview

The first two chapters are for those readers who just want the bare essentials. They contain the topics that you need to know to begin using Photoshop Elements right away. Chapter 1, "Introducing Photoshop Elements 3," is a brief introduction to Elements and what the program can do for you. The second chapter, "Just the Facts—The Basics of Using Elements 3," covers basic stuff, such as the layout of the program, tool names, and how to do basic stuff like auto-fixing photos, printing, or attaching your photo wonders to an email.

Since the most common problems faced by photographers has to do with lighting or color, the next two chapters show you how to use Elements not only to correct common lighting problems but also to control the color in your photographs, allowing your colors to be both correct and vivid. These chapters also show how you can correct a myriad of other common photo problems, including the all-important topics of improving image composition with both size and content, as well as adjusting and enhancing your photos.

With all of the digital photos that have accumulated and will continue to accumulate in your computer, you will need to know how to organize them. Chapter 5 is all about organizing your photo collection. How this organization is accomplished depends on the type of computer that you have. For Mac users, you will learn all the tricks and techniques to get the most out of your File Browser while Windows users will discover how to use the new Photo Organizer. This naturally flows into the two chapters that follow: Chapters 6 and 7.

The first half of the book mostly focuses on making your photos look good. Chapters 6 and 7 are about all the fun things that you can do with Elements whether it's moving people from one photo to another or replacing an overcast sky. Chapter 6, "Dazzling Effects and Techniques," is by far the largest one in the book and it is jam-packed with many step-by-step projects. Chapter 7, "Fun with Type, Shapes, and Cookie Cutter Tools," explains all the different text effects that are possible with Photoshop Elements 3. This chapter teaches you how to add titles to photos for a more professional look, how to add cartoon-like thought balloons to pictures, and shows you how you can turn photos into different shapes.

I refer to the next two chapters as the photographic repair shop and it covers two important topics: retouching and repairing photographs. In Chapter 8, "Retouching Photos Like a Pro," you'll learn how easy it is to remove blemishes and other defects with the stroke of a brush tool. You'll also learn how to smooth skin to take years off a face and to reshape body parts to compensate for bad camera angles during shooting. Chapter 9, "Scan and Repair Photographs," is an important chapter in which you discover how to salvage photographs that you might have thought were beyond repair.

Making panoramas is one of my favorite subjects so I spend way too many pages showing you how to photograph and then use the PhotoMerge command in Elements to make stunning panoramas.

The last chapter is all about sharing photos. Whether you are printing the photos and mailing them or creating a slide show and burning it onto a CD, this chapter shows you how easy it is to make photo creations that are super easy and yet look very professional.

Step-by-Step Tutorials

As someone who has sat in more than his fair share of photo-editing classes, I know that anything I learn by watching someone else do, that it doesn't stick. If I actually do the procedure or technique being described, I have a much better chance of recalling it later when I need to use it. This book contains a lot of step-by-step tutorials—to let you work along with those tutorials, the sample files are available for download at www.peachpit.com/50coolways.

Acknowledgments

This is the part of the book that reads like a speech by an Oscar winner. Let's face it, when you see your favorite actor or actress on the silver screen, you don't see the hundreds of people that are needed to make the movie. Now that movie credits include everyone involved in a production, you get a better idea of just what it takes to create a movie. This book represents the combined efforts of a large cast of hard-working craftspeople and artists. If I listed everyone who made a contribution to this edition, it would take up a large number of pages. So like a winning speech at the Academy Awards with a three-minute time limit, here are the people (coworkers and friends) that I want to recognize for their efforts.

First of all, I want to thank the crew on the Adobe Photoshop Elements development team who worked long and hard to create this version of Elements. Special thanks to Adobe's Mark Dahm who patiently listened to my ranting and raving during the early stages of the product development.

Several folk at Peachpit Press really had to go above and beyond to get this book into your hands. I want to thank my editor, Karyn Johnson, who put in some long, long hours to get all of the parts of the book together. I also want to thank our hard-working copy editor, Emilia Thiuri; proofreader, Haig MacGregor; and Myrna Vladic and the group at happenstance type-o-rama, for their expertise in production. Others at Peachpit who made this book possible include Stephanie Wall and Nancy Davis. My good friend Steve Bain once again agreed to go through the manuscript to ensure that all of the content and tutorials work the way they are supposed to.

I especially want to thank all of the people that let me use their pictures in the book, especially Cooper Morin. I must also include thanks to my family who puts up with my long absences while I work on writing books. Well, my time is up, and my final thank you is to all of those who buy these books because without you, all of this effort would be for naught.

1   Introducing Photoshop Elements 3

If this is the first time you've used Photoshop Elements, let me tell you a little about what you can expect from this program. A few years ago, Adobe realized that a growing number of consumers were demanding professional-level photo-editing tools, but did not want or need many of the features in Photoshop, the industry standard for photo editing. As digital cameras have improved every year, so has the need for better tools to manipulate and output the resulting photographs. Photoshop Elements specifically addresses the needs of photographers, especially digital photographers.

What is Photoshop Elements?

In short Photoshop Elements is a powerful image editor that will meet all of your digital photography needs. You can use Elements to do the following, and more:

- Import images from your digital camera (or card reader) into your computer.

- Crop, enhance, and color correct your photos.

- Manipulate your photos. It is a universal law of photography that the best-looking photo of you is coupled with either someone you are no longer attached to, or the worst possible picture of a loved one. Elements can change all that with the sweep of a mouse.

- Share your photos with everyone you know. Whether you want to print your photos and mail them, email them, or make an electronic slide show, and more, Elements gives you the ability to do it quickly, and more importantly, do it automatically.

What's the Difference between Photoshop and Photoshop Elements 3?

This is one of the most asked questions I encounter. It is easy to think of Elements as a stripped-down version of Photoshop because the two programs look and act in a similar fashion. The first time I met the product manager for Elements I think I referred to it as a "crippled version" of Photoshop. I couldn't have been further from the truth. I think of Elements as Photoshop repurposed for the digital photographer. Elements offers most of the professional-level tools found in the more expensive Photoshop. The major difference between Elements and its more famous cousin is that Elements focuses on simplifying the process of digital photo editing. Are there features in Photoshop CS that I wish were in Elements? Sure there are. Are those additional tools worth the extra dollars? Not for a majority of users.

What's New in Version 3.0?

This question is very popular among owners of previous versions of Elements. It's generally asked because current owners are wondering if there are enough new goodies to justify paying for the upgrade. The change that has drawn the greatest attention is that the Mac and PC versions are no longer identical. The PC version now includes a full-featured photo organizer in addition to the photo editor. This difference between platforms is not important if you own a PC. If you own a Mac, it's not fun. Overall, version 3 of Elements has added some powerful new tools for the digital photographer. So, if you own a previous version and take photos with a digital camera, the decision to upgrade is compelling. Here is a brief summary of features and tools that are either new or have been improved upon in Photoshop Elements 3.0.

Photo Organizer (Windows)

In the first two versions of Photoshop Elements, image files were managed using the File Browser, which still exists in this version, but as a photo manager File Browser is pretty limited. Let's face it, now that you have a digital camera, you probably have accumulated several hundred images scattered throughout your hard drive. The new tool, named Photo Organizer (**Figure 1.1**), may appear familiar to many of you. That's because it is an improved version of Photoshop Album 2. It isn't integrated into Elements but runs as a separate application alongside Elements' Editor. For the PC users, you now have two programs to work with instead of only one—Elements' Editor (called Standard Editor) and Photo Organizer. This may sound more complicated, but it really helps when working with your ever-expanding library of digital photos. Even though they are separate programs, you can seamlessly move images between the two applications with the click of a button.

Using the Photo Organizer, you can import photos directly from your digital camera and assign keywords to photos (like vacation, Disneyland, Christmas, and so forth) at the same time. When you try to find that particular photo at a later date, you can search and sort images by date or subject matter. Since it is a visual database, the results of your search appear as a series of thumbnails like the ones shown in **Figure 1.1**. There are also a lot of additional cool features that you can use to share your photos electronically, such as the ability to make a Web page or a professional-looking slide show, plus the backup and archiving of your photo collection to a CD or DVD. There is so much that you can do with this feature that I have dedicated an entire chapter (Chapter 5) to it.

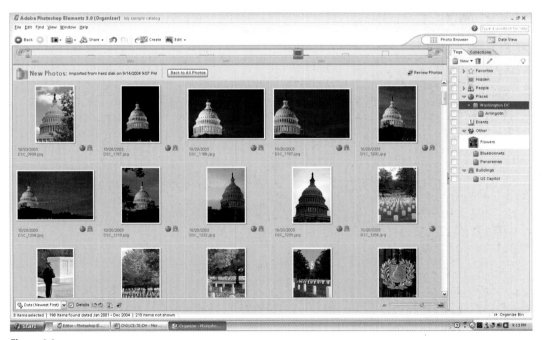

Figure 1.1
The new Photo Organizer is an excellent image manager.

Where Is the Mac Version of Organizer?

Many people I have talked to during testing have asked why Adobe didn't include a version of Photo Organizer in the Mac version. While I can't give an official answer, I can provide a reasonable guess: The decision not to produce a Mac version of Photo Organizer was strictly a business decision on the part of Adobe. The Windows version uses an enhanced version of the existing Photoshop Album product, but since there isn't a Mac version of Album, the cost of creating one could not be justified.

Which leads to the next question: Why didn't Adobe make a Mac version of Photoshop Album? I believe the reason there isn't a Mac version of Album has to do in part with the introduction of iPhoto by Apple. The existence of this product would have made it difficult for Adobe to see a return on their investment of development dollars. Even though many Mac users I have spoken with have pointed out that iPhoto is not as robust or feature-laden as Album, iPhoto is adequate enough for a large percentage of Mac users and therefore good enough to thwart potential sales of a Mac version of Album. Adobe, like any other company, is in business to make a profit for its stockholders. That means making products for markets that will result in sales. If Adobe makes products that don't make a profit, then they will join a host of other software companies that didn't.

To paraphrase *The Godfather*, "It's not personal, Mac users. It's strictly business."

File Organization on the Mac

Since the Mac version of Elements 3 doesn't have Photo Organizer, Adobe has added some additional features to compensate for the lack of an organizer. These additions include a full-featured version of the File Browser from Photoshop CS (the Windows version of File Browser doesn't have all the bells and whistles of the CS version), additional Web Photo Gallery templates, a Picture Package editor, and several other enhancements that won't be available on the Windows version. Still, if you are a Mac person you may be wondering why it appears that Adobe forgot about you. First of all, they didn't forget. This Organizer-less version topic came up a lot during product testing, and I have included my analysis of Adobe's actions in the sidebar, "Where Is the Mac Version of Organizer?"

Camera RAW Support

This is a great feature, inherited from Photoshop CS, that gives Elements users the ability to open RAW format files made with a digital camera, without needing to use software provided by the camera manufacturer or by a third party. If the term RAW is new to you, here is a brief description.

The RAW format is the format preferred by professionals and serious amateur photographers. Most high-end consumer cameras and all professional digital cameras support this format, which is the unprocessed image produced by the camera sensor. The RAW format has been compared to unprocessed film, in that when the RAW format file is opened using the Camera RAW plug-in feature, you have much more control over many aspects of the image (color temperature, color noise and contrast, to name a few). Most importantly the image can be saved as a 16-bit-per-channel image, which gives greater latitude when enhancing a photo. When any RAW format file is opened, the Camera RAW control panel opens (**Figure 1.2**), and you can fine-tune your digital photos before loading them into the Elements workspace.

Figure 1.2
The Camera RAW plug-in feature gives you the highest degree of control over your digital photos.

Digital Noise Removal Filter

Photos taken with digital cameras under low-light conditions using high ISO settings (equivalent to exposure speed of film) have more than their fair share of noise appearing in the resulting image. Noise appears as a blotchy area on a solid blue sky or as multi-colored little dots, especially in darker regions of a photo. Up until now the only remedy was to buy one of several third-party Photoshop plug-in filters (some of which cost more than Elements). With Elements 3, there is now a digital noise removal filter built right into the program. The new Filter reduces both unwanted noise resulting either from high ISO settings or low lighting conditions.

The Healing and Spot Healing Brushes

Another great tool brought over from Photoshop is the Healing Brush, and something new, the Spot Healing Brush. With these tools, you can quickly remove dirt, scars, blemishes, defects, scratches, tears, creases, and more. For those not familiar with the Healing brush, it acts in a similar fashion to the Clone Stamp tool. It copies pixels from one part of an image to another, except that once the Healing Brush has copied pixels to part of an image, Elements evaluates the affected area and the surrounding pixels, and then blends all the pixels together. The Spot Healing Brush is even simpler in its operation: Just click on the spot or defect you want to remove, and Elements evaluates the area under the tool, then makes all the pixels look the same. The crease and dirt on the old photograph shown in **Figure 1.3** were cleaned up in less than two minutes using both the Healing and Spot Healing brushes.

Figure 1.3
The damage to this photo was quickly and easily repaired using the Healing and Spot Healing Brush tools.

Quick Fix Mode

All of the controls you need to correct or enhance a photograph are in view on the right when you enter the Quick Fix mode (**Figure 1.4**). When you click the Quick Fix button, the Quick Fix screen fills the display. From here, you quickly apply multiple changes and review the result in real time. Quick Fix includes a new auto adjustment technology that improves shadows and lightness automatically. In addition to the correction and enhancement controls, horizontal or vertical viewing options are available so you can see the effects of the changes as they are being made. You can pull images into Quick Fix from the photo bin to make fast edits without leaving Quick Fix mode.

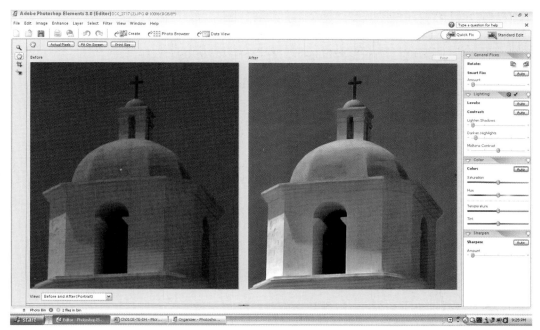

Figure 1.4
The Quick Fix mode is a fast way to enhance or correct photos.

Shadows/Highlights

Another feature that has found its way over from Photoshop is the Shadows/Highlights command, which selectively adjusts shadow and highlight areas of photos to correct unwanted lighting problems. To see how well it works, look at **Figure 1.5,** which was taken on an overcast day in Chicago. In the "before" shot, the underside of the archway is so dark you can barely see the giant 30-foot wreath. By adjusting the controls of the Shadows/Highlights command, the darker areas are made lighter, while the lighter areas either remain unchanged or darkened as necessary.

Color Replacement Tool

This tool helps you quickly select either specific colors or a range of colors in a photo, and then replace those colors with different colors. My favorite application of the tool is when it comes time to pick out a new color of paint for a room or the outside of your home. By using the Color Replacement tool to replace the existing colors with the desired new ones, you can see what your house will look like with those new colors before you paint it (**Figure 1.6**).

Figure 1.5
Before: The wreath in the archway is lost in the dark. After: Adjustment of the Shadows/Highlights command recovers the lost details of this shot.

Figure 1.6
Before: Original Photo. After: The selected colors are replaced with new ones.

The Cookie Cutter Tool

Here is a tool with a silly name that is loads of fun to work with. The Cookie Cutter tool cuts and crops photos into custom shapes in the blink of an eye. Its operation is simple. Just select the shape you want to use to crop the image to and drag the shape over the subject to be cropped. When you let go of the mouse, the image is floating on a layer in the custom shape that was used. When this new tool is combined with Layer Styles you can quickly create cool projects like the one shown in **Figure 1.7**.

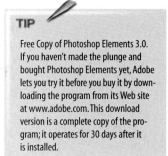

TIP

Free Copy of Photoshop Elements 3.0. If you haven't made the plunge and bought Photoshop Elements yet, Adobe lets you try it before you buy it by downloading the program from its Web site at www.adobe.com. This download version is a complete copy of the program; it operates for 30 days after it is installed.

This is only a partial list of the new features in Photoshop Elements 3.0. Add to it all of the tools and features that were improved—for example, pressure tablet support, batch processing, and printing, to name just a few—and it becomes apparent that this is the most improved release in the short history of the product.

Figure 1.7
The Cookie Cutter tool cuts and crops photos into desired shapes.

Hardware Requirements for Elements 3.0

As Elements continues to improve, the minimum hardware and operating system requirements change as well. Like most Mac applications written today OS X v.9 is no longer
supported. The following hardware requirements are the minimum needed to operate
the system:

Mac

- PowerPC G3, G4, or G5 processor
- Mac OS X v.10.2 through v.10.3
- 256 MB of RAM
- 200 MB of available hard-disk space
- Color monitor with 16-bit color or greater video card
- A monitor resolution of 1024 by 768 pixels or greater
- CD-ROM drive

To this list I would make the following recommendations in order of importance:

- 24-bit/32-bit color instead of 16-bit
- 512 MB RAM instead of 256 MB

Windows:

- Intel Pentium II processor 800 MHz or greater
- Windows Millennium Edition, Windows 2000, or Windows XP Home/Professional
- 256 MB of RAM
- 200 MB of available hard-disk space
- Color monitor with 16-bit color or greater video card
- A monitor resolution of 1024 by 768 pixels or greater
- Internet Explorer 5.0, 5.5, or 6.0 (updated with applicable Service Packs)
- CD-ROM drive

To this list I would make the following recommendations in order of importance:

- 24-bit/32-bit color instead of 16-bit
- 512 MB RAM instead of 256 MB

Summary

Now you know a little bit about Elements and what is necessary to run it. In the next chapter, we'll cover the basic stuff you need to know to do the projects and exercises described in the remainder of this book. Although there may seem to be way too many palettes, tools, and other items to recall, remember that you can get great results from this program by using only a few of the important ones.

2

Just the Facts—The Basics of Using Photoshop Elements 3

This is a chapter for those in a hurry. It is a no-frills chapter about how to do the most common tasks using Photoshop Elements. It takes you from downloading the photo to sharing the photo with others.

Opening Elements—So Many Choices

When you launch Photoshop Elements 3 a welcome screen appears on the screen, presenting you with several choices to make. The screen that appears depends on the operating system being used. **Figure 2.1** shows the screen that appears when Elements is opened on a Mac.

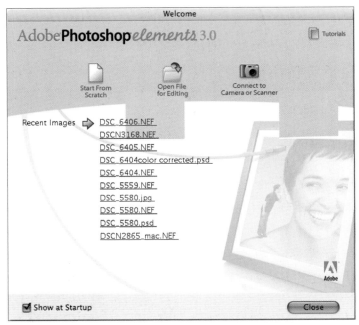

Figure 2.1
The welcome screen on a Mac offers several choices when Elements is launched.

When Elements is launched on a Windows computer, a different welcome screen appears with many more choices to make (**Figure 2.2**). So why are they so different?

The Windows version of Photoshop Elements is actually two programs: Editor and Organizer. Each has two modes of operation.

The Elements Editor (Windows and Macintosh)

Although there are minor differences, the Editor portion of Elements exists on both platforms and both have two modes of operation: Standard Edit and Quick Fix.

Standard Edit mode—This is the traditional editor workspace (**Figure 2.3**), which is familiar to Photoshop Elements users. From this workspace you can do just about anything to your images.

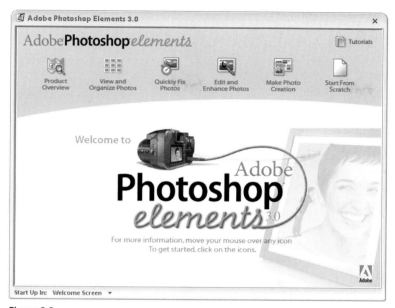

Figure 2.2
The welcome screen for Windows offers even more choices.

Figure 2.3
The Standard Edit mode is the traditional workspace of Elements.

Quick Fix mode—When the Quick Fix button in Standard Edit is clicked, the screen is filled with a workspace optimized to quickly fix an image with the most commonly used controls on the screen and a real-time selectable preview display (**Figure 2.4**).

Figure 2.4
The Quick Fix mode offers all the controls needed to quickly enhance a photo.

The Elements Organizer (Windows only)

The Elements Organizer is a new addition to Elements 3. It is an updated version of Photoshop Album. The Organizer offers lots of cool creation tools for making slide shows, photo calendars, and much, much more. Like the Editor, it also has two modes of operation:

Photo Browser—This is an image management application that helps you to organize your photo collection and provides a visual display of the photos in the catalog (**Figure 2.5**).

Date View—This is a unique method of viewing photos in a calendar style format (**Figure 2.6**).

Figure 2.5
The Photo Browser is a great way to visually manage your photos.

Figure 2.6
Date View offers a unique way to display images sorted by date.

Welcome Screen (Windows)

The welcome screen in Windows has seven opening options; however, it isn't evident which choices correspond to which parts of the programs. Here is a quick summary of where those choices take you:

- View and Organize Photos—Opens the Photo Browser mode of the Organizer
- Quickly Fix Photos—Opens Editor in Quick Fix mode
- Edit and Enhance Your Photos—Opens the Editor
- Make Photo Creation—Opens Organizer
- Start from Scratch—Editor with the New dialog open

In addition to the five operational choices are two other choices that are self-explanatory: Tutorials and Product Overview.

Deciding What Appears When You Start Elements

In earlier versions of Elements you could choose to display the welcome screen or not. In Elements 3 you can select one of three options to appear when the program begins.

At the bottom-left of the welcome screen is an option list (**Figure 2.7**) from which you can choose what is displayed when you start Elements. You can open the welcome screen from within Elements by choosing Window, Welcome Screen.

Now that you know the basic parts of the application, let's see how it works.

The Fast Track Method

Here's the quickest way to get pictures from your camera ready for printing. It involves only five steps:

1. Move the photos from the camera to the computer
2. Rotate the picture (if necessary)
3. Crop the photo (if necessary—and it probably is)
4. Enhance the photo
5. Save and share the photo

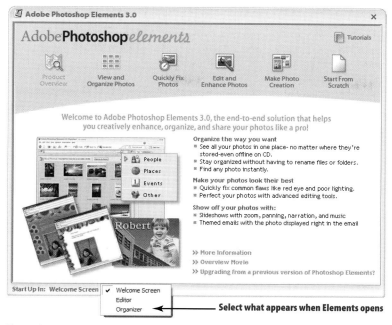

Figure 2.7
From here you can select what launches when Elements is started.

Connecting Camera and Computer

You need a way to get your pictures from the camera into the computer. To do this, you need a connection between the camera and the computer using one of the following connection types:

- Dedicated card reader

- Physical connection to the camera (called tethering)

The type of connection used determines how long it will take to move pictures from your camera to your computer. Card readers are faster than almost any other connection and very inexpensive.

TIP

A computer treats a digital camera and a card reader the same.

Whichever connection you use, when you attach the reader/camera to the computer, the operating system detects it and, depending on which platform you have, it presents you with some choices.

Connecting to a Windows Computer

When you attach a camera or card reader to a Windows computer, it is detected, and a window opens, offering a list of choices (**Figure 2.8**) for what application you want to use to work with the images.

Figure 2.8
Windows asks you what action to take after plugging in a camera or card reader.

Choose Photoshop Elements and another dialog opens (**Figure 2.9**).

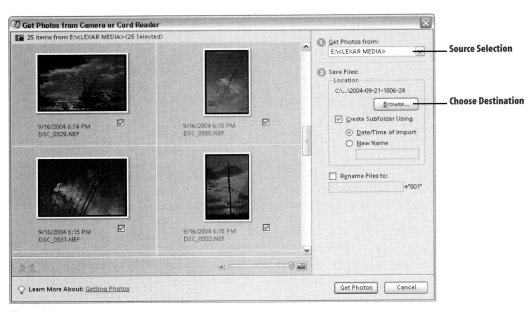

Figure 2.9
The Adobe Photo Downloader automates the transfer of your photos into Elements.

Connecting to a Mac Computer

There are a few differences when connecting to a Mac. When you connect either the camera or a card reader, the OS X operating system assumes you want to import your photos into iPhoto, so the first thing to do is to change the settings:

1. Launch Image Capture from your applications folder when neither a camera nor a card reader is connected.

2. Select Preferences from the Image Capture menu to open the Image Capture Preferences dialog. Click the Camera pane and browse to locate Photoshop Elements 3 for the When a camera is connected setting (**Figure 2.10**). Click OK to apply the change.

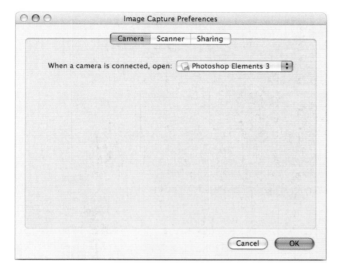

Figure 2.10
This dialog controls what application starts when a camera or card reader is connected to the Mac.

Transferring Photos into Elements (Windows and Macintosh)

Transferring the photos is as simple as 1-2-3. Here is how it is done:

1. Select the source—use a camera or card reader.

2. Choose a place to put the files—There are several options here. Pay close attention to the Create Subfolder option. If this option is checked each time you copy photos into Elements, it will put the pictures into separate folders labeled by a date/time stamp or a name you assign to them.

3. Transfer the photos—Click the Get Photos button to begin the transfer.

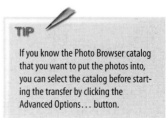

TIP

If you know the Photo Browser catalog that you want to put the photos into, you can select the catalog before starting the transfer by clicking the Advanced Options... button.

When the transfer of photos is complete, the Photo Downloader will ask you if you want to delete the photos on the camera memory card. This is up to you, but I recommend you make a habit of first making sure the photos have transferred without any problems, and then clear the memory card using the camera.

Opening the Photos

Once the photos are in your computer, there are several ways to get into Photoshop Elements to work on them:

- From the Photo Browser (Windows only)—Select the photo you want and click the Standard Edit button or use Ctrl+I (**Figure 2.11**).

- From the File Browser—Double-click on the thumbnail.

- From the Menu bar—Choose File, Open and locate the image or images you want.

Click this button to send photos to the Editor

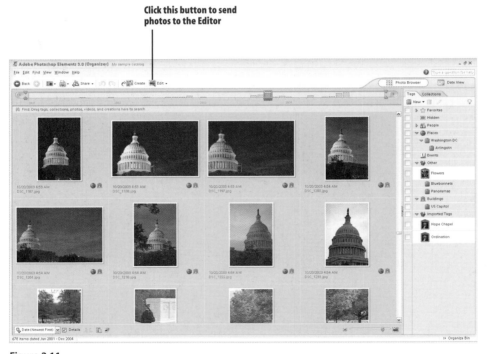

Figure 2.11
There are several ways to open images from the Photo Browser.

Rotating the Photos

This is the first and most common correction you'll make with Elements. Anytime you take a photograph with the camera in portrait orientation, it needs to be rotated. For the record, when we talk about the orientation of the camera, we mean what part of the image is on top—the wide part or the narrow part. **Figure 2.12** shows the same subject taken using two orientations: landscape and portrait.

With Photoshop Elements, you can rotate a picture in several ways:

- Using Photo Browser (Windows)
- Using the File Browser
- Using the Rotate command
- Automatically rotates photo if your camera includes orientation data

Figure 2.12
The left photo is taken in landscape orientation; the right photo is taken in portrait orientation.

Rotating Images with Photo Browser (Windows)

Rotating a photo by using the Photo Browser is the simplest and quickest way. Simply select the thumbnails of the photos you need to rotate, and click the button for the desired rotation direction at the bottom of the Photo Browser (**Figure 2.13**).

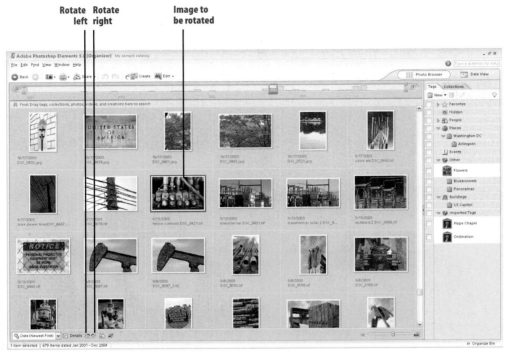

Figure 2.13
The icons at the bottom of the Photo Browser provide a fast and easy way to rotate your photos to the correct orientation.

Rotating with the File Browser (Windows/Macintosh)

Rotating a photo by using the File Browser is a two-step process. The Browser rotates the thumbnail, and the next time the file is opened the image is rotated.

1. Right-click (Option-click for Mac) the thumbnail you want to rotate.

2. Choose the rotation direction from the menu that appears (**see Figure 2.14**).

TIP

You can select and rotate multiple photos if you Ctrl-click (Command-click) the desired thumbnails in the browser.

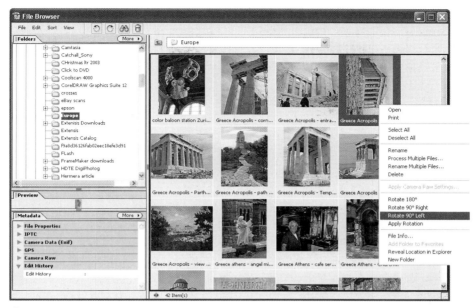

Figure 2.14
The Photo Browser provides a way to rotate multiple photographs.

Rotating a photo using the File Browser causes a dialog to appear (**Figure 2.15**). It tells you that you are not actually rotating the image, but rotating the thumbnail.

The next time Elements opens the image, it will rotate it to match the thumbnail. There is a trick to this, however, you must save the file when you close it. If you don't save it, the rotation is lost. You also need to take note of the Don't Show Again check box in the lower-left corner of the dialog. Unless you really want this warning appearing every time you rotate a photo, I recommend that you check this box.

Figure 2.15
This dialog lets you know that you are only rotating the thumbnail and not the photo.

The Rotate Command—One Photo at a Time

It isn't necessary to use the Photo Browser or the File Browser to rotate images. You can also choose Rotate from the Image menu and select the rotation that turns your photo right side up.

Cropping

Now that your photos are all pointed the right way, the next step is to crop them (**Figure 2.16**). Generally, people don't think about cropping their photos because of the feeling that they want to keep every part of the photo. The truth is that most photographs are greatly improved by removing the part of the scene that distracts the viewer's eye. You can crop photos using the Crop tool (C) ⊿ . Its operation is pretty obvious. The part that requires judgment on your part is what to crop and what to leave in the photo.

Using the Crop tool is simple. After you select the Crop tool, drag it over the part of the image that you want to keep. When you release the mouse button, the crop marquee appears as a bounding box with handles at the corners and sides. You can use these to adjust the crop marquee. When the photo is cropped the way you want it, double-click the image. It crops according to your specifications.

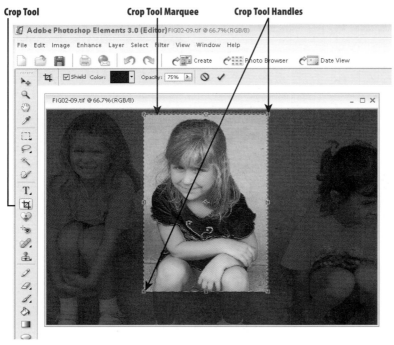

Figure 2.16
The Crop tool provides a quick and simple way to improve the composition of most photographs.

Why Crop Before Adjusting Photo Exposure?

There's a very good reason why you need to crop your image before making any tonal or color corrections. The automatic correction features of Photoshop Elements read the information contained in the entire image to determine what and how much correction to apply. The automatic correction tools attempt to correct the color and/or exposure of all parts of the photo.

For example, in **Figure 2.17**, the boys on the right are in the shadows while the boy on the left is in bright sunlight. In cropping, I want only the two boys in the shadows to remain. If Auto Smart Fix (Ctrl+M) (Cmd+M) is applied before it's cropped, Elements tries to balance out the dark (shadow) and bright (highlight) portions of the photo using a part of the photo that we will ultimately remove. The resulting photo still has the boys in the dark—so to speak (**Figure 2.18**). If the photo is cropped before Auto Smart Fix is applied, the resulting photo looks better (**Figure 2.19**).

Figure 2.17
The subject we want is in the shadows.

Figure 2.18
Applying Auto Smart Fix before cropping has almost no effect.

Figure 2.19
Applying Auto Smart Fix after cropping produces desired results.

What to Crop

This chapter only covers the basics, so consider these general rules when you decide what to remove from your photos:

- Decide what the subject of the photo is and remove anything that distracts from the subject.

- Avoid placing the subject in the center of the photo. This is called the rule of thirds and it is covered in more detail in Chapter 4, "Making Your Photos Look Professional."

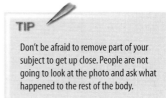

TIP

Don't be afraid to remove part of your subject to get up close. People are not going to look at the photo and ask what happened to the rest of the body.

Here is an example of the aforementioned points. The girl in **Figure 2.20** is lost in the larger photo. By cropping the photo to what's shown in **Figure 2.21**, the girl becomes the focus of the photo. Rather than crop the photo so she is in the center, the photo was cropped so she was in the left third of the photo.

Figure 2.20
The subject is lost in the larger photo.

Figure 2.21
Cropping away the excess focuses attention on the girl and her windswept hair.

Enhancing Your Photos

I wish that you could just click a single button in Elements that automatically makes your picture perfect. The reason this button doesn't exist is because the computer doesn't have any way of knowing what's right and what's wrong with your photo. While that single button doesn't yet exist, Elements provides several different automatic tools that can improve your photos.

Auto Smart Fix: One-Stop Image Correction

Auto Smart Fix (ASF) is a new feature of Photoshop Elements 3.0. It applies many different types of adjustments with a single action. It is located in the Enhance menu. Unlike Quick Fix, which is a mode that has several interactive adjustment sliders, ASF is completely automatic—which is both good and bad.

Applying Smart Fix to a photo can instantly make the photo look better. **Figure 2.22** is an example of Smart Fix working perfectly. The original photo (photo on the left) was slightly overexposed and had a bluish color cast to it. As you can see in the photo on the right, Auto Smart Fix made the image appear more vibrant.

The fully automatic approach is bad when the application of ASF makes the photo worse. Since it is completely automatic, there are no options. If ASF doesn't improve the photo, you need to Undo (Ctrl+Z/Cmd+Z) and use another tool. An example is shown in **Figure 2.23**, which is slightly underexposed. Application of ASF causes the carpet and the dark hair to become visible but the faces of the children now appear washed out.

Figure 2.22
When Auto Smart Fix works, it works great.

Figure 2.23
Here (before and after) is an example of when Auto Smart Fix adjusts the image and it doesn't work as well.

There is no way to tell in advance what type of images will be improved by ASF and which ones won't. I estimate that about seven out of ten are visibly improved. The images that have dark backgrounds typically aren't good candidates for ASF.

If your image isn't improved using Auto Smart Fix, there are many other ways and tools to fix it, which are discussed in the next chapter.

Sorting Out the Good from the Bad

Some images cannot be salvaged. Either they are all black, all white, or most commonly, the auto-focus on your camera got faked out and the photo is a complete blur. I recommend that you make a habit of deleting these photos. If you don't, the number of these images grows at an alarming rate. Like all things in Elements there are several ways to delete photos. To delete a photo using the File Browser:

1. Select the thumbnail of the photo you want to delete in the File Browser.

2. Press the Delete key and a warning message appears to make sure you want to delete the photo (**Figure 2.24**). Click Yes, and the photo is moved to the Recycle Bin (Windows) or the Trash (Mac).

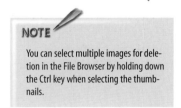

NOTE

You can select multiple images for deletion in the File Browser by holding down the Ctrl key when selecting the thumbnails.

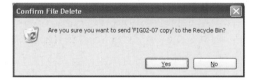

Figure 2.24
This warning appears when you attempt to delete an image.

Sharing Your Photos

According to most industry studies, the most common method of sharing photos is by email. The problem most people have is that the photos produced by their digital camera are so large, they gag their email service provider. So to send photos by email, they must be resized. The cool part is Elements will do it all for you. Here is how to share your photos via email:

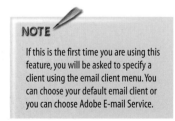

NOTE

If this is the first time you are using this feature, you will be asked to specify a client using the email client menu. You can choose your default email client or you can choose Adobe E-mail Service.

1. Open the photo that you want to send to someone and choose File, Attach to E-mail..., which opens a dialog (**Figure 2.25**). You can add additional photos by clicking the Add button.

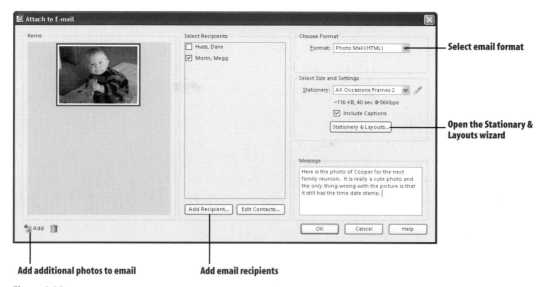

Figure 2.25
The Attach to E-mail dialog.

2. Add the name and email address of the recipient by clicking the Add Recipient button. The name then appears in the Select Recipients list.

3. Selecting Format, Photo Mail (HTML) works with most systems, but if you get replies telling you that the intended recipients couldn't open or see the photo then I recommend you choose Individual Attachments.

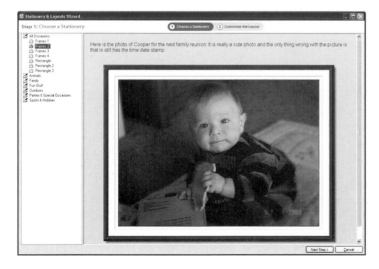

Figure 2.26
The Stationary & Layouts selection.

4. Now is the fun part: Click the Stationary & Layouts button, opening a wizard style selection that takes you step by step through the options of creating a really cool email (**Figure 2.26**). When you finish you are returned to the Attach to E-mail dialog, where you can add a message to the email.

5. Clicking OK launches your default email service and the email appears ready to send. At this time, you can add additional email recipients from your email address book. Click the Send button, and you have created a really cool email (**Figure 2.27**).

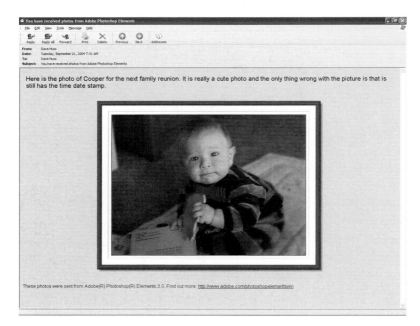

Figure 2.27
The completed and delivered email.

Summary

Now you know how to do the quick and slick stuff with Elements. In the next chapter we will learn some more of the tools and how to go beyond the basics. You will discover some new automatic tools and learn how to fix those photos that couldn't be enhanced with the Auto Smart Fix.

Making Photos Look Their Best

Now that digital cameras are being used by most consumers, you can go to your favorite photo developer, plug your camera memory card into a kiosk, select your favorite shots, and—Presto!—you have photographs. Although I can understand the appeal of popping in the media and receiving prints, I always want to fiddle with my photos a little (sometimes a lot) before I show them around. In this chapter, we'll discover how easy it is to make your photos look better before you share them, whether it is by email or by printing them.

There are only a few steps that are involved in making your photos look great, and while the steps are listed in their recommended order, it is not necessary to do them all—or any of them. After all, some pictures look perfect right out of the camera—not often, but it happens.

So, we'll begin with the first step, improving the composition.

Better Photos Through Cropping

There are basically two reasons to crop a photo: To improve the composition of the subject in the photo, and to change the aspect ratio to fit a standard photo size, if you plan to make prints of the photos. We'll begin by looking at how to crop for composition.

Cropping Controls What the Viewer Sees

To demonstrate how important cropping is in creating the overall visual impact of a photo, look at the original photo in **Figure 3.1**. I took this photo when our friends celebrated their 25th wedding anniversary by renewing their wedding vows with their nine children in attendance.

If I do a tight crop as shown in **Figure 3.2**, the real subject becomes the young man who is embarrassed by the sight of mom and dad smooching.

Figure 3.1
A typical wedding photo, right?

Figure 3.2
Cropping changes the whole mood and subject of the photo.

Simple Rules of Composition

The rules for good composition apply to both taking the original photo and cropping it. You should either try to fill the frame with the subject (**Figure 3.3**), or follow the "rule of thirds," which is discussed later in the chapter.

Figure 3.3
Cropping the photo to fill the frame is an effective solution.

The advantage of filling the frame with your subject is that it's simple to do. Here is how it is done:

1. Select the Crop tool 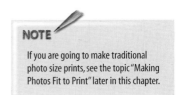.

2. Click and drag the tool over the area to be selected. The area being removed will appear dark (**Figure 3.4**).

3. Adjust the handles to fine-tune the area to be cropped. You can move the entire crop selection marquee around the image by clicking inside the crop selection and dragging it to a new position.

4. When the composition looks right, either double-click inside the cropped area or click the Commit checkmark in the Options bar.

NOTE

If you are going to make traditional photo size prints, see the topic "Making Photos Fit to Print" later in this chapter.

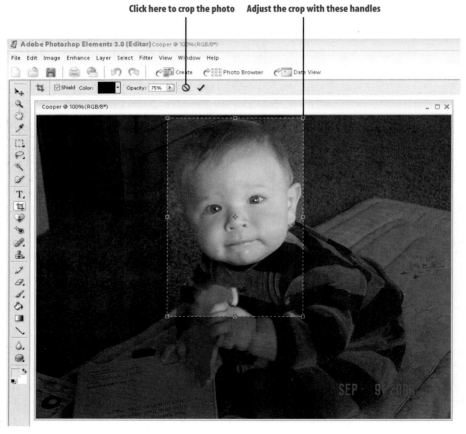

Figure 3.4
The darkened areas indicate what the cropped photo will look like.

Figure 3.5
The *rule of thirds* is an age-old guideline for creating professional-looking photos.

The Rule of Thirds

With the rule of thirds, you mentally divide the crop area with two evenly spaced vertical lines and two evenly spaced horizontal lines (**Figure 3.5**), creating a grid of nine sections. To create a pleasing composition, the primary focal point of the image should fall at one of the line intersections. Avoid placing the focal point in the dead center of the image, as this generally creates a bland composition.

Another school of thought of the rule of thirds is that in a landscape orientation, the subject should be placed along one of the two imaginary horizontal lines, and in a portrait the subject should be placed along one of the imaginary vertical lines. That said, the example shown in Figure 3.5 breaks this rule. The boy trying to run up the slide is along the horizontal, but the photo is in a portrait orientation. Why? To make the point that these guidelines are just that—guidelines. Don't become a slave to them.

Making Photos Fit to Print

Most digital cameras create pictures with different ratios of height to width (called an aspect ratio) than traditional 35-mm film cameras. This difference is important. It determines what will and will not appear in the printed photo.

The dimensions of standard 35 mm film are 36 by 24 mm, which translates into an aspect ratio of 3:2. In contrast, typical digital camera sensor dimensions are 1600 by 1200, 2048 by 1536, 2272 by 1704, and 2560 by 1920 pixels (not mm). All of these dimensions represent an aspect ratio of 4:3. This means that your digital camera pictures are taller or wider than those you used to take with your film camera. This makes a difference on what eventually ends up in your prints, and you should keep it in mind when cropping photos for printing.

Figure 3.6 is the original digital image of a dad and son at the son's wedding. When printed as a 4 by 6 photo, the edges of the photo are cut off (**Figure 3.7**). The loss isn't critical, but this small loss can become critical if your subject matter goes from edge to edge in a photo.

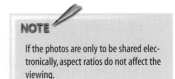

NOTE

If the photos are only to be shared electronically, aspect ratios do not affect the viewing.

Figure 3.6
Digital camera image of father and son fills the frame.

Figure 3.7
When limited to traditional photo dimensions, the edges of digital photos are lost.

How to Crop to the Correct Size

If you know that the photo is going to be printed, you can set the crop tool to the correct dimensions so it will be cropped to the correct aspect ratio. I have included a photo to use for this exercise on the Peachpit Press Web site. Locate and download **US_Capitol.jpg**.

Here is how it is done:

1. Open **US_Capitol.jpg** and select the Crop tool (C).

2. In the Options bar, click on Preset Options, and a list of pre-defined photo sizes appears (**Figure 3.8**). Select Crop Tool 6 in. x 4 in.

3. Click and drag the Crop tool into the image. The aspect ratio of the tool is locked at the preset you selected. In my example (**Figure 3.9**), I cropped out the construction fence at the bottom.

4. When you have the image cropped the way you like it, click the Commit checkmark in the options bar, and your photo is ready to be printed without unexpected loss of material at the edges.

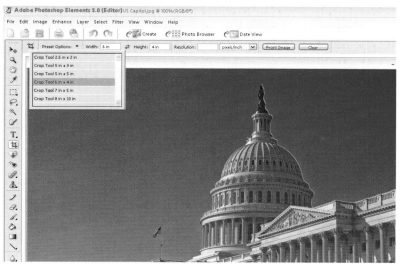

Figure 3.8
The Preset Options list provides presets for all of the traditional photo sizes.

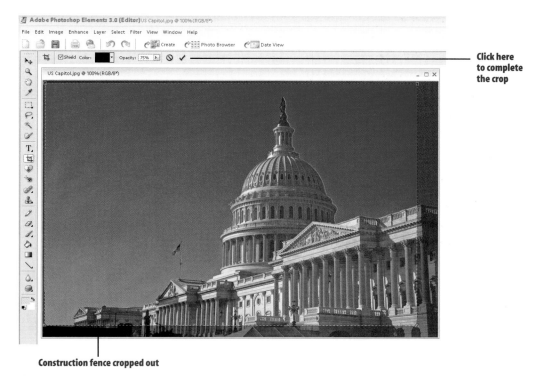

Click here
to complete
the crop

Construction fence cropped out

Figure 3.9
The crop is limited to the aspect ratio selected in the Preset Options.

Fast Facts about Cropping

Here are some quick facts and tips about using the Crop tool that you should know about. Refer to the Crop Tools Options bar shown in **Figure 3.10**.

- When you're finished using a preset crop setting, make it a habit to clear the setting by clicking on the Clear button in the Options bar. If you don't, the next time you use the Crop tool to make a freehand crop, you'll wonder why it doesn't work correctly.

- To flip the width and the height settings in the Options bar, click the icon between the two values.

- Pressing the Escape key clears the selected cropping area.

- The Front Image button makes the width and height values of the Crop tool the same as the currently selected image. This is really handy when you want to crop several images so that they are all the same size.

Now that we know something about composition and cropping, let's learn about Quick Fix mode—everything you need in one location.

Cropping Versus Picture Size

If you watch TV or go to the movies, you have probably seen a critical scene where someone asks a technician to zoom in on some part of a video or satellite photo, at which point, my favorite line is said: "Now enhance it." Amazingly, the blurred license plate or face or whatever suddenly comes into crystal-clear focus. Don't believe it— it only happens in the movies. The point is, when you crop away a large part of a photo to create the composition you want, be careful that you haven't reduced your photo to the size of a postage stamp. There are times when you must crop out a large percentage of a photo to get the composition that you want. At times like this, having a camera with a large sensor (4 or more megapixels) comes in handy.

If you want only to show the picture on the Web, the image size can be relatively small. If, on the other hand, you want to print a photo, you need to have enough remaining size to print the image at a resolution of 150 dots-per-inch (dpi) to get a crisp and clean photo.

Swaps height and width

Figure 3.10
The Crop Tool Options bar.

Quick Fix: One-Stop Image Correction

Quick Fix has been completely overhauled in Photoshop Elements 3.0, and it is now one of the two modes of operation in Editor—Standard Edit and Quick Fix.

Clicking the Quick Fix button in the Standard Edit mode switches over to the Quick Fix mode, taking over the entire screen (**Figure 3.11**). From here you can do just about everything relating to image enhancement including rotation, cropping, red eye removal, and both color and lighting adjustments. It even has Auto Smart Fix, which we learned about in Chapter 2. The Quick Fix mode takes sort of a Swiss Army knife approach to image correction and, like that famous knife, it has more features on it than you may ever use.

Rather than describe how the parts of Quick Fix operate, the exercises in the remainder of the chapter will let you use Quick Fix to solve several common photo problems. Before we can begin, let's see where everything is located.

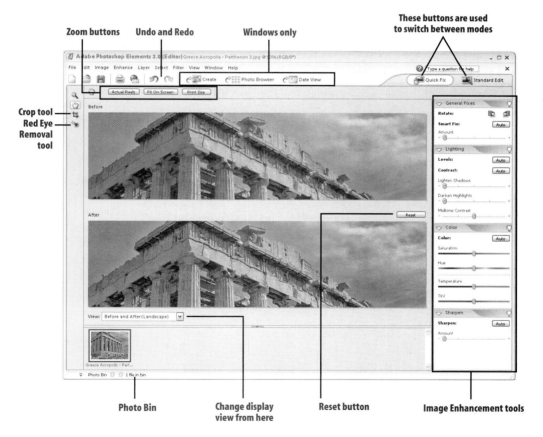

Figure 3.11
The Quick Fix mode provides all the image enhancement tools you need in a single area.

The Quick Fix Layout

The Mac and Windows version of Quick Fix look nearly identical, with the exception of three buttons in the Menu bar—Create, Photo Browser, and Date View—that do not exist on the Mac version. Most of the tools shown in Figure 3.11 are self-explanatory but there are a few that I need to point out.

- View. This feature allows you to select one of the four display views (**Figure 3.12**). The Before and After view is your best choice because you can see the changes being made. Make sure to use the orientation that matches your photo. If you choose otherwise, Elements makes the preview areas much smaller so they fit the chosen orientation, making them much harder to see.

Figure 3.12
Select one of four preview views when working in Quick Fix.

- Photo Bin. This feature is new to Elements 3.0. In earlier versions, when you minimized a photo, it became a floating title bar cluttering up the workspace. Now, when an open image is minimized by clicking the Minimize button (in the upper-right corner of the image window for Windows, or the amber button in the upper-left corner for Mac), it is moved out of the workspace and to the Photo Bin. See the sidebar "Taming the Wild Photo Bin" for information on how to use it.

- Reset. The Reset button clears all of the changes made to the image you are working on. If you just want to remove the last change applied, use the Undo button in the Menu bar.

- We'll cover the other tools as we use them. So let's take this baby for a spin.

Taming the Wild Photo Bin

Usually, most Windows users' first encounter with the Photo Bin is by accident. Typically, when the cursor gets too close to the bottom of the Windows workspace, the Photo Bin suddenly pops open seemingly out of nowhere. The Mac doesn't have auto-hide (be thankful), so users do not have this problem. The Photo Bin is a handy space allowing multiple images to be open without cluttering the Elements workspace. Here are some simple rules so you can understand how it works and how to use it:

- All open images that are minimized go to the Photo Bin.

- The Photo Bin can be minimized and opened from the Window menu (Window, Photo Bin). It can also be opened and closed by clicking on the icon in the lower-left corner of the Photo Bin (the icon is there even when it is closed).

- To prevent the Photo Bin from popping open every time your cursor gets in the lower part of your workspace, right-click on the Photo Bin and uncheck auto-hide (Windows only).

Enhancing a Lifeless Photo

Many times I have taken a photo of something that really got my attention at the time I took the photo, but when I look at the image later, I am disappointed and question what ever prompted me to take the photo in the first place. Let's see how Elements can put some life back into a lifeless photo. The first photo you need is **Balboa_park.jpg**.

1. Open the image **Balboa_park.jpg**. Click the Quick Fix button in the upper-right corner of the Editor.

2. Change the View to Before and After (Portrait), and then choose Fit On Screen (Ctrl+0/Cmd+0) (**Figure 3.13**).

3. Click the Auto button next to Contrast, and the image will immediately improve.

TIP

Close the Photo Bin to have an even, large preview area.

Fit On Screen

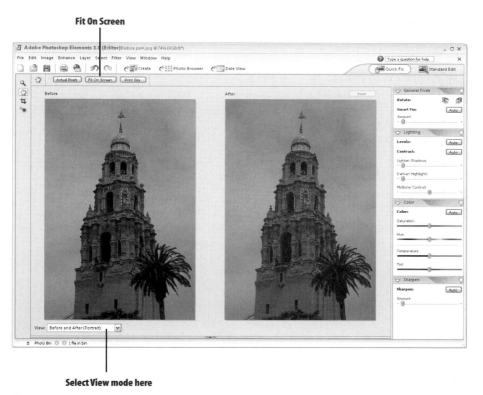

Select View mode here

Figure 3.13
Adjust your View and Zoom settings to get the best preview of the changes being made.

4. Now move the Lighten Shadows and Dark Highlights sliders as indicated in **Figure 3.14**.

5. Click the Auto button in the Sharpen section. The image is done. Click the Standard Edit button, and you're returned to the Standard Edit mode of the Editor. Notice that the adjustments applied in the Quick Fix mode now appear in the Undo History palette (**Figure 3.15**). The before and after appears in **Figure 3.16**.

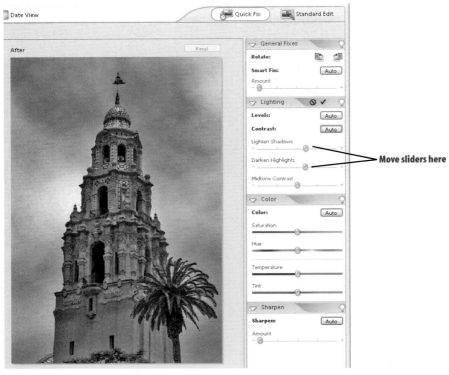

Figure 3.14
Adjusting the Shadows and Highlights brightens up the image even more.

Something to Try

Repeat the previous exercise as written, except at Step 5 click the Auto button in the Color section. What happened? Elements tried to make all three color channels (Red, Green, and Blue) the same. The result was the colors went askew. Sometimes this action works great, but sometimes it can wreck an image. There is no way to predict the outcome, just make a habit of applying the Auto color correction, and if it doesn't work, undo it. We'll learn more about this in the next chapter.

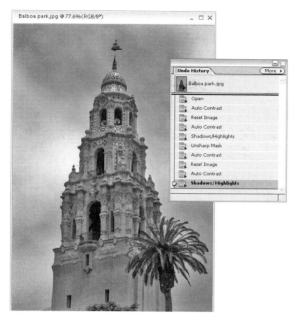

Figure 3.15
The effects applied in Quick Fix appear in the Undo History palette.

Figure 3.16
This before and after sequence shows how much of a change Quick Fix mode made to the photo.

Shedding Light on Dark Photos

Quick Fix can be used to recover underexposed photographs, like the one shown in **Figure 3.17**. This type of problem is quite common. The wreath (which is over 20 feet tall) is in the shadows of a deep arch. As a result the outside area is properly exposed but the area under the arch is almost pure black. This exercise uses the photo **Chicago_wreath.jpg**.

1. Open **Chicago_wreath.jpg** and open Quick Fix.

2. In the Contrast section, click the Auto button for Levels. See the sidebar "Auto Contrast Vs. Auto Levels" later in the chapter.

3. Move the Lighten Shadows slider until it is under the middle of the word Shadows. The wreath is now visible (**Figure 3.18**).

4. The colors are a little weak, so to finish up, move the Saturation lever until the slider just begins to come under the Auto button. You can make small adjustments to Hue, Temperature, and Tint to make the colors just the way you like them.

Figure 3.17
The wreath is hidden in the shadows.

Figure 3.18
The wreath that was in the shadows is now visible.

5. You can return to Standard Edit and save the changes, or save the file while in Quick Fix.

Figure 3.19
The tools in Quick Fix quickly recovered the wreath in the shadows.

Auto Contrast Vs. Auto Levels

These two automatic tools at times act in contradictory ways, so here is a brief explanation of how they work and differ to help you get the most out of using them. Auto Contrast redistributes the pixels between shadows and highlights, which improves the photo without affecting the colors. Auto Levels does the same thing, except it redistributes the pixels on each color channel individually, which usually produces a color shift—in most cases toward blue. So if you want to improve contrast without affecting the color, use Auto Contrast. Depending on the color composition of the image, Auto Levels can sometimes do a better job than Auto Contrast. The only way to know is to try it. If it doesn't work, click Undo.

The Auto Levels and Auto Contrast tools can be accessed in Quick Fix mode, and from the Enhance menu when in Standard Edit mode.

Getting the Red Out

Red eye is a problem that occurs often in flash photos—even though your camera may have a red eye reduction feature. See the sidebar "What Causes Red Eye?" It is a problem that can make even a sweet young girl (**Figure 3.20**) look like she is possessed.

Fortunately, Adobe's newest incarnation of the Red Eye Removal tool in Elements 3.0 makes the correction of red eye a very simple job, as you will discover in the next exercise. You will need to download the image **Red_eye_girl.jpg** from the Peachpit Press Web page. The Red Eye Removal tool is available in both Quick Fix and Standard Edit mode.

1. From the Standard Edit mode, open the photograph **Red_eye_girl.jpg** (**Figure 3.20**).

2. Select the Red Eye Removal tool (Y) in the Toolbox.

3. With the Options bar set to the default values (both are 50 percent), click on the red part of one eye. After a moment the red will be replaced with a much darker color. Repeat with the other eye. The red eye is gone (**Figure 3.21**).

What Causes Red Eye?

Red Eye occurs when taking photos of people or animals using flash lighting. It never happens with natural lighting, such as the sun. Factors that produce red eye in your final picture are when the angle between flash and camera lens is too narrow, the ambient lighting is too dim, or your subject has had a few drinks. This explains why photos of a bunch of men on a hunting trip, as they are sitting around a campfire, can produce examples of red eye that look like a scene from a sci-fi movie. The reason for increased incidence of red eye when the subject is in the dark is that the subject's pupil has dilated to adjust to the darker environment. So when you take a flash photo, the light from the flash reflects off of the retina in the back of the eye. The light is reflected and is picked up by the camera. What you are actually seeing is the reflection of blood in the eye.

Click on the red of her eyes

Red Eye Removal tool

Figure 3.20
Red eye makes cute people look totally bizarre.

A Greater Red Eye Challenge

As great as the Red Eye Removal tool worked in the last exercise, you might be wondering, does it work that well every time? There will be situations when the Red Eye Removal tool needs some help. Which is why I included the next exercise, in which you will learn how to correct an extreme red eye problem.

1. Download and open the file **Red_eye_maximum.jpg** (**Figure 3.22**). Now this is either a serious red eye problem, or she really is possessed.

Figure 3.21
With two clicks of a mouse, the red eye is removed.

Figure 3.22
Some extreme cases of red eye are hard to correct.

2. Select the Zoom tool (Z) and zoom in so her two eyes fill the screen (**Figure 3.23**). With the default settings, click the Red Eye Removal tool first on the lower-left eye and then on the other. The first eye on the left looks passable but the right eye has red eye so extreme that she looks like she has an eye disease. Undo the last red eye you applied using Ctrl+Z (Cmd+Z).

3. Zoom in on the right eye by dragging a rectangle across it with the Zoom tool.

4. Select the Red Eye Removal tool and change the settings in the Options bar. Make both settings 100 percent. Click inside the eye again. It looks better (**Figure 3.24**), but it still needs improvement.

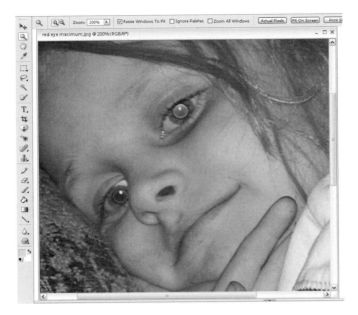

Figure 3.23
Even the Red Eye Removal
tool needs some help at times.

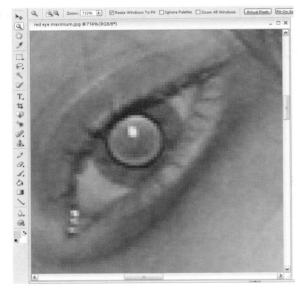

Figure 3.24
Increasing the Red Eye
Removal tool settings to their
maximum almost solves the
problem.

5. Select the Brush tool (B). In the Options bar, change the Mode setting to Saturation, and from the Brush Presets, select the Hard Round 9 Pixel brush. Use the brush and paint over all of the areas of color—they will become gray. The pupil area is still too light (**Figure 3.25**).

6. To darken only the lighter area, we need to use the Burn tool (O). Change the settings in the Options bar to the same brush (Hard Round 9 Pixel), the Range to Highlights, and the Exposure to 90 percent. Paint over the light areas, but not the glint of white in the center, until the bright areas are lessened (**Figure 3.26**).

7. Change the Zoom to Fit on Screen to see the challenging red eye problem has been corrected.

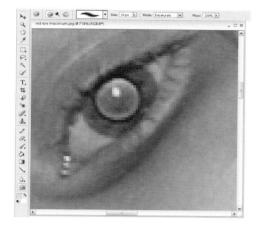

Figure 3.25.
With the color gone, the pupil area is still too light.

Burn tool　　　**Don't darken the pupil's glint**

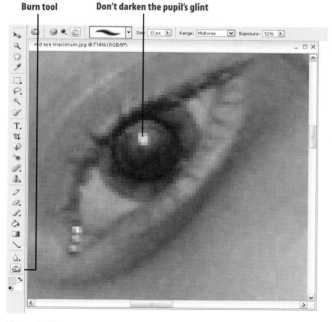

Figure 3.26
The Burn tool is used to darken just the bright areas without darkening the rest.

The Best Zoom for Previewing Effects

When you are viewing the photo on your computer screen at anything other than 100 percent, the image that you see is not an accurate representation of the actual photo. Without getting too technical, at all zoom settings other than 100 percent (called Actual Pixels in Elements), the computer is not showing you the actual pixels in the image. To create the requested viewing zoom level, the computer is making an approximation of the pixels.

Although viewing at this zoom level might not fit on your screen, always change the viewing to the Actual Pixels when evaluating critical changes. You can select Actual Pixels in several ways. From the View menu, you can select Actual Pixels from the Options Bar when the Zoom tool is selected, or you can use the keyboard shortcut Alt+Ctrl+0 (Cmd+Option+0).

Figure 3.27
It took a little work, but one of the worst possible red-eye problems has been corrected.

Sharpening—The Last Step

After you are happy with the color and other adjustments that you made to the photo, you should sharpen it. Here are a few things to know about sharpening photos.

- If the photo is out of focus, after you apply sharpening, it will still be out of focus.

- Photoshop Elements (and Photoshop) offers several different types of sharpening. Make it a habit to use the Unsharp Mask. The Auto setting for sharpening in Auto Fix uses the Unsharp Mask. See the sidebar, "Unsharp Mask: Great Tool with a Weird Name."

- Apply sharpening last, after you have done everything else.

- If you are going to change the size of the image, don't apply sharpening until you have the image at its final size.

How Sharp Is Sharp Enough?

How much sharpening should you apply? It depends on what you are sharpening. Don't you just love that answer? I should run for a political office. It's true, though. If you are sharpening a portrait of a middle-aged person, sharpening will bring out all the details (wrinkles) in his or her face, so you wouldn't necessarily want too much, if any, sharpening. If you are applying sharpening to man-made objects, such as buildings or cars, you can get away with almost any amount. You know you have applied too much sharpening when lighter parts of the image begin to lose their details and become solid white. This phenomenon is called a blowout and should be avoided.

Another potential problem when sharpening a photograph, negative, or slide that was scanned is that sharpening emphasizes all the dust, hair, and other debris on the photo or scanner glass. **Figure 3.28** shows part of a photograph scanned using a flatbed scanner. If you look close you can see the debris that was embedded in the print.

Unsharp Mask: Great Tool with a Weird Name

The term Unsharp Mask is actually the name for the original process, which dates back almost 100 years. There are two Unsharp Mask filters in Elements. In the Quick Fix mode, it is a single slider with an Auto button. In Standard Edit mode, it is in the Filter menu under Sharpen. You will discover Unsharp Mask at the bottom of the drop-down list of all the other Sharpen filters. The three dots (ellipsis) that follow the name indicate that a dialog box is associated with the filter. (Only the Unsharp Mask filter has a dialog box.)

When the Unsharp Mask dialog appears, you'll see three adjustment sliders: Amount, Radius, and Threshold. Three controls that interact with each other can seem complicated, so for most sharpening, I recommend that you keep the Threshold at 0 levels, the Radius at a value of 1, and begin with the Amount slider at 100 percent and move it until the image looks right. If you are working on really large images (made by a 4+ megapixel camera), you may consider increasing the radius to a value of 2.

Figure 3.28
While some debris is noticeable after scanning, it can be corrected with the spot healing brush.

This is especially noticeable if a photo has many dark areas, such as someone wearing a dark suit or dress. Apply too much sharpening to Figure 3.28 produces a snowstorm of junk (**Figure 3.29**). To demonstrate a point and create the image shown in Figure 3.29, I applied the Unsharp Mask at an insane setting—Radius of 6 at 200%.

Sometimes even a moderate amount of sharpening can light up all the debris that you should have cleaned off the photograph and/or scanner before scanning it.

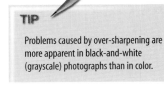

TIP

Problems caused by over-sharpening are more apparent in black-and-white (grayscale) photographs than in color.

Figure 3.29
Applying too much sharpening amplifies the appearance of every defect in the photo.

Summary

Now that you know how to do the quick and slick photo fixups, the next chapter deals with the all-important topic of color and how to remove unwanted color casts, plus a lot of other color issues.

Color Challenges and Solutions

In the previous chapters we learned how to solve some of the more common problems faced with digital photography. In this chapter, you will discover some of the more advanced techniques used to correct, enhance, and even change colors.

TIP

To ensure the most accurate color possible, regardless of the software platform you are using, your monitor should be operated in subdued light; strong, direct light should not reach the screen. Dark areas of the display screen should appear dark to the eye. Total darkness is unnecessary and undesirable.

Monitor Calibration Solutions

The software-based calibration solutions are only as good as your eyeball— which is about a hundredth as accurate as a color-measuring device (colorimeter) attached to the face of your monitor. A few years ago, these devices and their software cost several thousand dollars. Suppliers of color-calibration equipment saw that with the increasing popularity of digital photography, there was a need to have a calibration solution that was more user friendly to the pocketbook. So now you can get several excellent hardware-based solutions for several hundred rather than several thousand dollars. There are links to the major suppliers in the support section of Adobe.com under Support.

WARNING

If you are using a third-party color calibration/color management system, don't use Adobe Gamma. They will interfere with each other and could make the colors more inaccurate.

Calibrating Your Monitor

Before we can begin working seriously with color, you need to make sure that the colors in your monitor are calibrated. Without calibrating the colors in your monitor, you may waste a lot of time fine-tuning colors in your image only to see a completely different set of colors displayed when the image appears on another monitor or is printed. Color mismatch problems are especially acute when using older CRT monitors because the color phosphors inside a CRT change with age.

There are two ways to calibrate your monitor: You can use a software-only approach, or you can use an external calibration device in combination with your monitor. See the sidebar "Monitor Calibration Solutions."

Why Calibrate?

Monitor color calibration is not just for professionals. If you take the 5-10 minutes required to run the calibration software provided by Adobe (or that is part of Mac OS X), you will stand a better chance of receiving color prints that look closer to what you see on the screen than if you didn't calibrate.

Whether you are using Windows or Mac, there is a wizard style-calibration routine available to calibrate the colors in your monitor. The Windows platform uses an Adobe application called Adobe Gamma that was installed in your system at the time you installed Elements. Mac users have similar software called Display Calibrator Assistant that is part of OS X.

Before You Begin (Windows Only)

If you have an LCD (flat panel) monitor on a PC, you must ensure that the display driver (also called a color profile) provided with your monitor is installed. It was probably on a CD that came with your monitor. Here is how to check that the correct color profile is installed:

1. Right-click on your desktop and choose Properties.

2. Click the Setting tab, click the Advanced button, and then choose the Monitor tab. The name of your monitor should appear, and it should not say *default monitor* or *Plug-and-play monitor* (Figure 4.1).

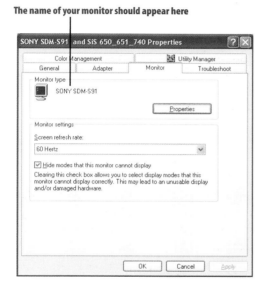

The name of your monitor should appear here

Figure 4.1
Ensure the correct color profile for your display is installed.

3. If you see the word *default monitor* or *Plug-and-play monitor* in this window, your computer system does not have the correct color profile installed and is using a generic Windows display driver. To get the best possible calibration using Adobe Gamma, you should have the correct drivers installed.

If the correct color profile is not installed, and you haven't a clue where the original CD that came with the monitor went to, you can go to the monitor's manufacturer support page and download it. In almost all cases, the drivers are self-extracting and self-installing.

Let's begin with learning about how to use Adobe Gamma.

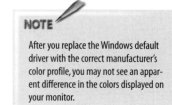

NOTE

After you replace the Windows default driver with the correct manufacturer's color profile, you may not see an apparent difference in the colors displayed on your monitor.

Defining Accurate Color Using Adobe Gamma

While Adobe Gamma is a wizard-style application, I have included some basic information about starting and using it. Here is how to calibrate your monitor:

1. Go to Start > Control Panel > Adobe Gamma. This launches the opening window (**Figure 4.2**). Choose Step by Step (Wizard) and click Next.

2. In the Description text box (**Figure 4.3**), the name that appears should be the name of the color profile installed for your monitor, especially if it is an LCD flat panel display. Having a display driver for older CRTs isn't as critical, as colors tend to shift with age, making the original color profile less accurate. If a generic default monitor name appears, type in your own name for the profile. I recommend a name such as the brand of monitor you are using and the date.

TIP

The date is important with CRT-based monitors so you can know how long it has been since it was last calibrated.

Figure 4.2
Adobe Gamma is a wizard-style tool for calibrating your monitor.

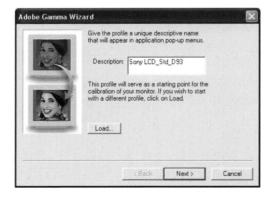

Figure 4.3
Give your color profile a name.

3. The next screen is for setting up your contrast and adjusting your brightness. Be aware that if you are calibrating the LCD panel on your notebook, you may not have a contrast adjustment. Just make sure your brightness is set to maximum. When you have made the adjustments, click Next.

4. Selecting phosphors comes next (**Figure 4.4**). If you are using an LCD panel, it will say Custom, and will advance you to the next screen. There may be a long list of monitors with strange-sounding names but unless you can actually find your specific monitor profile, go with Trinitron for a CRT monitor and click Next.

5. The Gamma setting has two options (**Figure 4.5**). You can make the adjustment using a single gray screen, or you can adjust each color channel individually. My recommendation is to use the single gray color swatch if your monitor is an LCD, and the individual channels if it is a CRT type. That's because the color balance between individual color channels in an LCD monitor rarely changes, as often happens with a CRT. To adjust the Gamma, you need to squint your eyes (no kidding) and adjust the sliders until the colors (or the background and foreground of the gray color swatch) appear to blend. They won't be exactly the same but get them as close as possible. Don't change the Windows Default setting. Click Next.

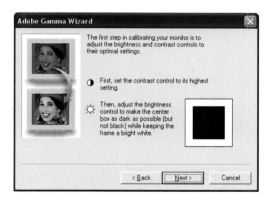

Figure 4.4
Pick a Phosphor Setting for your CRT monitor (not for LCD monitors).

Figure 4.5
The Gamma setting is used to balance the colors to produce accurate, neutral colors, which is important.

6. One of the last screens (**Figure 4.6**) lets you pick the Hardware White Point, which means you are determining if you want areas of pure white to have a cooler (slightly bluish), neutral, or warmer (slightly redder) appearance. You can even click the Measure button, which will open another screen with instructions on how select the white point. I recommend taking the default (which is the neutral setting) and moving to the next screen (not shown), which just confirms that you want to use the white point you selected in the previous screen.

7. From this screen, you can see the change produced by the profile you just created by clicking the Before and After button (**Figure 4.7**). As you click between them, the effect of the original or the profile you just created controls the screen appearance. If you want to change some of the choices you made, use the Back button and make the changes. If you are satisfied with the new profile, click Next, and you will be asked to name the new color profile before saving it (screen not shown). Wait! Didn't we name it at Step 2? I think the program suffers (and always has suffered) from short-term memory loss. So pick a name using my suggestions from Step 2 and save it. Before closing Adobe Gamma, make this program the default color profile for Windows. That's it! You are all calibrated. It took less than five minutes and it was free.

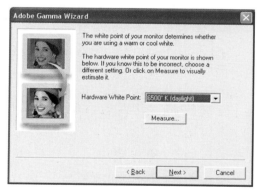

Figure 4.6
Selecting the white point controls the overall cooler or warmer appearance of images on your screen.

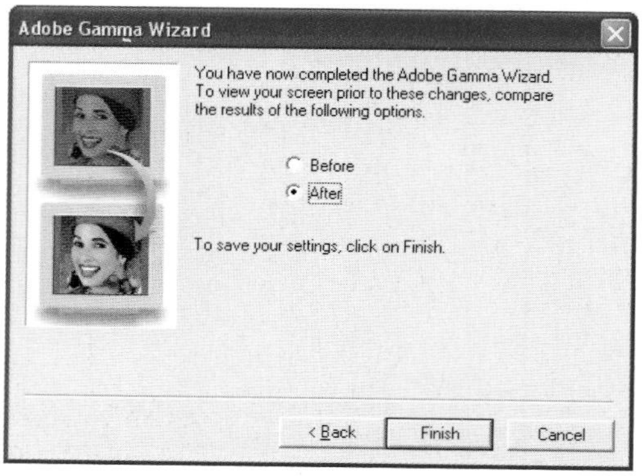

Figure 4.7
From this screen you can compare the appearance of the original and the calibrated color profile.

Calibrating Your Mac with Display Calibrator Assistant

The calibration utility that is part of Mac OS X is called Display Calibrator Assistant, and it operates in a manner very similar to Adobe Gamma. Here is how it works:

1. Choose System Preferences from the Apple menu. Click the Displays icon, followed by the Color tab, and then click the Calibrate button, opening the Introduction screen (**Figure 4.8**). Click the Continue button at the bottom right to move to the next screen.

2. The next screen (**Figure 4.9**) asks you to adjust the brightness and contrast of your display to ensure it is properly set up before you attempt to calibrate the color.

3. There are several screens that follow (more if you have chosen Expert mode) that are similar to the one shown in **Figure 4.10**. Although each screen controls a different aspect of the calibration process, they all require you to adjust the controls (both left and right) to get the apple to blend with the background color. You need to squint your eyes and adjust the sliders individually, until the apple icon and the background match.

4. Select Target Gamma (**Figure 4.11**). This setting determines how bright your monitor appears. Unless you have a specific reason for doing otherwise, you should choose the default 1.8 setting for a Mac.

How Often Should I Calibrate My Monitor?

For most home systems you should calibrate your CRT monitor every four months. If you are using a flat panel LCD display, you can usually go as long as a year between calibrations. If you are using a third-party calibration hardware/software device, it will automatically remind you to recalibrate every 30 days.

NOTE

If you choose the Expert mode from this screen, there will be a few more steps, and the resulting profile may be more accurate.

Figure 4.8
The Introduction screen for Display Calibrator Assistant.

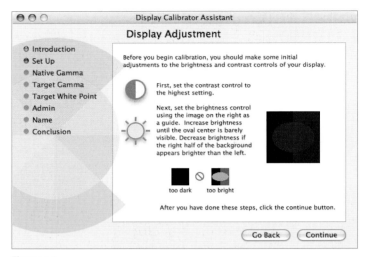

Figure 4.9
Adjust display contrast and brightness.

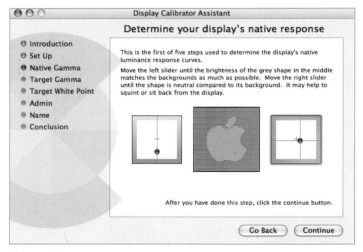

Figure 4.10
One of several Gamma adjustment screens that are part of the calibration process.

5. The next screen (**Figure 4.12**) selects what is called the target white point. The white point controls whether or not areas of pure white have a cooler (slightly bluish), neutral, or warmer (slightly redder) appearance. The higher the numbers, the cooler the colors, with lower numbers producing a warmer white. While you can change this any way you like, I recommend using the native white point by checking the box shown on the screen.

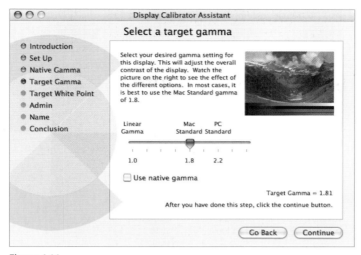

Figure 4.11
Choose the default Mac setting of 1.8.

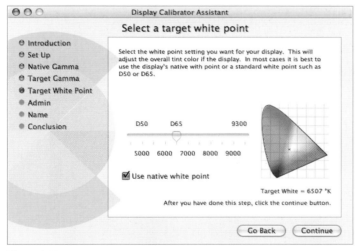

Figure 4.12
White point selection controls the overall cooler or warmer appearance of images on your screen.

6. Once you have completed the calibration, you need to name the monitor's color profile that you have just created (**Figure 4.13**). I recommend a name such as the brand of monitor you are using and the date. Adding a date to the name is especially important for CRT monitors, whose colors tend to shift with age. You may see an additional screen asking if you want to share the color profile you just created with others on your network, which is an entirely different subject (sharing profiles) and beyond the scope of this book.

7. You're finished. After you're done, the last screen (**Figure 4.14**) displays a lot of really cool, albeit incomprehensible, technical information about the color profile you've just created.

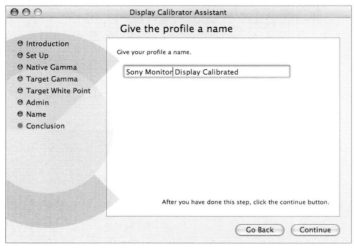

Figure 4.13
Use a name that represents the monitor used, and the date if it is a CRT.

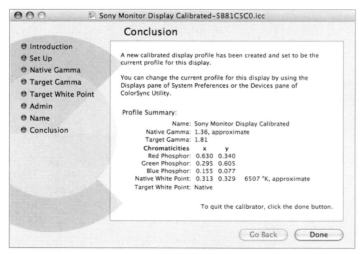

Figure 4.14
This screen displays enough technical information about the color profile you just created to satisfy the most technical of users.

Tackling Color Casts

A color cast is a shift of the overall color in an image toward cooler or warmer colors. If you are out in the Texas Hill Country on a bright sunny summer day, everything you see has a bluish tint to it. It's true, but you don't notice it because your brain filters it out and the colors seem normal. Your camera isn't as smart as your built-in optical system, so the camera captures all the colors, including those that you don't want. **Figure 4.15** is a roadside photo of some wildflowers exactly as it came out of a very expensive digital camera.

Using Elements 3.0, I was able to recover the beauty of the scene I saw the day I took the photo (**Figure 4.16**). All the information was there; it just needed to be rearranged a little.

Figure 4.15
This photo has a cool color cast that detracts from the photograph I visualized when I originally chose to take the picture.

Figure 4.16
With the color cast removed, and a few other color enhancements, this photo looks more like the scene I saw when I took the photograph.

Other Causes of Color Casts

If you notice that the images you bring in from your digital camera have aconsistent reddish or greenish cast, then the color space information provided by your camera may be causing the problem. See the sidebar "What Is EXIF Camera Data?" for more information. To see if this is the cause of your color casts, change the camera data EXIF settings in Preferences. Here is how it's done:

1. Choose Edit, Preferences, Saving Files (**Figure 4.17**).

2. Check Ignore Camera Data (EXIF) profiles and click OK.

By having Elements ignore the EXIF data settings your image isn't altered in any way. It is just telling Elements to either use the EXIF color information or not in calculating the way Elements displays the image. It does not affect any of the EXIF data (type of camera, date photo was taken, camera settings).

In the next section you will discover how to remove color casts caused by both overcast days and sunny days. We will begin with a simple one—an overcast day. Download the photo, **Classic_yacht.jpg**, from the Peachpit Press Web site.

What Is EXIF Camera Data?

Besides the photo, nearly all cameras store additional information such as the date and time the image was taken, aperture, shutter speed, ISO, and most other camera settings. This data, also known as "metadata," is stored in a special file called the EXIF (Exchangeable Image File) header. EXIF data are very useful because you do not need to worry about remembering the settings you used when taking the image. Later you can analyze on your computer which camera settings created the best results, so you can learn from your experience. If you're not familiar with the term colorspace, it is a complicated mathematical model used to define how colors appear. The EXIF standard only allows two values for the EXIF colorspace: sRGB or NONE. The sRGB colorspace of some camera manufacturers is different from the sRGB in Elements often. When this happens it often causes colors to display inaccurately, often appearing as a red or greenish color cast. To prevent this, you must set Elements to ignore the EXIF color information.

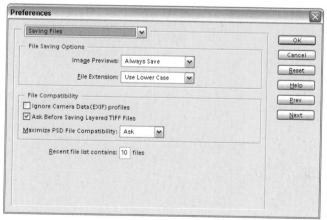

Figure 4.17
The option to Ignore Camera Data (EXIF) profiles is found in Preferences.

Removing the Gloom from Overcast Days

The first photo we'll work with was taken in San Diego in June. There is a thick marine layer that hovers over the city for several weeks in June. This phenomenon is so consistent every year that the locals refer to those overcast days as the "June Gloom." The photo of the yacht was taken during the gloom, and as a result, it looks like there is a dirty film over the entire photo. So, let's see what we can do to make it look better.

1. Open **Classic_yacht.jpg** (**Figure 4.18**).

2. First, apply Auto Contrast (Enhance, Auto Contrast). The effect is immediate (**Figure 4.19**). The colors appear brighter and no new color shifts were introduced. See the sidebar "Auto Levels Vs. Auto Contrast" in Chapter 3 for more information about color shifts.

Figure 4.18
Good subject, diffused lighting (no harsh shadows), but the overcast skies make the color in the image appear flat.

Figure 4.19
Auto Contrast brightens the image up considerably, but there is still a color cast.

3. There are several ways to remove the color cast. Auto Color Correction will work because there is so much white in the image, but let's learn to use a different tool. To use it, select Enhance, Adjust Color, Remove Color Cast. A new dialog opens, and when you place the cursor over the photo, it becomes an eyedropper. Click the eyedropper on the spot indicated in **Figure 4.20**, and the color cast disappears. Click the OK button on the dialog to finish the color cast removal.

Figure 4.20
The Color Cast Removal tool is one of several ways to remove a color cast from a photo.

How to Use the Remove Color Cast Command

Remove Color Cast works on a simple principle. You look at the photo and determine what color should be neutral (white, black, or gray). When you click the eyedropper cursor of the Remove Color Cast tool on a spot of color that you think is neutral, Elements calculates the color cast by reading the color that you selected as neutral, and generates what it thinks is the color adjustment correction necessary to remove the color cast. That's if you pick the right color.

Here are some areas to avoid when selecting samples. Don't include dark shadows and bright spots of white (blowouts). Typically you don't want to select any part of an image's border, but if you have a photograph that has changed colors with age, sampling its originally white border works great. If the first point you sample doesn't work, click the Reset button in the dialog and try another. Be aware that there are some images that have no usable neutral colors and in such cases this tool won't work. When that happens, don't waste a lot of time trying to make it work, move on to another method.

4. The color cast is gone but the shadows are still pretty deep and dark. To correct this we need to use the Shadows/Highlights tool. Choose Enhance, Adjust Lighting, Shadows/Highlights, which opens its own dialog (**Figure 4.21**).

5. Change the Lighten Shadow setting to 40 percent. This is enough to lighten the shadows between the yacht and the ferry. If it was increased much beyond 40 percent the contrast on the photo would fade as all of the darkest areas began to lighten up. To partially compensate for the loss in contrast caused by lightening the shadows, you must next increase the Midtone Contrast to +10 percent. We don't use the Darken Highlights slider for this image. The before-and-after photos are shown together in **Figure 4.22**. Click OK to complete the correction.

Figure 4.21
The Shadow/Highlights tool brings out detail hidden in the shadows.

Figure 4.22
A gloomy photo becomes a much more vivid one in five steps.

Correcting the Sunny Day Blues

The most common color challenge you will encounter is removing the bluish color cast that affects digital photos taken on bright sunny days. There are several ways to remove a sunny day color cast. The first exercise teaches you how to use the Color Variations to correct a bluish color cast using the photo **Blue_cast_steeple.jpg** from the Peachpit Press Web site.

1. Open the image **Blue_cast_steeple.jpg**. This photo (**Figure 4.23**) was taken on a bright sunny afternoon with a cloudless sky. The reflection of the blue sky produces a bluish cast on the entire image.

Figure 4.23
The bright blue summer sky gives the photo a bluish color cast.

Colors and Their Opposites

You may know that digital color images are composed of three primary colors, Red, Green and Blue (RGB), which appear at the top of the Color Variations dialog (**Figure 4.24**). What you may not know is that each primary color has an opposite color (called a secondary color): They are, respectively, Cyan, Magenta, and Yellow (CMY). The secondary colors are listed in the Color Variations dialog as Decrease Red (cyan), Decrease Green (magenta), and Decrease Blue (yellow) at the bottom of the Color Variations. The relationship between colors is as follows:

- Increase Red to decrease Cyan, decrease Red to increase Cyan

- Increase Green to decrease Magenta, decrease Green to increase Magenta

- Increase Blue to decrease Yellow, decrease Blue to increase Yellow

2. Choose Enhance, Adjust Color, Color Variations. When the dialog opens (**Figure 4.24**), click the Increase Red preview thumbnail one time and then click Darken thumbnail before clicking OK. The blue color cast is removed (**Figure 4.25**).

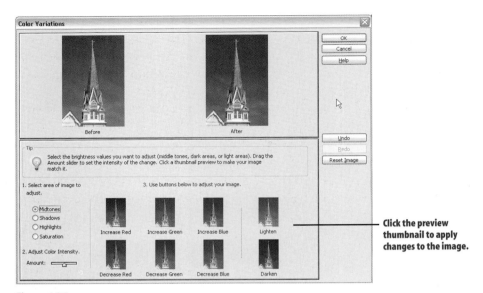

Figure 4.24
The Color Variations dialog.

Click the preview
thumbnail to apply
changes to the image.

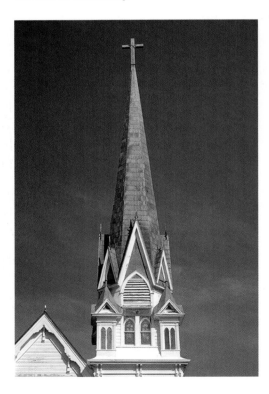

Figure 4.25
Color Variations removes the blue
color cast in a single action.

Understanding How Colors Work

So, why didn't we use Auto Color Correction as we did earlier in the chapter? Because if you use it or Remove Color Cast with the photo used in the previous exercise, there will be little to no change (try it). Unlike the other color correction tools, Color Variations is not an automatic tool and it requires that you make decisions about which color to change. To do that successfully means you need to understand a little about how colors act and react with one another. See the sidebar "Colors and Their Opposites" to learn more about how colors act and react with each other.

The color cast in the photo (Figure 4.23) appears as a faded blue, indicating it most likely is a cyan color cast, and not blue. This is why we added Red to the photo in the previous exercise, to reduce the cyan in the photo. Color Variations is a good tool to correct photos taken on bright sunny days.

More Practice Removing a Color Cast

Now that you have learned how to do some easy color cast removal, are you up for a challenge? The next photo was the one shown earlier in the chapter (Figure 4.15). When I took the photo of the field of wildflowers, the scene was stunning, but the resulting photo wasn't. Using any of the previously used automatic color correction tools do not restore the original colors. In this exercise we are going to learn a little bit more about using the Color Variations feature and how to use it in combination with other tools to achieve the desired effect. To do the following exercise requires that you download the file, **Blue_cast.jpg**, from the Peachpit Press Web site.

1. Open **Blue_cast.jpg** and let's evaluate it before starting. Like so many digital photos taken on sunny days it has a bright cyan color cast and is mildly overexposed, which washes out colors (**Figure 4.26**).

2. Choose Enhance, Adjust Color, Color Variations. Look at the small previews at the bottom (**Figure 4.27**). On the left side of the dialog, make sure Midtones is selected. The Adjust Color Intensity slider determines how much of the selected change is applied every time a preview panel is clicked. To see how much effect

Figure 4.26
This photo has a cyan overcast and is slightly overexposed.

can be applied, move the slider to the extreme right. For this exercise, move it back to about the middle.

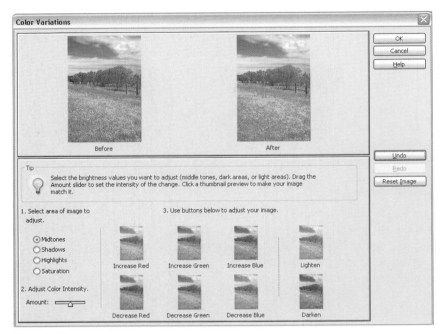

Figure 4.27
The Adjust Color Intensity slider determines how much correction is applied each time one of the preview windows is clicked.

3. Click once on Increase Red. Move the slider to the left until it is under the letter "I" of Intensity. Click on Darken.

4. On the left of the dialog, click the Saturation button, and the dialog changes. Move the Adjust Color Intensity slider back to mid-position and click on More Saturation. Click the OK button, and the color adjusted image appears (**Figure 4.28**). I warn you, the colors won't look very natural—be patient.

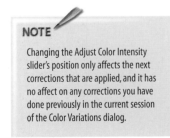

NOTE

Changing the Adjust Color Intensity slider's position only affects the next corrections that are applied, and it has no affect on any corrections you have done previously in the current session of the Color Variations dialog.

Figure 4.28
After applying Color Variations, the colors appear to have a reddish cast.

Figure 4.29
Applying Auto Color Correction finishes the job, and the original vivid colors are restored.

5. Choose Enhance, Auto Color Correction. Wow! The colors look much better (**Figure 4.29**). I deliberately added too much red to the image (remember that red is the opposite of cyan) because I know that applying the Auto Color Correction will push the image toward cyan, while adjusting everything else in the photo. There are other combinations to achieve the restoration of correct color to the photo, but this combination is my favorite, and it works almost every time.

Putting It All Together

When trying to correct an unwanted color cast, here is a recommended order of things to try:

1. Auto Contrast. Apply the Auto Contrast first. Sometimes (not often) this corrects the problem.

2. Auto Color Correction. This works most often when there are large amounts of white in the image. If it doesn't work, Undo (Ctrl+Z/Cmd+Z) it, and go to the next step.

3. Remove Color Cast. If Auto Color Correction didn't work, there is a good chance Remove Color Cast won't work either, but you should give it a try if the photo has small areas of white in it.

4. Color Variations. This is the tool that will correct the majority of your color problems. Experiment with it, trying different combinations of colors, and adding changes to Highlights and Shadows on the left side of the dialog.

Adding a Color Cast for Effect

Sometimes you will want to add an overlay color (color cast) to produce an effect. For example, you can add a color tint to make a photo look old or rustic. To do this exercise, you will need to download the file **Old_lantern.jpg** from the Peachpit Press Web site. Adding a color cast is done using the Colorize option of the Hue/Saturation command. Here is how to do it:

1. Open the file **Old_lantern.jpg** (**Figure 4.30**).

Figure 4.30
A rusty lantern.

Accurate Colors Vs. Desired Colors

When correcting or enhancing colors in a photo, there are two general schools of thought: The first is, make the colors accurate so the colors in the photo appear exactly as they appeared when you shot the photo. The other approach is to enhance or correct the colors in the photo so they appear as you imagine they should appear. Photojournalists are strong advocates of accurate color. They eschew any attempts to alter the reality expressed by the photo. Nearly everyone else just wants their photos to look good when they show them to others, and so any color changes that make the photo look better are acceptable. So if you're not a photojournalist, have fun enhancing, changing, and replacing colors in your photos, and don't let anyone make you feel guilty about doing it—even a photojournalist.

2. Open Hue/Saturation (Ctrl+U/Cmd+U). When the dialog opens, check the Colorize check box. Moving the Hue slider controls what color the overall image will have, while the Saturation slider determines how much or how little of the color tint will be applied. For this exercise, choose a Hue setting of 30 and a Saturation setting of 25 (**Figure 4.31**). In most cases you will not change the Lightness setting. Click OK to apply the change.

Figure 4.31
Using the Colorize option changes the appearance of the lantern.

3. As a finishing touch, give the photo an antique appearance by choosing Filter, Brushstrokes, Ink Outlines… and apply the default setting. The finished image is shown in **Figure 4.32**.

The Colorize option isn't limited to making photos look old. It is an excellent tool to create effects for photos that will be used as backgrounds for reports or presentations like the one shown in **Figure 4.33**. The exercise for creating that image is found in Chapter 6.

Figure 4.32
Applying the Ink Outline filter completes the transformation to an antique photo.

Figure 4.33
Colorize can be used for a variety of effects, like this one.

Replacing Colors

Photoshop Elements has a tool called Replace Color that can be really handy for times that you want to change a limited range of colors. The next exercise uses the file **House.jpg**, which can be downloaded from the Peachpit Press Web site. Have you ever tried to pick a new color to paint your house or room and tried to visualize what the new color will look like after it is applied? This next exercise will show you how to accurately see what the final result will look like, without painting one brushstroke.

1. Open the file **House.jpg** (**Figure 4.34**).

Figure 4.34
Photo of the current paint job on the house.

2. Choose Enhance, Adjust Color, Replace Color, and a dialog appears on the workspace. Change the Fuzziness setting to 40 (**Figure 4.35**).

3. Ensure Selection under the preview window is selected. Place the cursor over the photo (the cursor has become an eyedropper) and click on a sample of the color that you want to replace, as shown in **Figure 4.36**. You have selected the initial color to be replaced.

Figure 4.35
The Replace Color dialog.

Click here first   **Preview shows what colors have been selected.**

Figure 4.36
Click on the color that you want to replace.

4. As you can see in the preview box, only a small portion of the colors were selected with the first sample. To include the other shades of colors on the house siding, hold down the Shift key and click on all of the other points shown in **Figure 4.37**. Each time you Shift-click on a different shade of the color, it gets included in the colors to be replaced. If you look at the preview window in the dialog, you'll also notice that some areas other than the house siding have also been included. Since we just want to see how the replacement colors look, it isn't important to keep the color off of the grass. See the sidebar "Learning More About Using Color Replacement" for more information on how to prevent this.

5. This is the fun part. Move the Hue slider back and forth and watch the color of the house siding change as you do (**Figure 4.38**).

6. When you have the replaced the colors, click OK to apply the changes. In this example (**Figure 4.39**), I am now sure that I do not want that color of blue on the house.

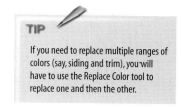

TIP

If you need to replace multiple ranges of colors (say, siding and trim), you will have to use the Replace Color tool to replace one and then the other.

Shift-click on these spots

Preview shows colors that have been selected

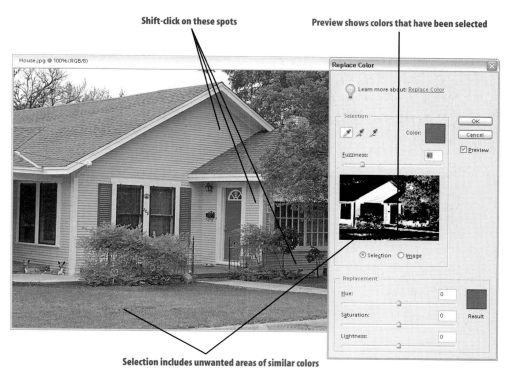

Selection includes unwanted areas of similar colors

Figure 4.37
Shift-click on the additional shades of colors that you want to include.

Figure 4.38
The Replace Color dialog.

Learning More About Using Color Replacement

There are two keys to using Color Replacement: Selecting the existing color and creating the replacement color.

After selecting the initial color with the eyedropper cursor, there are several ways to increase the range of colors selected. Moving the Fuzziness slider to the right increases the range of colors to be replaced, while moving it to the left limits the range of colors selected for replacement. The small preview box indicates the areas of the photo that are selected. Areas that are white are selected, while the darker areas are not. The problem with increasing the range of selected colors using the Fuzziness slider is a tendency to include colors you don't want. The best way to increase the range of colors to be replaced is to hold down the Shift key while clicking on additional shades of the color you want to include for replacement. Conversely, holding down the Ctrl (Cmd) key while clicking on a color will remove the color from ones already selected.

Sometimes the colors selected aren't the ones you want included. In the previous example, the sidewalk, the chimney, and a small patch of the lawn got selected because they had colors similar to the side of the house. The easiest way to deal with this is by creating a rough selection with the Polygon Lasso tool in the Tools palette that excludes nearby areas of similar color.

There are two ways to define the replacement color. You can move the Hue, Saturation, and Lightness sliders until you get the combination you like. This technique will not work on white, black, or gray (they are all neutral colors). To select a specific color, click on the Result color swatch in the lower-right corner of the dialog, and the Color Picker dialog will open. From here you can find any color under the sun.

Figure 4.39
The replaced color on the house which I do not want.

Summary

There is so much more that you can do with color that it could fill an entire book. While this topic will appear in other sections of the book, for now you have learned enough to be creative with color in your photos and be able to solve a majority of your color-related problems. Now that you know how to fix all of these photos, in the next chapter you will discover how to organize them.

5 Organizing and Managing Your Pictures

One of the advantages of a digital camera is the freedom to take as many photos as you like without the additional costs of film and developing. This advantage can also turn into a nightmare unless you have a way to organize and manage your photos. With so many places for the photos to hide—external hard drives, Zip drives, CD-ROMs—it's a wonder that we can ever find the photo we are looking for. In this chapter, you will discover how to use several of the tools available in Elements to organize your photos, and more importantly, how to locate a specific photo when you need it.

Basics of Image Organization

There are two visual file management tools in Elements—the File Browser and the Photo Organizer (Windows). Before we start seeing how to use these tools, we must first consider some ideas about general file organization of images.

Use Folders to Categorize Photos

Regardless of the tools that you choose to organize your photos, I strongly recommend that you keep photos categorized in folders rather than dumping them all into a common folder on your hard drive. The best time to do this is when transferring the photos from your camera to your computer. I recommend maintaining a master folder on a hard drive in which you keep all the digital photo folders.

Because I use Photo Organizer, this named folder division approach to organizing photos isn't mandatory because the software knows the names and locations of all the photos. Even though I am using Organizer, I still maintain the images in separate folders in case something catastrophic, like a virus attack, were to happen to the catalog file. In such a situation it would be difficult to reconstruct the grouping of the photos without a fundamental folder organization like the example shown in **Figure 5.1**.

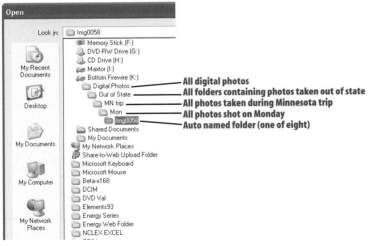

Figure 5.1
Organizing by event, place, or location serves as a good foundation for any image management plan.

Organization Workflow

I am not an organized person. My office stands in mute testimony to that fact. I would have included a photo to prove my point but the publisher said that we would have to include warning labels on the book. My lifetime motto is: If a cluttered desk is the sign of a cluttered mind, what is a clean and empty desk the sign of? I say all this so you don't think the following recommendations are the ravings of an obsessive, neat person and, therefore, probably won't work for you.

As we saw in Figure 5.1, I use nested folders (folders placed within folders) to further group my photos together. The example is not something I created to demonstrate a concept. It is actually part of my 35,000+ image library located on one of my external hard drives. Here is how that particular organization came to be.

When I was in Minnesota taking photos for four days, I took my notebook—of course—to capture and catalog all of the images I shot each day. Keep in mind that I probably shoot more photos in a day than most vacationers shoot in several weeks. On my notebook, I created four daily folders, one for each shooting day.

> **TIP**
>
> Another way to name daily folders is not by days of the week (which tends to be forgotten on a vacation) but by the day number of the trip. For example, day two, day four, etc.

Every evening I would sit in the motel room and do the following:

- Download the images from my camera into the daily folder.

- Review the photos, deleting the bad ones (there were many) and identifying particularly good ones, which I then put into a Keeper folder. I have a Keeper folder in each daily folder. Usually, but not always, I copy all of the keepers into a Keeper folder for the trip.

- Backup the daily folders onto a CD-ROM.

Upon returning home from my trip, I transferred all of the daily folders from my notebook computer to my main system and into a folder named MN trip, in the Digital Photos folder.

When there were several folders for out-of-state locations, I created an Out of State folder and moved all of the folders that did not contain Texas photos into it. For more information about moving and copying folders in Windows, see the sidebar, "Move and Copy— What's the Difference?"

Be Ready to Modify Your Changes

I shared my workflow with you so that you could understand that while my image file organization has become quite complex, it began as a simple system and grew as the collection grew.

Sometimes you will reorganize your folders and discover that it doesn't work as expected. When this happens, rearrange again. For example, I initially kept all my Texas photos in folders named after the cities in which they were shot. Texas is my home state, and at one point there were several hundred folders under Texas. I tried several schemes until I came up with a sub-grouping that divided the state into established regions—Southern, Central, etc.

Folder Naming Suggestions

The easiest folder names are those named for an event (for example, Amanda's Wedding, Baby's First Birthday). Don't clutter the folder name with a date unless it's necessary; usually, just the year (State Track Meet 2004) is sufficient.

For photos not related to specific events, use location (Hawaii 2004) or subject matter (for example, Blue-bonnets or Clouds).

NOTE

If you have more than one subject, location, or event on your camera when you download the images, I strongly recommend sorting out the photos and placing them in their own folders rather than trying to give a folder a very long combination name, such as Billy Bob's wedding 2003/Wild Reception Party 2003/Divorce Proceeding 2004.

Naming Pictures—A Real Timesaver

All digital cameras automatically assign numbers to photos when the pictures are taken. Some cameras reset the number counter each time the media is removed from the

Move and Copy—What's the Difference?

When you are relocating folders either on a Mac or a Windows computer, you may have two options—to Copy or to Move the folder. To Copy the folder means that a duplicate of the folder and its contents is created. To Move a folder means that the folder and its contents are duplicated and then the original is deleted. In Windows, the operating system provides the Copy and Move commands. When using the Move command you should be aware that Windows verifies the copy that was made before deleting the original. Moving folders within one another in My Computer or Windows Explorer only requires that you drag one folder into another. If you want to move a file from one hard drive to another or one networked computer to another, you can right-click the folder you want to move and drag it to the destination. When you let go of the right mouse button a sub-menu pops up. The two top choices are, Copy Here and Move Here.

On a Mac, you can move one folder into another by simply dragging the file or folder into the destination folder. To copy a file or folder you need to hold the Option key while dragging the file or folder. The plus (+) symbol accompanying the icon indicates the file or folder being dragged is a copy.

camera. This can be a problem because the result is many photos files with a label similar to DCN_0001.JPG.

Regardless of how your camera works, you may want to give your pictures unique names that describe the picture. This brings up another potential headache. Say you have six pictures of Uncle Bob sitting in front of a fireplace. Two possible solutions can prevent duplicate filenames. You can use sequential numbers following the description (for example, Uncle Bob fireplace 01, Uncle Bob fireplace 02, and so on).

TIP

Most digital cameras offer a menu option to turn off the feature that resets file numbering when the media is removed. By not resetting the picture-number counter each time, each photo has a unique number—until you reach 9,999.

The second solution has to do with the way I manage my photos. Because I usually like to keep the original photo files under the original number assigned by the camera, I give the picture file a name by adding a descriptive name in front of the number. For example, Uncle Bob's photos would be Uncle Bob fireplace DCN0001, Uncle Bob fireplace DCN0002, and so on. I recommend this method because after I apply all changes, enhancements, or corrections to the named copy of the photo, I have the original file name as part of the completed photo name, allowing me to locate the original picture file when necessary—and believe me, it is often necessary. Without the number, you'd have to wade through dozens of images trying to see which original image is Uncle Bob fireplace 01.

Now that we've covered some image management fundamentals, let's learn how to use the tools in Elements to organize and manage your photos. We'll begin with the File Browser.

Using the File Browser

As you may recall, the Mac version of Elements 3 doesn't have a Photo Organizer but it does have a full-featured File Browser (**Figure 5.2**) that is almost identical to one that ships with Photoshop CS. The File Browser in the Windows version (**Figure 5.3**) is a much abbreviated version in part because many of the features of the File Browser are available in the Photo Organizer.

TIP

If you use Elements 3 on Windows, I strongly recommend that you invest some time learning to use the Photo Organizer—even if you are accustomed to using the File Browser. I believe Photo Organizer will be the tool that Adobe concentrates on in future releases of Elements.

The File Browser allows you to view, navigate, organize, and locate photos on your computer. As mentioned earlier, the Mac version (Figure 5.2) has more features than the Windows version (Figure 5.3). Still, both operate in the same way.

Figure 5.2
The Mac version of File Browser is a full-featured visual organizer tool.

Major Parts of the File Browser

Because the File Browser can do so much, it may appear a little complicated the first time you see it or try to use it.

The File Browser is divided into four major areas: Folder palette, Thumbnail preview, Preview palette, and Metadata palette. The following list is a more detailed explanation of these palettes, with a few additional features noted:

- Menu bar. The File Browser has its own menu bar which is different from the standard Elements menu. It's easy to pick the wrong one, for me at least. Only the Mac version has the Automate choice in the Menu bar.

- Shortcut buttons. This is the quickest way to use some of the most commonly used features. Again there is one more icon button on the Mac.

Menu bar   **Shortcut buttons**   **Thumbnail preview**

Folder palette

Preview palette (nothing selected)

Metadata palette

Figure 5.3
The Windows version of File Browser doesn't have all of the features found on the Mac version.

- Thumbnail preview. Adobe calls this the Main Window. Call it what you want, the thumbnails of the images in the selected folder appear here, given time. More on that later.

- Preview palette. It shows a preview of the image currently selected in the Thumbnail preview area.

- Folder palette. From here you can navigate to, and select, the folder you want to work with.

- Metadata palette. More technical information than you ever want to know about.

- Keywords palette (Mac only). Part of the Metadata, it is used to assign and sort images based on keywords.

How File Browser Works—In a Nutshell

The File Browser is opened through the Elements Editor menu bar (File, Browse Folders…), or you can use the keyboard shortcut (Shift+Ctrl+O/Shift+Cmd+O) if you can remember it. Here is how to use it in four easy steps.

1. Open the File Browser.

2. Navigate to, and select, the desired folder in the Folder palette by clicking on it. At this point the thumbnails begin to appear in the Thumbnail preview. How long it takes depends on several factors. See the sidebar, "Why and When Thumbnails Are Slow."

3. Open the image you want by selecting its thumbnail (you can select more than one thumbnail) and pressing the Enter (Return on Mac) key, or by double-clicking on the thumbnail. The images are opened in the Editor.

TIP

Cache files of the thumbnails take up drive space. While individually they aren't really big, a lot of them do add up. If your drive space is limited, you may want to eliminate these files in folders you rarely visit. Elements has several ways to manage these files. See Cache files in the index of the Adobe online help for details about managing the files.

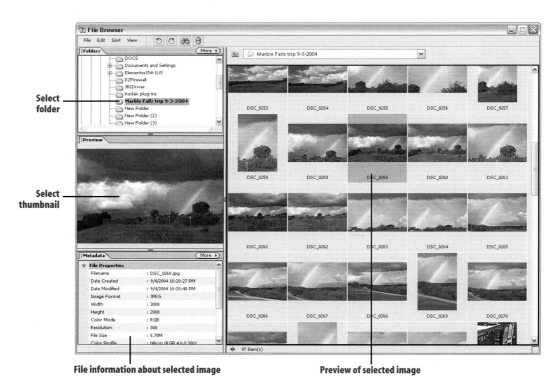

Select folder

Select thumbnail

File information about selected image

Preview of selected image

Figure 5.4
Selecting and opening images using the File Browser.

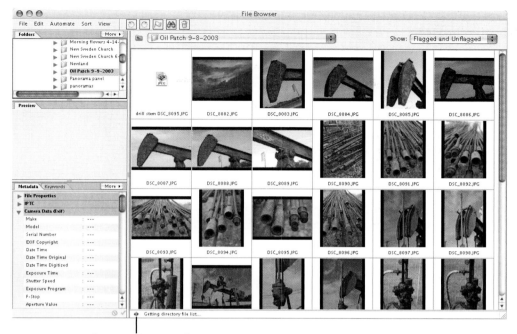

Message area tells you that the Browser is hard at work

Figure 5.5
The message area informs you when the Browser is busy building thumbnails.

Why and When Thumbnails are Slow

The first time you select a folder to view, the File Browser must generate the thumbnails you see in the Thumbnail preview area. How long it takes depends on two main factors: how many images are in the folder and the size of the images. If you open a folder with several hundred images taken with a 5-megapixel digital camera, Elements will devote a lot of your computer resources to read each file and create the thumbnails. As a result, Elements may seem to be stuck and non-operational while it is creating the thumbnails. The good news is that this only happens the first time the folder is opened. At that time Elements creates a file of the thumbnail images (called a cache file) and keeps it in the folder, so the next time you open the Browser to that folder, it only has to read the existing cache file that it calls a directory list. The only indication that the thumbnails are being created is a flashing hard drive light (PC) or, on either platform, the message area at the bottom of the Browser (**Figure 5.5**) will display a status message. Be aware that while Elements is hard at work building thumbnails, it will pretty much ignore anything you try to do to get its attention until it is finished. If the Browser is opening an existing cache file the message will say Getting directory file list.... This action is finished very quickly. If you see the message, Getting (filename) thumbnails, it could take a while.

Changing Your View of Thumbnails

The first time you open the File Browser, it is usually at its default setting. The File Browser is a powerful visual tool that can be rearranged and displayed in a variety of ways to make it fit your needs. One option is to change your view of thumbnails.

To fit more images into the Thumbnail preview area, you can change the size of the thumbnails using the View menu (**Figure 5.6**)

Figure 5.6
The View menu gives you many options to control the size and number of thumbnails displayed.

While each of these options are covered in the online user guide, there are a few choices on the list that are worth special mention:

- Refresh (F5). This is the most important one of the lot. Clicking refresh makes Elements reread the contents of the selected folder (not just the cache file). Any images that were added since the folder was selected are added. So when you are looking in a folder for an image that you know you just put there, press the F5 key and see if it suddenly appears.

- Unreadable Files. With this option unchecked only files that can be opened by Elements will appear in the Thumbnail preview area.

- Flagged and Unflagged Files (Mac only). Flagging a file by clicking on the Flag shortcut button is a quick way to select and control the display of a group of images. It is very handy for quickly marking photos either for deletion (losers) or particularly good ones (keepers). The display of flagged or unflagged files is more quickly accessed in the Show: selection field in the upper-right corner of the Browser.

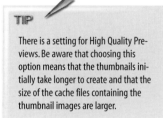

TIP

There is a setting for High Quality Previews. Be aware that choosing this option means that the thumbnails initially take longer to create and that the size of the cache files containing the thumbnail images are larger.

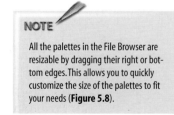

NOTE

All the palettes in the File Browser are resizable by dragging their right or bottom edges. This allows you to quickly customize the size of the palettes to fit your needs (**Figure 5.8**).

- Thumbnail size. This is pretty self-explanatory except for the Custom setting. When you choose Custom, the size of the thumbnail is controlled through the settings in Preferences (Ctrl+K/Cmd+K) and then by choosing File Browser from the list (or by pressing Ctrl+9/Cmd+9) to view specific File Browser Preferences regarding thumbnail size (**Figure 5.7**). See the Adobe online help file for details about the other setting options.

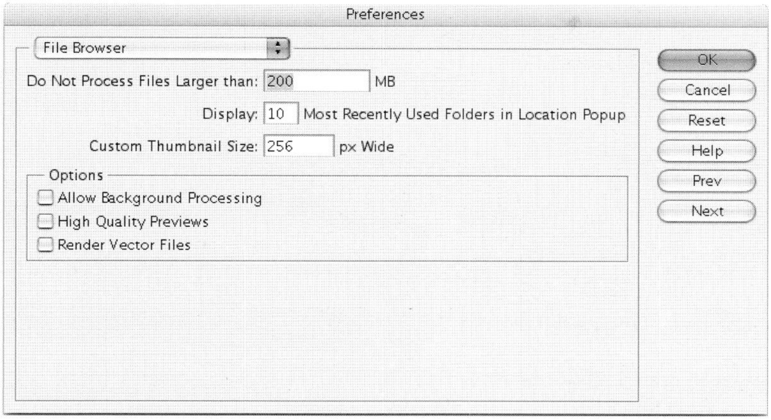

Figure 5.7
The File Browser Preference settings.

Using File Info to Add More Information

You can use the File Info feature of Photoshop Elements to input additional information to the photograph. With an image open, selecting File, File Info opens a dialog that provides five selectable pages for information (**Figure 5.9**). The Description page displays a wealth of information (that you must add) including copyright, title, comments, and so on. If you choose to make the image copyrighted, a copyright symbol appears in the title bar whenever the image is opened.

Rotating Photos in the File Browser

Two of the shortcut buttons at the top of the File Browser allow you to rotate the thumbnails either left or right to their correct orientation (it isn't called clockwise and counter-clockwise because many people have never seen an analog clock). When you choose to rotate from the File Browser, you get a message box telling you that this action only rotates the thumbnail, and for the actual image to be rotated you must open it in Elements. At this time, the image will open with the rotation applied and then you must save the file. Sound complicated? You bet. Rotate the images in Elements Editor and the next time you open the File Browser, click Refresh (F5) and the thumbnails will reflect the rotation. In the long run, it is a much simpler way to do it.

Figure 5.8
The File Browser palettes can be resized to almost any size by dragging the right or bottom edges of the palettes.

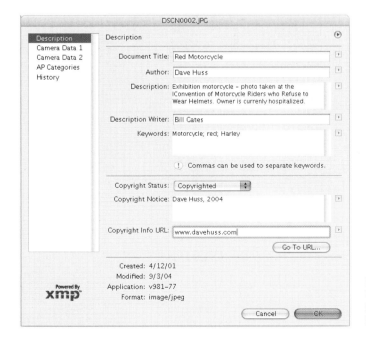

Figure 5.9
Use the File Info feature to store important information with the image.

The remaining pages in File Info are mostly read-only data. The two Camera Data pages provide a wealth of technical information about the image that was provided by the camera when the image was shot (**Figure 5.10**). Sometimes, these pages are blank because the information was either not recorded by the camera, the image was scanned, or (something that's quite common) the data was lost when the file was copied by an application that doesn't preserve the image data.

The Power of Keywords

Keywords are description words or phrases used to identify subjects or component parts of an image. In Photo Organizer, the keywords are called Tags or Subcategories. Regardless of whether you are using Browser or Organizer, the success of organizing your collection is determined, in part, by your choice of keywords (or tags). **Figure 5.11** is an example of effective keyword assignments.

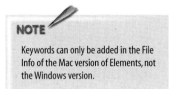

NOTE

Keywords can only be added in the File Info of the Mac version of Elements, not the Windows version.

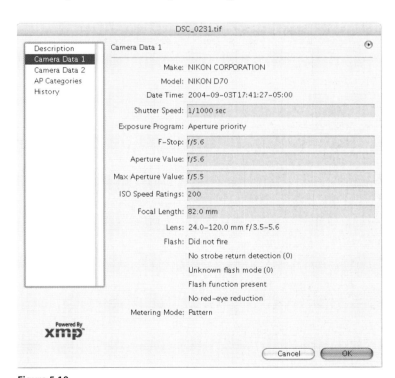

Figure 5.10
The Camera Data pages display a wealth of technical information about the actual photograph—if the camera recorded it.

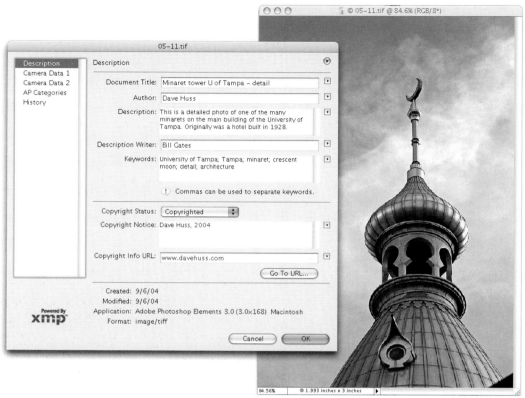

Figure 5.11
Keywords should identify major components of a photo to make it easy to find a photo.

Choosing the Right Keyword

When adding a keyword, ask yourself this question: Will I ever search for this photo using this keyword? In Figure 5.11, six keywords were assigned:

- University of Tampa, Tampa. Location is usually a strong keyword. In this case, the minarets are unique to Tampa and their University. If I wanted to find this photo I would first search using the keyword *Tampa*, which would give me a lot of hits, but it would include all of the minaret photos.

- Minaret. This might seem to be the best choice, but I probably wouldn't search on it. Why? Because minaret is not a common word to me and it's possible that I spelled it wrong when the keyword was added (Elements doesn't offer a spell checker—that's a hint, Adobe). I would first search on the location, even though it would produce many more hits that must be searched through, to find the minaret photos.

- Architecture, Detail. I use these two keywords a lot. Any photo of a building that is not a barn (remember, I live in Texas) is assigned this keyword. The keyword detail means it was a close-up shot of a portion of the subject.

- Crescent Moon. This is one of those once-in-a-blue-moon keywords you add that might cause the photo to turn up when you least expect it, but need it for a project.

Shakespeare said "Brevity is the soul of wit," and in like manner, the same can be said for the assignment of keywords. Only include those keywords absolutely necessary to group or locate a photo. In the previous example (**Figure 5.11**), the other possibilities that were not included were:

- Moroccan. The style of the hotel (it originally was built as a hotel) was Moroccan.

- Plant. The name of the building is Plant Hall.

- Aluminum. The minaret is constructed using aluminum.

- Clouds. Yep, there are clouds in the photo.

- Pole. That's what's under the crescent moon.

These are just a few of the many keywords that could be assigned. The only reason that you would want to include such a large number of keywords is if you are selling the photo to a stock photography house. They identify every possible item in the photo with a keyword. **Figure 5.12** is a screen shot of one of my Washington D.C. photos on Ablestock.com (www.ablestock.com). It is a photo of the interior of the old U.S. Library of Congress. As you can see, they assign a large number of keywords. Some of the keywords are beyond me. For example, have you found the *plinth* yet? Bottom line, only assign essential keywords that will help you—not others—find a photo later on.

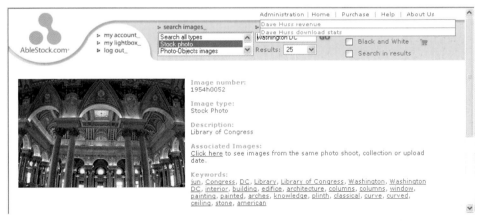

Figure 5.12
Stock photography houses assign many, many keywords to increase the chances of the photograph being found.

Now let's learn how to add keywords using the File Browser on the Mac. If you use Windows, skip forward to the section on using the Photo Organizer later in this chapter.

Adding Keywords to Photos with File Browser (Mac Only)

For Mac users there are two ways to add keywords to an image: using File Info, which we discussed earlier, and the Keywords palette in Browser. The advantage of using the File Browser is that you can add the same keyword to multiple photos at the same time—a real time saver.

Up until now we have been talking about keywords. If there were no other level of organization other than single keywords, the keyword list would be miles long. Adobe provides a way to group keywords together. Called Keyword Sets, they allow higher-level grouping (**Figure 5.13**). Keyword organization is limited to two levels, Keyword Sets and Keywords.

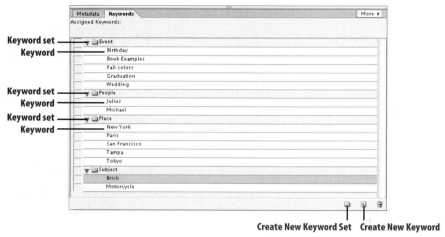

Figure 5.13
Keyword Sets make more efficient organization of keywords possible.

Adding a Keyword Set

Here is how it is done:

1. Open the File Browser and select the Keyword palette.

2. Click the New Keyword Set button (Figure 5.13). A flashing blank appears in the Keywords palette.

3. Name your keyword set and press Return. You just made a Keyword Set.

TIP

Keep your most frequently used keywords in their own Keyword set which makes it much easier to access them from a single location instead of moving up and down the Keywords palette.

Adding Keywords

Keywords are added in much the same way as Keyword Sets.

1. Open the File Browser and select the Keywords palette.

2. Select the Keyword Set into which you want to add the new keyword.

2. Click the New Keyword button (Figure 5.13). A flashing blank appears in the Keyword Set.

3. Name your keyword and press Return.

NOTE

When you select multiple images, the warning message shown in **Figure 5.14** appears before the keyword is assigned to the images. You may want to turn this feature off.

Assigning Keywords to Images

Once you have the keywords you want to use, here is how to assign them to images:

1. Select one or more files by clicking on the thumbnail. Use Cmd-click or Shift-click to choose multiple images. Use Shift to select contiguous, Cmd to select non-contiguous, or Cmd+A to select all images (standard Mac and Windows conventions). Use Cmd+A to select all images currently in the thumbnail view.

2. In the Keywords palette, click the box next to the name of the keyword you want to add, or double-click the keyword. When the keyword has been assigned, a check mark appears in the box next to the keyword once the image is selected.

TIP

You can add an entire Keyword Set to a selected image or multiple images by clicking the box next to the name of the keyword set, or double-clicking the keyword group.

NOTE

When you import an image that already has keywords, those keywords appear in the Other Keywords category until you re-categorize them.

Searching for Keywords

Now that you have made the effort to add all of these keywords to your images, the next step is searching for a photo, or group of photos, using keywords. Your searches are not just limited to keywords, you can also search by file name, file creation date, or one of a dozen other attributes. Using the file browser, you can run very specific searches by adding up to three different search criteria to narrow your search.

It's actually quite simple. Here is how it's done.

1. From the File Browser, click the Search button 🔍 or from the File Browser menu bar, choose File, Search.

2. In the Search dialog (**Figure 5.15**), choose a source folder from the Look In menu. By default, the menu displays the currently active folder. Click the Browse button to go to a different folder.

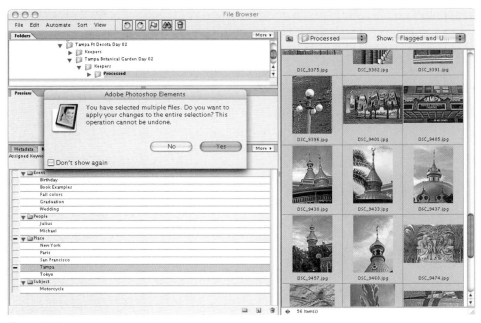

Figure 5.14
Assigning keywords to multiple images produces a warning message until you turn it off.

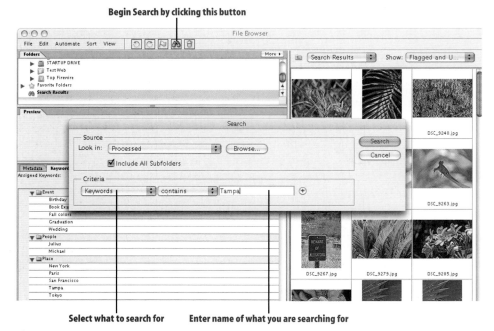

Figure 5.15
The Search dialog.

3. From the leftmost Criteria menu, choose what type of data you want to search for. If it is keywords, then select it from the drop-down menu.

4. Enter the text of what you are looking for in the text box at the right. In the case of keywords, it would be the name of the keyword you are in search of.

5. Click Search. After it has finished searching, the File Browser displays the photos that match the search criteria.

That about wraps up the File Browser, and it is time to move on to the Photo Organizer.

Using the Photo Organizer

I want to repeat a few things here before we get started just in case you started reading the book on this page. Photoshop Elements 3 (Windows) is really two programs— Elements Editor and Photo Organizer. Photo Organizer is a separate program that, when launched, can run at the same time that Elements 3 Editor is running. While both programs work seamlessly with one another, they are two separate programs.

Organizer: An Overview

Photo Organizer is an updated version of Adobe Photoshop Album. If you are familiar with Album, you will feel really comfortable with the operation of Organizer.

Photo Organizer has two modes of operation: Photo Browser (**Figure 5.16**) and Date View (**Figure 5.17**). We will be doing most of our work in Photo Browser mode. So let's take a closer look at it.

A Quick Tour of Photo Browser

You can use the Photo Browser to view just about any form of media that is available today. You can see all of your photos, video clips, and even audio files. From the Photo Browser, you can download photos from your digital camera, photos from your scanner, a CD, or DVD, to name only a few sources. Like the File Browser, you can organize items into categories by attaching tags to the images, and you can also quickly move an image from the Photo Browser into the Elements Editor with the click of a button.

NOTE

To search all of the subfolders that may be in the selected folder, make sure Include All Subfolders is selected.

TIP

While text entries used for searching are NOT case sensitive, the search engine doesn't catch spelling mistakes. For example, if I searched for the keyword Menaret, the search engine wouldn't ask me if I meant Minaret like popular search engine Google does. It would report that there are no hits (on the misspelled word).

NOTE

As I have mentioned several times, but it bears repeating, the Photo Organizer is part of the Windows release of Photoshop Elements 3.0 but it is not included in the Mac version.

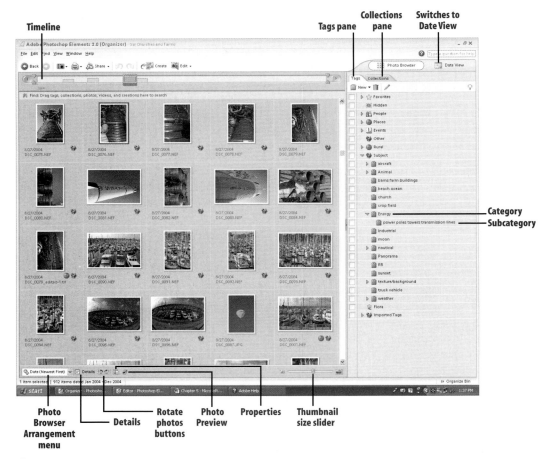

Figure 5.16
The Photo Browser mode of Photo Organizer.

There are several ways to open the Photo Browser. When you launch Photoshop Elements you can choose to go directly to Organizer from the Welcome screen. From the Elements Editor, just click the Photo Browser button in the shortcuts bar.

The following is a short list that describes the major components of the Photo Browser and gives a brief summary of what it does. We'll learn more as we actually learn to use them.

- Timeline. Probably one of the most useful features in Browser, the timeline helps you find photos by dates along the timeline.

- Date View. You can switch the Photo Organizer to Date View (Figure 5.17).

- Tags and Collections Panes. All of the tags, categories, subcategories (like keywords), and collections appear in one of these two areas.

- Photo Browser Arrangement menu. From here you can change the order of how thumbnails appear in the Photo Well. Their order of appearance can be according to date, when they were brought into Elements (import batch), or by the location of the folders containing the images.

- Thumbnail size slider. This controls the size of the thumbnails displayed in Photo Browser.

- Details. The details option shows or hides creation date, tags, and collections for items in the Photo Browser.

- Image Properties. When selected, the properties of any selected image, or images, appears on the lower-left side of the Browser window.

- Photo Preview. Clicking on this instantly produces a slide show for reviewing your photos.

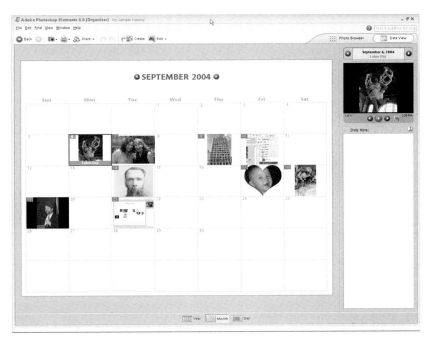

Figure 5.17
The Date View mode of Photo Organizer.

Putting the Photo Browser to Work

Since Adobe has included some excellent material in both the printed manual and the online help guide, I thought it best not to repeat what they have provided. Instead, let's concentrate on using the Photo Browser to organize and manage some photos by going through setting, organizing, and managing a typical photo catalog. If you want to go through the following step-by-step exercises, you can download the 16 photos used in the **Sample Image Folder** from the Peachpit Press Web page.

Creating a New Catalog

In Chapter 2 you learned how to move images to your computer. Now, we will learn how to move them into a catalog.

1. Open the Photo Organizer either by selecting it from the Welcome screen or clicking the Photo Organizer button above the Elements Editor menu bar.

2. When in Organizer, make sure you are in the Photo Browser view (Figure 5.16). How your Browser appears depends on settings from the last time it was used, so don't be concerned if yours looks different than the sample in Figure 5.16.

3. Choose File, Catalog, and the dialog shown in **Figure 5.18** appears. Click the New button which opens a New Catalog dialog. Name the catalog "My Sample Catalog" and click OK. You now have a new blank catalog (**Figure 5.19**).

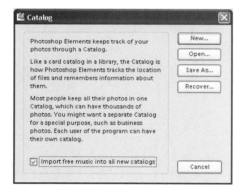

Figure 5.18
The Catalog dialog offers several cataloging options.

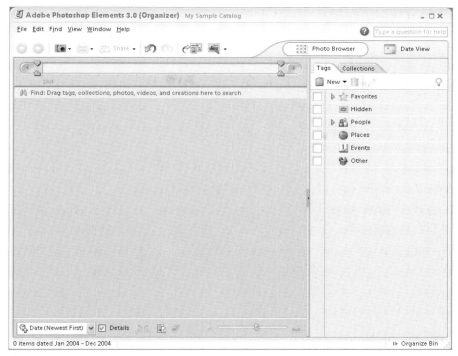

Figure 5.20
A new blank catalog waiting for you to fill it with photos.

Filling the New Catalog with Images

For this exercise, you will be loading a collection of 16 photos into the catalog you just created. Here is how to do it:

1. Click on the Camera Icon shown in **Figure 5.20** and select From Files and Folders… (Ctrl+Shift+G).

2. When the Get Photos from Files and Folders dialog opens (**Figure 5.21**), change the source location to the Download sample files folder you downloaded. Select all of the files in the folder by using Ctrl+A.

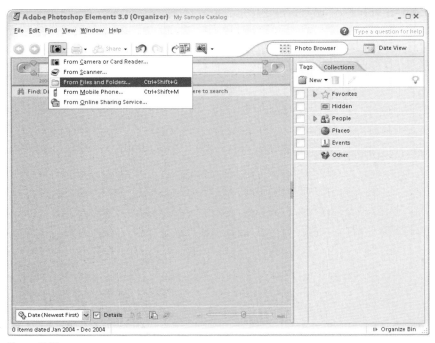

Figure 5.20
From here you can bring images into the catalog from many sources.

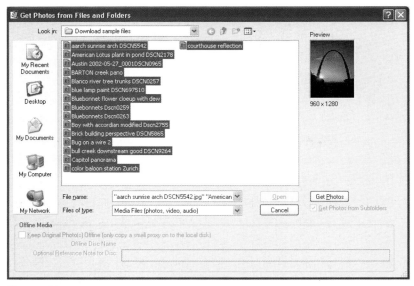

Figure 5.21
Select all the files in the Sample folder and click the Get Photos button.

3. When all the photos are selected, click the Get Photos button and after a few moments, you have a new catalog of images (**Figure 5.22**). A message box appears stating: "The only items in the main window are those you just imported. To see the rest of the catalog, click Back to All Photos."

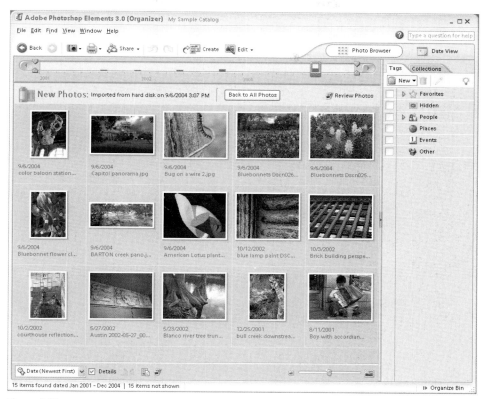

Figure 5.22
Your new catalog is filled with photos.

Working with Tags

Before we begin tagging images, you need to understand a few points about how they work. Tags are like keywords that you can attach to your images. Adding a tag doesn't alter the image to which it is attached, it just adds additional information that allows Photo Organizer to find and organize them.

It is important to know that Photo Browser doesn't move images around, but rather, keeps track of the photos right where they are. When working with File Browser, it was more effective to keep all of the files in groups of nested folders so it was easier for the

File Browser to search for them. With Photo Organizer, every time you get photos from a location that is on or attached to your computer, the Photo Browser makes a note where those files are located. Even though the thumbnails appear together in the Photo Well, they may actually be scattered throughout your system.

For example, after getting several hundred files from many different folders into a catalog, I create a tag called "Grace" and then attach it to every thumbnail that includes my daughter Grace. Later, by putting a check by her tag in the Tags pane, all photos with that tag, regardless of where the photos are stored on my system, appear in the Photo Well.

You can attach more than one tag to an item. For instance, you might have tags with the names of individual people, subject matter, locations, and events that you have photographed. By attaching multiple tags to your photos, you could search for these tags to make searches even more accurate. A recent example of this was when I was taking some photos of a hot air balloon race at Houston's NASA Space Center. While I was there, I took some great photos of a rocket they were refurbishing. I have taken many photos at NASA, so if I wanted to find those photos, I would select the NASA tag and the hot air balloon event tag. Only the NASA photos I took during that shoot would be displayed in the Photo Well.

Types of Tags

Everything having to do with tags is done in the Tags pane of the Photo Browser. When you created the new catalog, you may have noticed that there are, by default, four categories of tags in the Tags pane. They are:

- People
- Places
- Events
- Other

You aren't limited to using just these four general categories by any means. You can create your own categories and multiple levels of subcategories as well. In addition to the default tags and any that you create there are two special classifications of tags:

- Favorites. This category is my personal favorite (no pun intended). This is how you identify your really great photos (I call these keepers) and later you can find them by choosing what level of quality you have tagged them with. The Favorites contains tags with 1 to 5 stars indicated (**Figure 5.23**). An image can have only one favorite tag attached. After all, if you tagged an image as being a 5-star favorite, putting a 2-star favorite tag would be confusing at best.

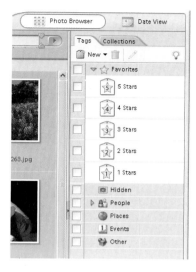

Figure 5.23
The favorite tag allows you to
keep track of your best work.

- Hidden. Items with a Hidden tag attached don't appear in the Photo Browser unless the Hidden tag is included as one of the search criteria. So if you mark a file with both a Most Embarrassing Moments and a Hidden tag, those holiday photos won't appear when the Most Embarrassing Moments tag is selected as long as the Hidden tag isn't selected.

Creating New Tags

The default set of tags aren't adequate to catalog anything. To create a catalog that meets your needs requires creating your own set of tags, which is quite easy to do. Looking at the photos in my sample catalog, there are four photos with flowers, so let's start by making a tag called Flowers. Here is how it is done:

1. With the Tags pane selected, click the New button from the toolbar, and choose New Tag from the drop-down menu (**Figure 5.24**).

Figure 5.24
Click the New button in the Tags
toolbar to create a new tag.

111

2. When the Create Tag dialog appears choose Category, then select the Other category from the drop-down list.

3. In the Name text window, name the tag Flowers, and click OK. The new tag appears in the Tags pane under Other (**Figure 5.25**). The icon for the new tag is a question mark and it will remain so until it is attached to a photo.

Figure 5.25
The new tag appears in the Tags pane under the Other category.

Attaching a Tag to a Single Photo

Now that you have made the new tag, here is how simple it is to assign it to a photo.

1. Click and drag the new tag you just created from the Tags pane onto the thumbnail of the close-up photo of a Bluebonnet flower. The question mark icon in the new tag is replaced with a tiny thumbnail of the flower and a small icon appears in the lower-right corner of the thumbnail (**Figure 5.26**). The icon that appears is the one that is assigned to the Others tag. If you place the cursor over the icon in the thumbnail's left-hand corner, the name of the attached tag appears (**Figure 5.27**).

New icon indicating that a tag has been attached

Figure 5.26
The tag is attached to the photo in a single action.

**Name of tag associated
with the photo**

Figure 5.27
Placing the cursor over a thumbnail's tag icon shows the names of the tags.

Attaching Tags to Multiple Photos

You can attach the same tag to multiple photos using the following technique:

1. Select all the photos in the Photo Well that you want to attach the Flowers tag to. Use Ctrl+click to select multiple photos. Each selected photo is highlighted with a blue border (**Figure 5.28**)

Figure 5.28
Ctrl+click to select all of the photos that will tagged.

2. Click and drag the Flowers tag on top of any of the selected thumbnails in the Photo Well. When you release the mouse button, the tag is applied to all of the selected photos (**Figure 5.29**).

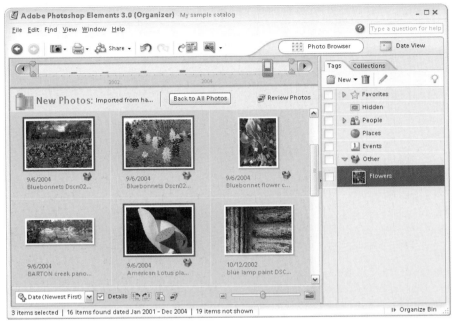

Figure 5.29
All of the selected photos are tagged.

Finding Photos Using Tags

Now that you have some of the photos tagged, let's use the tags to find the photos we want. Like everything else in Elements, there is more than one way to use tags to search for photos, but the following are the fastest and best ways to do it.

In the Tags pane, double-click the tag of the photos that you want to find. All the photos with that tag attached will appear in the Photo Well (**Figure 5.30**).

Another way to search for photos using a tag is to click the blank box to the left of the tag name. A binoculars icon appears and all of the photos that have this tag attached appear in the Photo Well.

TIP

Use the Green Back button under the word file in the File menu to return to the main collection of images after viewing the results of a tag search.

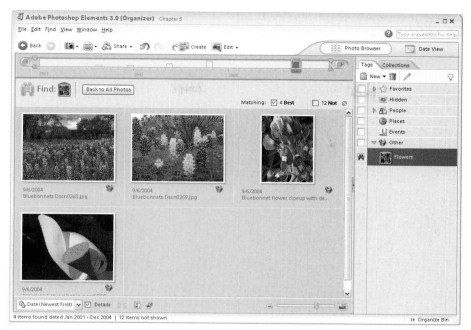

Figure 5.30
Double-click any tag in the Tags pane to see all the photos tagged with that tag.

Multiple Tag Searches

You can use the previous method to find photos using multiple tags. Just click the blank box next to all the tags that you want to use as search criteria. Elements will include all the photos that match any of the tags selected. When searching, a large number of photos could produce a lot of close matches with one but not all of the tags. Photo Browser lists the results in a way to help you narrow the search. To demonstrate, we need to create another tag.

1. Create a new tag named Bluebonnets in the Tags pane.

2. Select the three photos of the Bluebonnets (state flower of Texas) and drag the Bluebonnets tag onto them.

3. Click on the blank box next to the Flowers tag in the Tags pane. All four flower photos appear in the Photo Well. (**Figure 5.31**). Make a note in the Matching area that 4 photos are listed as best and 12 are not.

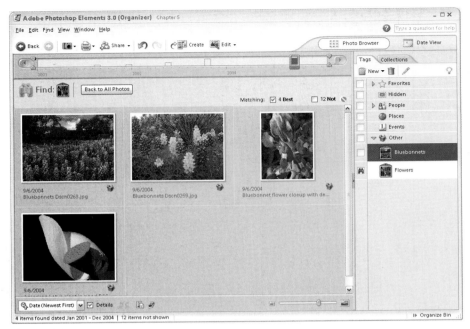

Figure 5.31
Selecting one tag makes four matching photos appear in the Photo Well.

4. Now click in the blank box next to Bluebonnets and see how the Matching changes to 3 best, 1 close, and 12 not. Click the Best to turn it off and click the Close to see the one photo that is a close match (**Figure 5.32**).

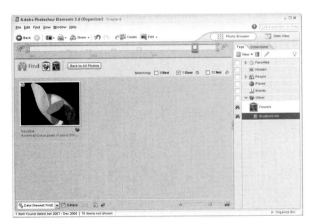

Figure 5.32
Photo Browser lets you refine the search results from multiple tags.

Changing Tags

As you create additional tags, you need to move folders into others to prevent the list of tags from becoming so long as to be unmanageable. Changing the hierarchy of tags in the Tags pane is really easy. Here is how to do it:

NOTE

If you want to move a subcategory tag from one folder to another you only need to drag the tag from one Tag folder to another.

- Using the tags made earlier, right-click on the Bluebonnets tag and select Change Bluebonnets tag to a sub-category (**Figure 5.34**). With the tag becoming a sub-category it no longer has a thumbnail.

Catalog Maintenance

Now you have your image catalog put together, and all of your photos are identified with tags. Most of the time you don't need to be concerned about your catalogs, but making regular backups of them is essential for protecting your photos in case something happens to your catalogs. This section covers some basic procedures to backup and maintain your image catalogs.

Working with Collections

The Photo Browser offers an additional way to rearrange your photos to create slide shows or bound books called Creations. When creating a slide show using tagged photos, you must accept the order in which they appear while a Collection allows you to rearrange photos to any order.

Figure 5.33
Combining tags by using sub-categories prevent overly long lists of tags.

Backing up Catalogs

Depending on how big your catalog is, backing it up can take a long time. So, when you open your catalog and see the reminder message asking if you want to backup your catalog now (**Figure 5.34**), most likely you don't want to do it right at that time. Here is how to do it when you do have the time:

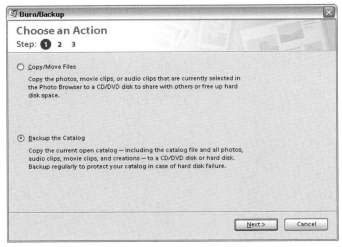

Figure 5.34
This dialog asks you if you want to backup your catalog (usually when you don't have the time to do so).

1. Choose File, Backup, and when the Burn/Backup dialog opens, the Backup the Catalog option should already be selected. (**Figure 5.35**).

Figure 5.35
Choose Backup the Catalog if it isn't already selected.

2. If any files in your catalog have been moved, it doesn't mean that they're lost, only that the catalog has lost track of their location. The most common cause of this problem is when the images are moved to a different location. Most of the time, Elements can find the missing files pretty quickly. If Photo Browser cannot find the files automatically, it will open the Missing Files Check Before Backup dialog that you can use to point Photo Browser to where the files have moved (**Figure 5.36**). If the files the catalog is looking for are actually gone, you can click the Remove from Catalog button, and Photo Browser will purge any references to the missing image files from the catalog. Once you have located missing files, you can continue making a backup.

Figure 5.36
The Reconnect Missing Files dialog box helps find missing files.

3. The Backup Options of the Burn/Backup dialog appears next (**Figure 5.37**). If this is the first backup you have done, you need to select Full Backup. Incremental Backup only copies files created or changed since the last backup.

Figure 5.37
The next step allows you to select what type of catalog backup to do.

4. The last dialog (**Figure 5.38**) allows you to select the output device or path. If you select a CD or DVD recorder (burner), the very first time you use it, Photo Browser will first run some data timing tests before backing up your images. If you are backing up to CD or DVD, and it requires more space than is available on the disc, the backup will pause, and you will be prompted for additional discs.

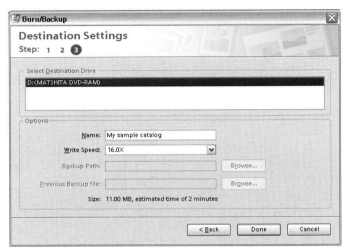

Figure 5.38.
This dialog allows you to select the device, or path, to which your catalog backup will be saved.

Moving Photos off of Your Computer

In the previous section you learned how the catalog can locate files that were inadvertently moved. So what do you do when you want to move older images off of the computer to make room for new photos? The Photo Browser has the option of copying or moving these files to a CD-ROM or DVD, using the Burn command. The advantage of using the Burn command is that the catalog knows where the files were moved to. The thumbnails remain in the catalog and if you select a photo that has been moved off of the computer, you will be prompted to insert the CD/DVD containing the requested file. Here is the procedure to move files off of your system.

1. Open the images that you want to copy or move in the Photo Browser.

2. Choose File, Burn (Ctrl+B), and the dialog that appears is the same as that which appears when selecting a backup (**Figure 5.39**), except that the option Copy/Move Files is selected.

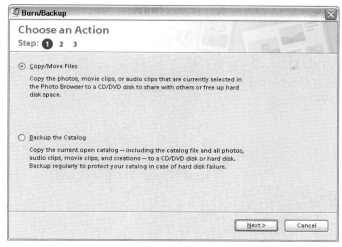

Figure 5.39
Choosing the Burn command offers the ability to move files off your computer to a CD/DVD.

3. The next dialog (**Figure 5.40**) features options to specify how files are to be moved offline and deleted from the original source.

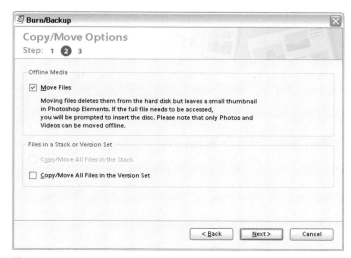

Figure 5.40
Choose if you want to move or copy the selected photos to a CD/DVD.

Recovering and Restoring Catalogs

So you're importing some photos into an existing catalog and your computer crashes. When you restart the computer and Photo Browser, you discover that the catalog you were importing the photo into is corrupted. If your catalog ever becomes corrupted, there is a tool in Photo Browser to recover it.

1. Choose File, Catalog... Click the Recover button which opens a message box (**Figure 5.41**).

Figure 5.41
The Recover feature can quickly restore damaged catalogs.

2. Click the OK button and Photo Browser repairs damaged catalogs.

There is so much more to the File Browser and Photo Browser that it could fill a book. To see what else these programs can do, take some time and review what Adobe included in the online help files.

In the next chapter, we will learn how to do even more cool stuff with Elements.

Dazzling Effects and Techniques

This chapter is a collection of things you can do using Photoshop Elements 3. It includes emphasizing a subject by creating a false depth of field, creating a hand-tinted look to your favorite photos, and isolating color for effect. You will also discover the fun of adding and removing objects or people from photographs, and converting photos into natural media paintings.

Emphasizing the Subject

Often times when you take a photograph of someone or something, the subject gets lost in the cluttered background like the photograph shown in **Figure 6.1**.

The secret to emphasizing the subject isn't done by eliminating the background, it is accomplished by creating a false sense of depth of field (DOF). If you're not familiar with the term, see the sidebar "Understanding Depth of Field." The typically wide-angle lenses of digital cameras tend to produce a wide depth of field and, as a result, the background is often in sharp focus. It is therefore necessary to use Elements to blur the background as it would appear had the camera produced it.

Figure 6.1
A cluttered background is distracting.

Understanding Depth of Field

Depth of field is an optical phenomenon produced by the camera lens. When a lens focuses on a subject at a distance, all subjects at that distance are in focus while subjects that are not at the same distance (that are either closer or farther away) appear out of focus. The zone in which the subject is in focus is referred to as the depth of field (DOF). If you are unfamiliar with photography, here is some useful information. The amount of DOF is controlled by the size of the aperture (f-stop), which, along with the shutter speed, is automatically set by your camera when shooting. If you are shooting pictures when there's a lot of light, the lens aperture is set to a small opening (large f-stop number) and the resulting DOF is at its greatest, meaning that almost everything is in focus. When there is low lighting, the aperture is opened to its largest size (smallest f-stop) and only the subject and very little else is in focus.

Creating a Depth of Field Focus Effect

In this exercise, you will learn how to make the background slightly out of focus to emphasize the subject. The procedure involves isolating the background with a selection, and then blurring it. The following exercise uses the file **Good_friends.jpg** which can be downloaded from the Peachpit Press Web site.

1. Open the file **Good_friends.jpg**.

2. Choose the Selection Brush tool in the Toolbox. Ensure the Mode setting in the Options bar is set to Mask. Paint the areas you want to preserve (**Figure 6.2**). See sidebar "Selecting Areas with a Brush" for additional information about making and using selections with the Selection Brush tool.

3. Choose Filter, Blur, Gaussian Blur. Change the blur setting to a radius of 6 pixels (**Figure 6.3**). Click OK to apply the blur.

Figure 6.2
Select the area to be preserved using the Selection Brush tool.

Figure 6.3
Applying a Gaussian Blur makes the background softly out of focus.

4. Another possibility you can try while the selection is still in place is to select Hue/Saturation (Ctrl+U/Cmd+U), and choose Colorize. Move the Hue slider until you have a background color that you like (**Figure 6.4**). Click OK. When you are finished with the selection, remove it (Ctrl+D/Cmd+D).

Selecting Areas with a Brush

The Selection Brush tool allows you to define areas of a photo that you want to protect from any action or effects applied to the rest of the image. The operation is simple. Paint the areas that you want to protect, but don't paint the areas to which you want to apply effects or changes. If you accidentally paint over an area, remove it by painting over it again while holding down the Alt (Option) key. The Hardness setting in the Options bar controls the softness of the selection edges. Although the size of the brush can be controlled using the settings in the Options bar, a more convenient way is to use the [and] keys to increase and decrease the brush size in increments. The best results are achieved using a pressure-sensitive tablet. See the section on setting up pressure-sensitive tablets later in this chapter.

Controlling the size of the selection brush is important for making the most accurate selections. When making a detailed selection, get in the habit of zooming in and working with a small brush size. Larger areas of the selection can be made quickly using larger brush sizes.

Figure 6.4
Applying the Colorize option is one of the many things you can do to an isolated background.

This technique of creating a blurred background is quick and effective. The only drawback is that it permanently alters the photo. So let's look at another way of doing it.

Another Way to Soften the Background

The problem with the technique we just looked at is that the background is permanently blurred. If at a later time you decide you want see the background, you must locate the original and start all over again. Here is a technique that takes a little longer to create a softer background but produces no change to the original image and allows you to change it at a later time.

To accomplish this feat of magic, we will need to use a Layer mask. If you have never heard of the term before, a Layer mask is a layer that hides or reveals portions of the layer above it. Clear as mud—right? It will make more sense as we go through the next exercise. For those of you that already know what a Layer mask is, you may be saying "Wait a minute…Photoshop Elements doesn't have the Layer masks feature." Actually, it does but it isn't called a Layer mask. Still, it acts like a Layer mask just the same. A rose by another name….

How to Make and Use a Layer Mask

You will need to download the file **Contented_cat.jpg** (**Figure 6.5**) from the Peachpit Press Web site. The photo is of a Siamese cat enjoying the warmth of both a wood stove and the sunlight from the windows on a very cold winter day in Nebraska. The subject is on the right third of the photo so the composition is good. The background is distracting (not to him) so we need to soften it. Here is how it's done.

Figure 6.5
This photo of the cat would look even better with a softly-blurred background.

1. Open the image **Contented_cat.jpg**.

2. Make a copy of the background. In the Layers palette, click on the background layer and drag it on to the Create a new layer icon (**Figure 6.6**).

3. Choose Gaussian Blur (Filter, Blur, Gaussian Blur). When the dialog opens, move the slider until the Radius is 8 pixels. Click OK (**Figure 6.7**).

Click and drag background to here

Figure 6.6
A copy of the background becomes the top layer.

Figure 6.7
Everything—including the subject—is blurred at this point.

4. Click the eye icon on the top layer to make the blurred image invisible (for the moment) and select the background by clicking on it. The currently selected layer becomes highlighted (**Figure 6.8**).

5. Choose the Polygonal Lasso tool (L) in the Toolbox (**Figure 6.9**) and make a rough selection that includes most of the background but not the cat or the sofa. It would look strange if the cat were sitting on a blurred sofa (**Figure 6.10**) Don't make your selection too close to the cat. This is because the background is relatively soft and thus, it isn't necessary to make the blurring meet tightly with the fur. The exception is the area near the left ear. Because there is a high contrast object near the ear, you need to make sure that it is blurred right down to the edge of the fur.

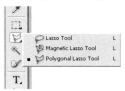

Figure 6.9
Choose the Polygonal Lasso Tool

Selected layer

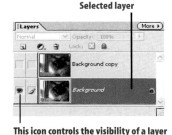

This icon controls the visibility of a layer

Figure 6.8
Hide the top layer and select the background.

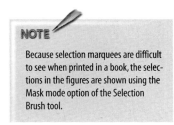

NOTE

Because selection marquees are difficult to see when printed in a book, the selections in the figures are shown using the Mask mode option of the Selection Brush tool.

Figure 6.10
Selecting the background is the first step.

6. To prevent a visible line where the blurring begins and ends, feather the selection (Select, Feather) and choose a Feather Radius setting of 10 (**Figure 6.11**).

Figure 6.11
Feather the selection.

7. Choose Layer, New Adjustment Layer…Levels. When the dialog opens, name the layer the following: Layer Mask. This isn't necessary but it is a good habit to give descriptive names so you will remember when you see the layer a year from now. Click OK. When the Levels dialog appears, click OK without making any changes. Your Layers palette should look like **Figure 6.12**. The selection that you made appears in the Layer mask thumbnail.

8. Select the top layer by clicking on it in the Layers palette (making it visible again). The entire photo then appears blurry again. Now comes the fun part. Choose Layer, Group with Previous. The layer's thumbnail has a small icon that appears to its left, indicating that this layer is linked to the layer below it. The background is now blurry and the foreground is in focus (**Figure 6.13**). To quickly move back and forth between blurry and non-blurry backgrounds, hold down the Alt (Option) key and click the eye icon on the background layer.

Adjustment layer icon

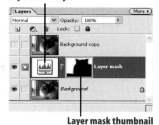

Layer mask thumbnail

Figure 6.12
The Layers Palette with a pseudo Layer mask.

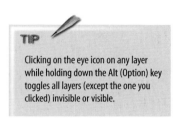

TIP

Clicking on the eye icon on any layer while holding down the Alt (Option) key toggles all layers (except the one you clicked) invisible or visible.

Blurred layer becomes transparent

Icon indicates this layer is grouped with the layer below

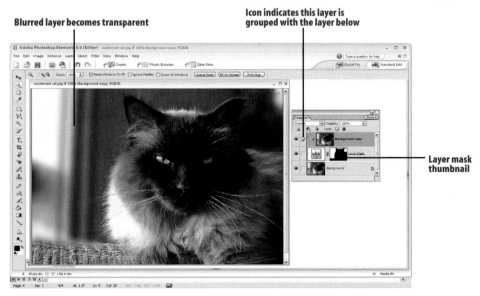

Layer mask thumbnail

Figure 6.13
The background appears blurred but the original is unaffected.

9. To demonstrate the flexibility of the Layer mask, click on the Layer mask thumbnail in the Layers palette to select it. Select the Brush tool (B) and with the foreground color set to black, place the cursor on the image and paint over part of the background as shown in **Figure 6.14**. The blurring disappears where you painted. A dark spot appears in the Layer mask thumbnail (within the Layers palette) in the area of the photo where you painted with the Brush tool.

Blurred layer becomes transparent

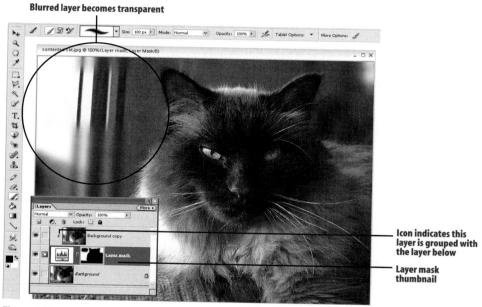

Figure 6.14
The top layer is revealed where the layer mask is painted.

10. To restore an area, all you need do is make the foreground color white (press the X key to eXchange the colors) and paint over the same area. The blurring of the top layer is once again visible.

So if areas painted on the Layer mask make the top layer transparent and painting the same area white makes it visible, what happens if the mask area is painted gray? I thought you'd never ask. Let's finish the exercise.

11. Select the Brush and choose one of the preset brush sizes (I used the 100 pix). To change the foreground color to gray, select Black and change the Opacity setting in the Options bar to 50%. Select the Layer mask thumbnail in the Layers palette and paint the couch that the cat is guarding. The Layer mask

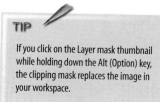

TIP

If you click on the Layer mask thumbnail while holding down the Alt (Option) key, the clipping mask replaces the image in your workspace.

thumbnail indicates a soft gray area where the couch is (Figure 6.15) and in the photo the couch appears slightly blurred. However, it is not as blurred as the background. The final image is shown in **Figure 6.16**.

Figure 6.15
Applying a 50% Black to the couch produces a soft blur effect.

Figure 6.16
A contented cat now has a soft background. All that's missing is…wait, nothing is missing.

Recapping the Layer Mask Exercise

Here is a summary of what you did in the Layer mask exercise and how it worked. When we created the Levels Adjustment layer, there was a selection already in place. The Adjustment layer used this selection for its own mask, which is why the selection appeared in the mask area of the layer.

When the Group with Previous command was applied to the top layer, its visibility became controlled by the mask area of the Adjustment layer.

Everywhere on the mask that was black, the blurred layer on top became invisible. Everywhere it was white, the blurred layer was seen.

Because you can paint directly on the mask area you can control what parts appear blurred and what parts don't. Here is how to do that:

NOTE

The actual mask in the Adjustment layer is technically called a clipping mask. The Adjustment layer, together with its clipping mask, operates as a Layer mask. I only mention this because you may come across the term clipping mask in some of the Elements online help files and user guide.

TIP

A quick way to evoke the Group with Previous command in the Layers palette is to place the cursor on the line separating the top layer and the Adjustment layer while holding down the Alt (Option) key. The cursor turns into a strange black ball and when it does, click on the line. The top layer is now linked to the Adjustment layer.

- To make part of the top layer visible, select the mask area in the Layers palette by clicking on it. Select the Brush tool and paint on the image using black. As you paint, the tiny thumbnail reflects the parts of the image that you have painted.

- To make part of the top layer invisible, do the same thing except use white.

- To make part of the top layer semi-transparent, change the brush color to shades of gray.

Finishing Up the Job

The image now has several layers. To preserve the image so that you can make more changes at a later date, save the image as a Photoshop (PSD) or Tagged Image Format File (TIFF). To save in another format that can be used to send to friends, you must first flatten the image (Layer, Flatten Image) and then save it in any format you desire. Now that you know how to make a Layer mask, let's see some other things it can be used for.

Making a Blended Photo Montage

Using the Layer mask we learned about in the previous exercise, you can also create a blended photo montage. By blended, I am referring to the gradual transition from one photo to the next. To be perfectly honest, you don't see many well-blended montages because the photos need to have a common theme. I have a large photo collection and it took me some time to come up with the photos we are going to use in the exercise.

To do this exercise, you will need to download the images **Dancing_couple.jpg** and the **Bride.jpg** (**Figure 6.17**). The photos are of a lovely couple who celebrated their 25th wedding anniversary by getting married again—this time with their nine children in attendance!

Figure 6.17
A Layer mask allows you to seamlessly merge two photos.

1. Open both images (**Dancing_couple.jpg** and **Bride.jpg**). Select the Move tool (V) in the Toolbox and then select the Bride photo.

2. Click inside of the bride photo and drag it over to the photo of the dancing couple. It becomes a layer in the photo. Position the photo so it is on the far left side of the image, as shown in **Figure 6.18**. Part of the left side will be off the edge—that's OK. Close the bride photo.

NOTE

I have already done some of the preliminary work necessary to make these photos blend together. One photo is oriented in landscape, while the other is a portrait shot. To make the portrait photo fit into the landscape photo, I used the Resize command (Image, Resize) to change the height of the portrait photo to match the height of the landscape.

Figure 6.18
Position the photo of the bride to the far left and a little above the bottom photo.

3. I think the photo looks good now, but let's make it even better. Select the Background layer in the Layers palette. Choose Layer, New Adjustment Layer... Levels. When the dialog opens, name the layer the following: Layer mask. Click OK. When the Levels dialog appears, click OK without making any changes.

4. Select the top layer (bride) and choose Layer, Group with Previous.

5. Click on the Layer mask thumbnail in the Layers palette to select it. If your foreground color isn't black, press the X key to swap the foreground and background colors. Next, choose the Gradient tool (G) in the Toolbox and from the Options bar choose the Foreground to Background preset (**Figure 6.19**).

WARNING

Whenever the Layer mask thumbnail of an Adjustment layer is selected, the default colors setting in the Toolbox is reversed. Clicking the thumbnail makes the foreground color white and the background color black.

6. Click at the point indicated in **Figure 6.20** and drag the Gradient tool reading to the endpoint shown in Figure 6.20. The result is shown in **Figure 6.21.**

Figure 6.19
Select the Layer mask thumbnail, the Gradient tool, and the indicated preset.

Figure 6.20
Drag a line between to create a gradient in the Layer mask

Figure 6.21
A nice blended photo montage but there is a small detail left to clean up.

7. The last thing to clean up is the faint vertical shadow from the original black bride background. With the Layer mask thumbnail still selected, choose the Brush tool and with the foreground color set to black, paint out the faint shadow line. The finished photo montage is shown in Figure **6.22.**

Figure 6.22
The final composition.

While working with a Layer mask takes more time, it give you much greater creative control than you would have had if you have outlined the subject (bride) with a selection tool and just pasted her into the other photograph. With the Layer mask, you can add or subtract pixels from the edges as much as you want because the original photos remain unchanged.

Now that you have got the hang of Layer masks, let's see what cool stuff can be done using just the Adjustment layers.

Isolating Colors for Effect

A favorite effect these days is to either remove all color from a photo and then selectively restore some of the colors to their original vivid hues, or replace the colors with slightly desaturated ones to make the photo appear hand-painted. It may sound complicated, but in truth both techniques are quite simple.

Removing and Restoring Color

You will need the file **Little_girl_with_pink_bow.jpg** to do this first exercise. Here is how it is done.

1. Open the file **Little_girl_with_pink_bow.jpg** (**Figure 6.23**).

Figure 6.23
This exercise begins with a color photograph of a young girl.

139

2. Choose Layer, New Adjustment Layer, Hue/Saturation. Use the default name and click OK. This opens the Hue Saturation dialog. Slide the Saturation slider all the way to the left and click OK. All color appears to be removed from the photo (**Figure 6.24**). Actually, the colors are still on the photo, but the Adjustment layer prevents them from being seen.

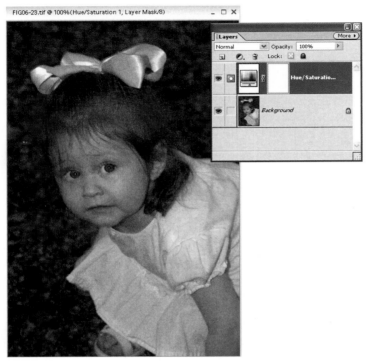

Figure 6.24
The Hue/Saturation Adjustment layer makes the colors in the photo invisible to the viewer.

3. Select the Hue/Saturation Adjustment layer thumbnail in the Adjustment layer. Press the X key to make the foreground color black if needed. Select the Brush tool in the Toolbox and paint the areas on the photo where you wish to restore the colors. If you accidentally paint outside of the area you want, change the color to white and paint over it to change it back. In this exercise, I restored the color to the pink bow and her blue eyes. (**Figure 6.25**).

TIP

Use the X key to quickly swap the foreground and background colors.

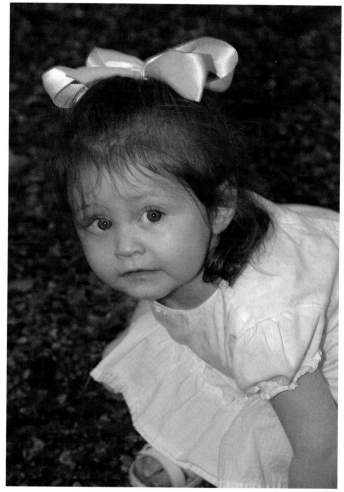

Figure 6.25
The Hue/Saturation Adjustment layer is used to selectively restore colors.

Creating Hand-Tinted Photos

One of the ironies of fads is how often the "new" look is an old look that a lot of people spent their lives trying to correct. I am referring to the technique of hand-tinting modern color photographs so that they appear like the hand-colored photos of bygone days before there was inexpensive color. When I graduated from high school back in the mid-sixties, all of the school photos were shot in black and white. If you wanted your senior portrait in color, someone hand-colored the black-and-white 8 x 10. Today we have cheap, accurate color photos. But what's popular? Hand-tinted photographs. There are some really great artists in my area that are making some good money at this trade. They apply tints on real black-and-white photos. Here is how you can do the same thing using Photoshop Elements. For this exercise, you will need to download the file **Little_girl_with_pink_bow2.jpg**. In case you are wondering, this photo has not been retouched—her eyes are really that blue.

1. Open the image **Little_girl_with_pink_bow2.jpg** (**Figure 6.26**).

2. Make a copy of the Background layer. Select the layer and apply the Smudge Stick filter (Filter, Artistic, Smudge Stick). Click OK in the dialog to apply the filter at default settings. The filter makes the photo look worse (**Figure 6.27**).

Figure 2.26
The original photo.

Figure 6.27
The Smudge Stick filter gives a mottled look to the photo.

3. In the Layers palette, change the Opacity setting to 50% to reduce the starkness of the Smudge Stick. Choose Layer, New Adjustment Layer, Hue/Saturation. Use the default name and click OK. The Hue/Saturation dialog opens. Slide the Saturation slider to the left to a setting of -60 and click OK (**Figure 6.28**).

4. Select the Hue/Saturation Adjustment layer thumbnail in the Adjustment layer. Press the X key to make the foreground color black. Select the Brush tool in the Toolbox and paint the areas of her face that you want to appear as hand-tinted. The key to achieve the effect is to just increase the saturation in areas that were traditionally emphasized—rosy cheeks, eyes, and lips (**Figure 6.29**).

Figure 6.28
The Hue/Saturation Adjustment layer reduces but doesn't remove all the color.

Figure 6.29
Restoring color to select areas gives a hand-tinted look.

5. To finish the effect, select the Burn tool. In the Options bar, change the Range setting to Shadows, and the Exposure to 50%. The Burn Brush darkens the selected range (shadows), which darkens the darker colors while leaving the pixels in the midtones and highlights unaffected. Paint her face and hair to darken the features. The final image is shown in **Figure 6.30.**

Figure 6.30
The finished photo.

Creating Painterly Effects

One of the great things about Photoshop Elements is all the cool stuff you can do to photos or other images by using the built-in filters. This chapter is all about getting your creative juices flowing. It is quick and easy to create some great-looking images after you learn how it's done (see **Figures 6.31** and **6.32**). You'll also learn a bunch of tricks to make ordinary images turn into jaw-dropping masterpieces. Enough chitchat, let's go to it.

Figure 6.31
The original photo has good composition.

Figure 6.32
Applying a few artistic filters produces a painted portrait.

Creating Painterly Masterpieces

A creative use of Photoshop Elements is applying painterly effects. The term painterly describes any filter or effect that turns photos into images that appear as if they were painted. Photoshop Elements contains a large selection of these filters to choose from. They have marvelous descriptive names like watercolor, stained glass, rough pastels, and chalk & charcoal. Many people have applied these filters to photos assuming they would magically transform them into natural media masterpieces. Not all photographs can be converted to painterly images though. To achieve the best painterly effects, the photo composition must be a good fit for the selected filter. The size of the photo also affects how well or how poorly the results.

NOTE

My conscience compels me to warn you that after you begin to creatively apply the Artistic filters in Photoshop Elements, you can become addicted and might spend hours, days, or even weeks in front of your computer going from one effect combination to another. You have been warned.

Probably the most important factor affecting the final result when applying the painterly effect has to do with the size of the original image in relation to the filter that you are using. Most of the painterly effect filters in Photoshop Elements use a fixed-sized brush when applying their painter effects; therefore, when the image is too large, the effects produced are small. Sometimes, they can be so small that they're not noticeable. Likewise, if the image is small to begin with, the photo can become unrecognizable after the filter is applied.

Figure 6.33 shows the original photo of some pelicans (the original photo is over 8 inches wide at 300 dpi). When the Watercolor filter is applied to it at its default setting, the effect is barely noticeable (see **Figure 6.34**). When I use the Resize command and change the resolution from 300 dpi to 72 dpi and reapply the same filter, the birds appear almost unrecognizable (see **Figure 6.35**).

Figure 6.33
The original photo of some pelicans catching some sun.

The reason why the size of the image alters the effects of most painterly filters is due to the filters applying their effects using a bitmap shape that is a fixed size. When the image is small, the bitmap shape is relatively large, and when the image is large, the shape is comparatively small; hence, there's little to no effect.

Figure 6.34
Applying the Watercolor filter to this large photo has little visible results.

Figure 6.35
With the image resized to make it much smaller, the same Watercolor filter makes the photo into a blurry mess.

Evaluating the Effects of a Painterly Filter

A tricky part of working with painterly effects is the effect that the zoom setting has on viewing the effects. Many times after applying a painterly effects filter, it might appear that the filter has had little to no effect. As previously mentioned, this might be because the image is so large that the effects are minimized. But, before jumping to that conclusion, make sure that you are viewing the results at 100% (called Actual Pixels in the View menu). **Figure 6.36** is a digital photograph of a farm to which the Watercolor filter was applied, viewed at a zoom level of 25%.

barns watercolor DSC_8572.jpg @ 25% (RGB/8)

Figure 6.36
Even though a watercolor filter was applied to this photo of a farm scene, it still looks like a photograph because the zoom view setting is at 25%.

When the zoom level is changed to Actual Pixels, the watercolor effect becomes more apparent (**Figure 6.37**).

Figure 6.37
Viewing the watercolor effect at 100% reveals the painterly effects that were not apparent at the lower zoom levels.

What Photos are Best Candidates for Painterly Effects?

As a rule, most of the painterly effects work better when the subject matter doesn't have a lot of sharp detail. **Figure 6.38** is the photograph of the girl with a pink bow we used in an earlier exercise. In this exercise, we'll change the photograph into what appears to be a painting that will be included in a family newsletter. You will also see an example where the application of the Artistic filter can be applied directly to the photograph to produce the desired effect.

1. Open the image **Little_girl_with_pink_bow2.jpg**.

2. Choose Filter, Artistic, Watercolor and a dialog opens (**Figure 6.39**). Make sure your settings are close to those shown in Figure 6.39, and then click OK to apply the filter.

3. Next we need to create the appearance that the photograph was painted on canvas. Choose Filter, Texture, Texturizer. When the dialog opens (**Figure 6.40**), choose the Canvas texture (although Sandstone looks good as well). Make sure the Relief setting (controls how high the apparent ridges in the canvas appear) is set to 2 or 3 to ensure a subtle effect, and click OK.

Figure 6.38
This photograph is a good subject for applying a painterly effect.

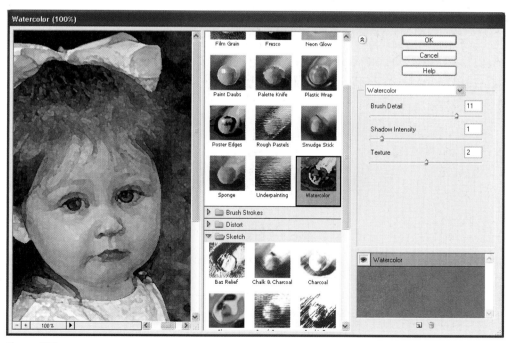

Figure 6.39
From this dialog you can see the effect and also select and apply any of the other Elements filters.

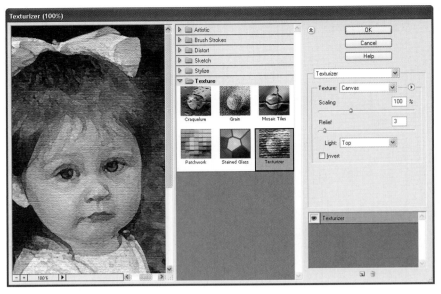

Figure 6.40
The Texturizer gives a great amount of control over the textures that are produced on an image.

4. To complete the illusion, let's give the painting a stroked-edge look. Open the Styles and Effects palette (Window, Styles, and Effects). At the top left, choose Effects. Select Frames on the top right (**Figure 6.41**).

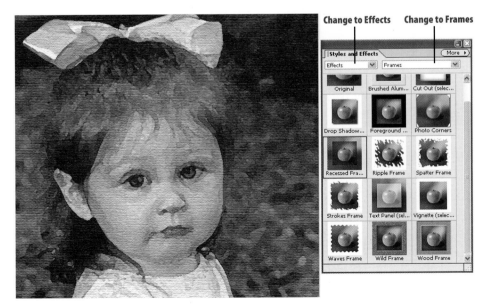

Figure 6.41
Select the Styles and Effects palette.

5. Locate the effect named Spatter Frame in the palette and double-click on it. Elements will add a layer to the image that creates the illusion. Flatten the image (Layer, Flatten Image). When the message box appears asking if you want to Discard Hidden Layers, click OK. The finished painting is shown in **Figure 6.42.**

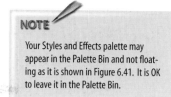

NOTE

Your Styles and Effects palette may appear in the Palette Bin and not floating as it is shown in Figure 6.41. It is OK to leave it in the Palette Bin.

Figure 6.42.
Using the painterly filters in Elements produces an image that appears to be painted.

Controlling Painterly Effects

There are many times when you apply a filter and it doesn't produce the desired effect. Often the problem is that the filter you used applied *too* much filter effect, making the image appear lost in the effect. In Adobe Photoshop, there is a command that lets you dial back the effect of the last command. It is called the Fade command and it's on the top of my list for goodies I want to find its way into Elements. Until Adobe adds the Fade command, here is how to produce the same effect using Elements.

To do the following step-by-step exercise, you will need to download the image **Profile.jpg** from the Peachpit Press Web site.

1. Open the image **Profile.jpg** (**Figure 4.43**). Create a duplicate layer by dragging the background over the Create a New Layer icon in the Layers palette (**Figure 4.44**).

Figure 6.43
The photograph with which we start.

Figure 6.44
Create a copy of the background.

2. With the Background copy still selected in the Layers palette, choose Filter, Sketch, Conte Crayon. When the filter dialog opens, ensure your settings are close to those shown in **Figure 6.45**, and click OK. Suddenly the color photo appears like a charcoal rendering.

Figure 6.45
Apply the Conte Crayon filter.

3. In the Layers palette, change the Opacity to 50%. The effect of the Conte Crayon has been reduced and it looks like a faded color print. Now for the magic: Change the Blend mode in the Layers palette to Luminosity (**Figure 6.46**).

4. To see the before-and-after differences, click on the eye icon to turn the Background copy layer on and off.

The appearance of the final image (**Figure 6.47**) was achieved by reducing the effect of the Conte Crayon filter using a pseudo-Fade command.

Figure 6.46
Reduce the Opacity and change the Blend mode.

Figure 6.47
The completed photograph.

The advantage of this method over the real Photoshop Fade command is that if the image is saved as a Photoshop Elements or TIFF file, the layers are preserved, the original image is left unaltered, and you can fine-tune the effect by changing either the Opacity settings, Blend mode, or both at a later time.

Other Painterly Effects

Often you will encounter photos for which you want to apply one of the effect filters in order to add "punch" to an otherwise flat image.

Figure 6.48 was taken at Pioneer Farms in Austin, Texas (where else?). It is a photograph of the bedroom of a log cabin built back in the mid-1800s. Although the photo looks fine, by using Fresco in the Artistic filers menu (at the default setting), the image appears more rustic (**Figure 6.49**).

Figure 6.48
The log cabin's interior is almost too perfect for the subject matter.

Figure 6.49
Applying the Poster Edge filter gives the photo a more rustic look.

The detail photo of an antique wood-burning stove in **Figure 6.50** is okay, but to bring out the details in the black wrought iron, I applied the Ink Outlines filter (Filter, Brush Strokes, Ink Outline…). In this case, the filter wasn't used to make the photo look like a painting, but to enhance the features of the stove's details to make it suitable for placement in a brochure. The application of the filter brought out the detail without adding enough of an effect to distract viewers (**Figure 10.51**).

For the record, you may have noticed some red and blue areas in the middle of the stove plate (that was me taking the photo). The easiest way to remove the color is to apply the Sponge tool (found in the Toolbox) using Desaturate at 100%. Did you also notice the modern screw is missing? I removed it with the Clone Stamp tool.

Figure 6.50
The detail is hard to see in this close-up photograph of an old wood-burning stove.

Figure 6.51
The application of the Ink Outline filter brings out the details in this photo.

Using Filters to Cover Up Poor Photos

Like it or not, in spite of your best efforts, some photos coming out of your camera are less than perfect. If it makes you feel better, I'm considered a good photographer and I am pleased if I get one great photo out of every fifty I take. Many times, the problem with your photos is out of your control. For example, the carpenter in **Figure 6.52** was in a dimly lit room with light streaming in from behind him. Dim lighting further complicated focusing with a digital camera. As it turned out, the only way to get the shot was to brace the camera against a barn wall and accept the blurriness that accompanies a photo taken at ⅛th of a second. The result was a blurry photo, but that doesn't mean we can't fix it.

Figure 6.52
Normally, a photo like this could never be salvaged, but with the Artistic filters, we can perform a little pixel magic.

The next exercise uses the image file **Carpenter.jpg** which can be downloaded from the Peachpit Press Web site.

1. The first step is to enhance the soft photo prior to applying any of the painterly filters. This is much like putting on stage makeup: It looks grotesque up close, but it looks great from where the audience sits. Apply an obscene amount of Unsharp Masking (Filter, Sharpen, Unsharp Mask) I recommend an amount of 200 percent at a 4-pixel radius. Then, apply an equally obscene amount of Contrast (+40) by selecting Enhance, Adjust Lighting, Brightness and Contrast. It's grotesque at this point (**Figure 6.53**), but it will look better, I promise.

Figure 6.53
Although the amounts of sharpening and contrast are way over the top, the photo was in such poor condition that it looks better.

2. Next, apply the Rough Pastels filter (Filter, Artistic, Rough Pastels) using the default settings.

Figure 6.54
Applying the Rough Pastels filter disguises many of the photo's defects with its painterly effects.

3. Because this man is working at a turn-of-the-century farm, we can apply one final, but optional, touch to make the photo really fit into a brochure about this place: Select the Hue/Saturation control (Ctrl+U/Cmd+U). Check the Colorize check box and change the Hue setting to 50. This creates a sepia-looking print that looks like it belongs in the Old West (**Figure 6.55**).

Figure 6.55
The Colorize feature of the Hue/Saturation command gives the photo an antique appearance.

Framing Your Work

When you go to all the trouble of creating the effect of an image being painted, it sometimes helps to frame the final work of the effect. Photoshop Elements has a collection of frames that are helpful in this regard. To be honest, I have seen better collections than the ones in this product, but I'm not complaining—they came free with Elements.

If you say the word frame, most people think of a wooden rectangle that supports and surrounds a painting or photo. The Frame effects that we used in an earlier exercise provided a rough-edged appearance of a painted work along the edges of an image.

Although the actual frames are somewhat plain, that doesn't mean you can't get creative with them.

The following exercise uses the file **Two_dogs.jpg** which can be downloaded from the Peachpit Press Web site. In this exercise, we will make a color-coordinated frame for the photo of the two dogs.

1. Open the file **Two_dogs.jpg**.

2. The frame we are going to apply uses the current foreground color for the color of the frame. We could pick a color using the Color Picker, instead we are going to sample a color from the photo. Select the Eyedropper tool (I) from the Toolbox. In the Options bar, change the Sample Size to 5 by 5 Average. This will produce foreground color that is an average of the color we choose. Click on any color in the photo that you would like the frame border to be. I chose the pink color in the sofa (**Figure 6.56**).

3. In the Styles and Effects palette (**Figure 6.57**), ensure the palette is set to Effects and Frames. Double-click on the Foreground Color Frame. A 3D-looking frame appears around the photo (**Figure 6.58**).

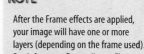

NOTE

After the Frame effects are applied, your image will have one or more layers (depending on the frame used). Don't forget to flatten (Layer, Flatten Image) or you might end up with a very large image file.

Color sample area

Figure 6.56
Use the Eyedropper tool to pick a frame color from the photo.

Double-click here

Set to Effects   **Set to Frames**

Figure 6.57
Styles and Effects palette.

Figure 6.58
The color-coordinated photo frame took less than a minute to create.

Figure 6.59
One of the Frame effects makes the photo appear to have photo corners on it.

Figure 6.59 is an interesting example where the photograph appears like it has photo corners on it.

Painterly Options with Plug-Ins

Several other programs use the plug-in architecture of Photoshop Elements to provide additional painterly effects. One of them, Virtual Painter, costs about half as much as Elements, but it does a fantastic job of creating the illusion of a photo being painted with natural media, such as oils or watercolor. A big advantage of Virtual Painter is its variable brush size that changes to accommodate the physical dimensions of a photo. I included several examples of art that I created using this plug-in (**Figures 6.60** and **6.61**). This program is available at www.jasc.com but it is just one example of many good methods for creating painterly effects.

Figure 6.60
The capitol building of Texas has great hinges on all of its doors. After I took a photo of one, I applied a painterly effect to it.

Figure 6.61
A photo of an oil pump where I applied Virtual Painter's colored pencil effect.

Removing Shadows from Under Hats

Before beginning the next major section which covers more advanced image manipulation, I want to cover the resolution of a common photographic problem that often occurs when taking photos of people wearing hats. If it's a bright sunny day, the smart move is to wear a hat. Unfortunately, the hat that protects the head also creates dark shadows over the face of the wearer as shown in **Figure 6.62.** The best way to eliminate the dark shadows is to prevent them when taking the photo. See the sidebar, "Removing Shadows with Your Camera Using Fill Flash." After the photo has been taken, here is how to do it using Photoshop Elements.

Figure 6.62
The hat protects the wearer from the harsh sun but the dark shadows prevent recognition.

Removing Shadows with Your Camera Using Fill Flash

The two major causes of shadows on the faces of your subjects are a bright light behind the subject (called backlighting) and wide-brimmed hats. Both produce dark shadows that make the subject all but unrecognizable. You could ask the person to take off the hat or face the light source but the result would be a well-exposed photo of someone squinting. There is a better way to preventing these shadows. It is easy and will not cause your subject to go sun-blind. When shooting on a bright sunny day and if there are shadows on the faces of your subject, find the flash control on your camera. It will be a button, knob, dial or an item in the LCD menu. Change the setting to Always On (it may be called Fill Flash). Even though it may seem odd to take a flash photo on a sunny day, you will love the results. The background will be properly exposed and the faces of your subjects will not be in shadows. Just a quick note, when you come indoors don't forget to turn the flash back to automatic.

If you want to work through this exercise, you will need to download the image **Couple_ wearing_hats.jpg** from the Peachpit Press Web site.

Here is the quickest way to eliminate the hat shadows—or any other annoying shadows, for that matter.

1. Open the file **Couple_wearing_hats.jpg.** Remember, our goal is to lighten only the area under the hats. Before Elements 3, the only solution would be to isolate the shadow area with a selection and apply tonal changes. That's still the best-quality solution, but for a tourist photo, the next step is the quick way.

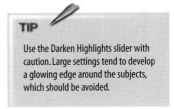

TIP

Use the Darken Highlights slider with caution. Large settings tend to develop a glowing edge around the subjects, which should be avoided.

2. Choose Enhance, Adjust Lighting, Shadows/Highlights and change the Lighten Shadows settings enough to reduce (but not eliminate) the shadows. Also, since there is so much white, move the Darken Highlights slider up just a bit. My settings are shown in **Figure 6.63.** Click OK. The shadows are still there but reduced.

3. Next, select the Dodge tool from the Toolbox. In the Options bar, change the brush size to 100 px, set the Range to Midtones, and put the Exposure at 15%. Now paint the shadow areas under the hats. Voila! That's all it took (**Figure 6.64**).

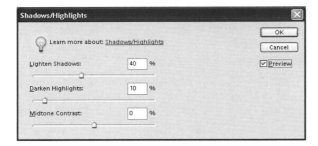

Figure 6.63
Adjust the Darken Highlights slider.

Rearranging and Replacing Objects in Photos

Rearranging objects in a photo is one of the most popular things users like to do with Photoshop Elements. We all have some favorite photos of ourselves or of a loved one that also includes someone we don't want in the picture. Before digital photo editing, removing the "jerk" from the photo was crudely resolved with a pair of scissors. In this section, we learn how to use the many Photoshop Elements selection tools to isolate the part of the photograph that needs to be removed or moved. Because these tools are critical to this type of photo editing, we spend more time learning how and when to use them.

Figure 6.64.
It took less than a few minutes to remove the shadows from underneath their hats.

Harnessing the Power of Selections

Until now, we used selections to isolate color or other image correction needs to a specific area of a photograph. We also used selections for creating special effects, such as a soft-focus background. Most of these selections were simple. To select a complex shape, such as a person or a pet, requires more precision. This is why Photoshop Elements provides a large assortment of tools that enable us to precisely select the portion of the image that we want to work on and protect other parts of the image. To be able to use these tools effectively, we will spend more time than usual learning just how selections work and how to use the tools.

Understanding Selections

As previously mentioned, Photoshop Elements has a large number of different tools whose only purpose is to define the part of the image where we want to work. The defined area is called a selection. All the tools used to make the selections are known as selection tools, with names such as Magnetic Lasso and Magic Wand. If this is your first time using Photoshop Elements, don't let the large number of selection tools and their strange-sounding names overwhelm you. We learn this one step at a time, beginning with a look at what a selection actually is.

The concept of selection is something that we all have used at one time or another. I have heard many analogies to the selection. Here are a few: If you have ever used a stencil, you have used a selection. The stencil enables you to apply paint to the part of the material while protecting the rest of the material. Another example of a selection that's closer to home (literally) is the use of masking tape to mask off parts of a room on which you don't want to get paint—which, for me, would be the whole room. Selections in Photoshop Elements act just like a stencil or masking tape when it comes to applying any effect to an image. So, let's look at the most basic of the selection tools: the Marquee tools.

Introducing Marquee Tools

The Marquee tools shown in **Figure 6.65** appear near the top of the Toolbox. They can be used to create selections in the shapes of rectangles and ellipses. If you access the Options bar, you can also create unique selections in fixed shapes.

Figure 6.65
The Marquee tools are the basic building blocks for many selections.

Although we used these tools in previous chapters, let's see how these basic selection tools can create some neat stuff. For the upcoming exercise, I recommend that you download the file **Sunflower.jpg** from the Peachpit Press Web site (**Figure 6.66**). After you do that, let's jump right in and create a visual effect by producing small glass balls filled with sunflowers. To make them, we use the Elliptical Marquee tool.

1. Open the file named **Sunflower.jpg.**

2. Select the Elliptical Marquee tool in the Toolbox by placing the cursor over the Marquee Tools button and clicking the small black triangle in the lower-right corner of the button. This opens the tool selection. When the pop-up menu appears, click on the tool to select it (**Figure 6.67**).

Figure 6.67
Select the Elliptical Marquee tool.

Figure 6.66
The original photograph
of a sunflower.

3. Place the cursor near the center of the photograph (not in the sunflower). Click and hold the mouse button and, while still holding the button, press and hold both the Shift and the Alt/Option keys. Drag the mouse outwards to form a circle roughly in the position that's shown in **Figure 6.68.** Release the mouse button and then release the keys. The edge of the selection is marked by a flashing black and white marquee that has come to be called "marching ants."

Selection marquee

Figure 6.68
The selection created is a
perfect circle surrounding
the sunflower.

4. Choose Edit, Copy (or Ctrl/Cmd+C). Only the contents of the photo inside the selection will be copied to the Clipboard.

5. Choose Edit, Paste (or Ctrl/Cmd+V) and the selection marquee disappears. Open the Layers palette to see the new layer (**Figure 6.69**). Because we will need the selection that was lost when we used the Paste command, choose Select, Reselect, and the marquee returns. We need this selection to be in place before we apply the next filter or the shape of the sphere will distort.

Figure 6.69
The Layers palette with the new layer added.

6. Select Filter, Distort, Spherize, and use the default setting of 100%. Click OK. The selection enables the Spherize filter to be applied to the top layer without distorting anything else (**Figure 6.70**).

7. Turn off the visible selection marquee (Ctrl/Cmd+H) to make it easier to see what we are doing next. Select the Dodge tool (O) from the Toolbox and, in the Options bar, select a soft brush that is 100 pixels. Make sure that the range is Midtones at 50 percent Exposure. To make this look like a glass sphere, we must lighten the edges. The one I am working on is shown in **Figure 6.71**.

TIP

The trick to this effect is to apply just the edge of the brush inside of the selection edge. As human viewers, we expect there to be more light reflected near the top upper-left part of the sphere, so apply additional stokes of the Dodge tool here.

Figure 6.70
Applying the Spherize filter.

Figure 6.71
Applying the Dodge tool along the edges defines the edge of the selection.

8. Select the Move tool (V) and, while holding the Shift key, click and drag the lower-right handle of the glass ball and make it smaller so that it looks like the one shown in **Figure 6.72.** When it's the correct size, double-click it to apply the resizing (called a transformation).

Figure 6.72
Resize and move the top layer.

9. Now for the fun part. In the Layers palette, select the background, deselect any selection that remains (Ctrl/Cmd+D) and apply the Polar Coordinates filter, which is located in the Distort category of the Filters menu using its Rectangular to Polar setting (the default) (**Figure 6.73**).

Figure 6.73
The finished sunflower in a glass ball on its layer is now independent of the background.

At this point, we have accomplished all we need to demonstrate the technique of selecting an image and using the clipboard to make it into a layer. I finished the image by using the Healing Brush tool to remove the hard vertical line that's produced by the Polar filter.

Next, I selected the sunflower ball and, with the Eraser tool (E) set to a low opacity (17%), I partially erased the background of the sunflower ball so that viewers could get the impression that they were looking through the glass. **Figure 6.74** shows the finished image.

Figure 6.74
This exercise looks like something Salvador Dali would have loved to create.

Using Marquee Tools: Some Tips and Tricks

So, what did we just do in the previous exercise? You used several keyboard combinations, which I didn't explain at the time. Here's what you were actually doing when you used those keys:

- Shift key—When enabled after the mouse button is pushed, the Shift key forces (constrains) the Ellipse tool to a circle and the Rectangle marquee to a square. If you don't do this, it is nearly impossible to get a square- or a circle-shaped selection.

- Alt (Option) key—Depressing this key after the mouse button is clicked makes the marquee produced by the tool expand outward from the center. If you didn't have this option, it could take forever to get the selection centered.

NOTE

At any point while creating a selection (without lifting your finger off the mouse), depressing the spacebar enables you to reposition the selection marquee by dragging it around with your mouse. Release the spacebar and you continue to create the marquee selection

The Marquee tool modifier keys are unique in that the action they perform is relative, depending if they are pressed before or after the mouse button is clicked. If the modifier key is pressed before the mouse button is pressed, the action changes.

The Marquee Tool Options Bar

If this is your first time working with Elements, the Marquee tools might seem to be limited. After all, how often will you need to select a square, rectangle, ellipse, or circle? In fact, you can create about any shape imaginable using these tools if you learn how to use some of the features found in the Options bar, shown in **Figure 6.75**.

Figure 6.75
The Options bar gives the Marquee tools greater capability.

Width/Height (Not Available in Normal Mode)

The Marquee tools interact with existing selections in four different ways. The default setting for the Marquee tools is New Selection. When New Selection is used, any time you make an additional selection, it replaces the current selection (if one exists). The ones you will use most often are the Add To and Subtract settings. Their operations are obvious, I hope. By using the Marquee tools in combination with these modes, it's possible to make almost any irregular shape imaginable. The last setting, Intersect with Selection, is unusual in that, when it is dragged over an existing selection, only the part of the selection that is under the new selection remains.

Feathering the Selections

Until now, we have been considering selections that have a hard and defined edge. The circle mask used in the previous exercise had an anti-aliased option, which feathered (smoothed) the edges of the circle we made (it also works with rounded rectangle selections). Times arise when you want to make a selection that has a soft edge. When you are removing someone or something from one photograph into another by using a feathered selection, the subject being moved blends into the picture more smoothly. Be careful with the amount of feathering you apply to the mask though. Usually, just a few pixels are sufficient. If you put in a large amount of feathering, the object looks like it has a glow or is furry. Feathering produces much softer edges when a subject is copied out of a photograph.

Although many things can be done with the Marquee selection tools, they represent really basic tools. When you need to create an irregular-shaped selection, consider the Lasso tools.

Rounding Up the Lasso Tools

The Lasso tools, which are located under the Marquee tools in the Toolbox, are a collection of three different tools that you can use to draw both straight-edged and freehand edges when making an irregularly-shaped selection. The three tools (shown in **Figure 6.76**) are the Lasso tool, Polygonal Lasso tool, and Magnetic Lasso tool.

Figure 6.76
Unlike the other Marquee tools, the Lasso tools enable you to define any irregular shape that you can draw.

Unlike the Marquee tools, which produce closed shapes, the Lasso tools let you draw a meandering path around a subject and, when you are done, you can either let go of the mouse or double-click it (this depends on the tool you are using) and Photoshop Elements will make a straight line back to the starting point to complete the selection.

The Lasso and Polygonal Lasso Tools

All these tools act in a similar fashion. In the grand scheme of things, the Lasso tool is designed to draw freehand selections and the Polygonal Lasso tool creates a selection made out of many straight lines. Well, in truth, the Lasso tool can act like a Polygonal tool when the Alt/Option key is held; in the same manner, the Polygonal tool operates like a freehand tool when the Alt/Option key is held. So why have both a Freehand and a Polygonal tool? It's a great mystery.

The Magnetic Lasso

The Magnetic Lasso tool is similar to its two Lasso-tool cousins, except it has the capability to automatically detect the edge (in most cases), which can save you so much work. And (do I need to say it?) if you hold the Alt/Option key, it becomes a Freehand tool just like the Lasso tool.

As previously mentioned, the idea behind the operation of the Lasso tools is for you to take your mouse and outline the part of the image you want selected. Most folks use one of the Lasso tools to isolate a part of a photograph so they can copy it into another image. Because you are essentially drawing an outline with a mouse, ask yourself this simple question: Can I sign my name with a mouse? If your answer is yes, you need a date. If your answer is no, and you are going to be creating many selections, seriously consider buying a graphics tablet. The industry standard for graphics tablets is Wacom Technology (www.wacom.com). These tablets used to be expensive, but now some models can be purchased for less than $100. Does this mean that you can't use Lasso selection tools without a graphics tablet? Of course not; it's just much easier if you have one. With that matter settled, let's consider some ideas on how to make better selections.

Getting the Best Selections (In the Least Amount of Time)

Whether doing art layout for work or for community projects (read: free), I have spent the past ten years making selections and the resulting composite images. In that time, I developed a short list of "do's" and "dont's" that I'll share with you to help you make great selections.

Do Make a First Rough Cut Selection

If the image is large enough so that it does not fit on the screen when you view it at 100% (Actual Pixels setting), shift the zoom level to Fit On Screen by either pressing Ctrl/Cmd+0 (zero) or double-clicking the Zoom or Hand tools in the toolbox and making a rough selection. It doesn't matter which selection tool you use. You just want to get as close as you can without spending too much time doing it. This selection gets you in the ballpark.

Zoom and Move

Set the Zoom to Actual Pixels. Use either Ctrl/Cmd+0 (zero) or double-click the Zoom or Hand tools in the toolbox. I know, the image no longer fits on the screen, but it doesn't matter. There are several ways to move around when you're this close, but the best way I know of is to press the spacebar so that your currently selected tool becomes the Hand tool (as long as you keep the spacebar depressed). This is a lifesaver when you are drawing a selection and you find that you have come to the edge of the part displayed on the screen. When that happens, press the spacebar, drag the image to expose more of the subject on the screen, and when you let go of the spacebar, you return to your selection just where you left it.

Adding Some and Taking Some

Using the Add To Selection and Subtract From Selection modes begin to shape the selection to fit the subject you are trying to isolate. Here is a trick that saves time when doing this. First, instead of clicking the buttons in the Options bar, use the key modifiers to change between modes. Pressing the Shift key changes the selection mode to Add To and pressing the Alt (Option) key changes it to Subtract From. Just remember that these modifier keys must be pressed before you click the mouse. Second, in the Options bar, pick Add To as a mode so you need only to use the modifier key when you want to subtract from the selection.

Get in Close

On some areas, you might need to zoom in at levels even greater than 100% (Photoshop goes up to 1,600%, which allows you to select microbes and stray electrons.) Now and again, you must return to Fit To Screen just to keep a perspective on this entire image. Speaking of keeping a perspective, while you are improving the selection keep in mind the ultimate destination for the image you are selecting. Here are some examples of factors that should affect the degree of exactness you want to invest in your selection:

- How close are the background colors of the image you are selecting and the current background colors? If they are roughly the same colors, investing a lot of time producing a detailed selection doesn't make much sense because a feathered edge works just fine.

- Will the final image be larger, smaller, or the same size? If you are going to be making the current image larger, every detail will stick out like a sore thumb. So, any extra time you spend to make the selection as exact as possible will pay off big. If you are reducing the size of the subject, many tiny details will become lost when it's resized, so again, don't invest too much time in the selection.

- Is this a paid job or a freebie? Creating a complex selection is a time-consuming process. I once spent nearly half a day on a single selection.

Let's Lasso Somebody

I can run on about these tools for many more pages, but I am not going to. I'm going to get some coffee while you make what is possibly your first freehand selection. This involves a groomsman named Jonathan in a cluttered church office wearing a ridiculously overpriced rental tuxedo. If his mother is going to frame this photograph, the background must be replaced with something less cluttered.

1. Download and open the picture labeled **Tuxedo_Jon.psd. (Figure 6.77)** I made this sample image much smaller than the original so it wouldn't gag your system.

2. Choose the Magnetic Lasso tool and get as close as you can to the edge of his tuxedo. Click and drag a line around him until it looks like the one that's shown in **Figure 6.78.** If you have any problems with creating the selection with the Magnetic Lasso tool, see the sidebar, "Controlling the Magnetic Lasso." After you are finished, Jon will be selected, but because we need to select the background, *invert the selection* by using Shift+Ctrl(Cmd)+I.

Figure 6.77
Great tux—but a cluttered background.

Figure 6.78
We can quickly select Jon from the background by using the Magnetic Lasso tool.

One of the ways to emphasize the subject is to blur the background using Gaussian blur, which we have done in earlier exercises. In this case, the problem with this method is that the background is so cluttered that by the time you get it blurred enough to do the job, it looks sort of surreal. On top of that, Jon and the couch on his right are the same distance from the camera, so it doesn't look right. Let's solve this by replacing the background with a different one.

3 Download and open the file **Background.jpg.** When it opens, select the entire image (Ctrl/Cmd+A), copy the image to the clipboard, (Ctrl/Cmd+C) and close the image. Don't save the changes when asked.

4. With Jon's photo selected, choose Edit, Paste Into Selection. Wow—the photograph has replaced the previously cluttered one! Select the Move tool (V) in the Toolbox, and move the background image around to position it, as shown in **Figure 6.79.**

Using a selection allows for a background replacement without losing the original background.

Figure 6.79
The new background is less cluttered than the original.

Controlling the Magnetic Lasso

The Magnetic Lasso tool is a great timesaver when it comes to making selections. Essentially, as you move the tool along an edge that you want to select, the tool is constantly looking for and creating a selection along the edge. On a high contrast, well-defined edge, it works better than advertised. On edges that are poorly defined, in that the colors inside and outside the edge are very near the same color, it needs some help from you.

Using the tool is relatively simple. Click once on the point where you want to begin the selection. This point is called a fastening point. Now, move the tool (slowly and without holding the mouse button) along the edge. Fastening points appear along the edge of the selection as the computer tries to automatically determine where the edge is. At some point, the computer will guess wrong. When it does, stop and press the backspace key.

Each time you press this key, Photoshop removes the last point on the selection. Continue to do this until you get to a point on the selection that is on the actual edge. You can try it again, but usually, when the Magnetic tool is guessing wrong, there's either a low-contrast edge or there is something nearby (not on the edge) that is pulling the tool away from the edge.

At this point, you have several choices. You can change the settings in the Options bar, click your way through it (I'll explain in a moment), or temporarily change Lasso tools. I rarely recommend changing the options settings. So, here is what I recommend you try. When you hit a rough patch, if the edge is irregular (lots of ins and outs), you can click each of the points that define the edge, which puts them closely together. Another option is to temporarily switch to the Lasso tool by holding the Alt (Option) key and dragging the mouse along the edge with the mouse button depressed. In images where the subject being selected is close to the color of the background so that it blends with the shadows or background, the Magnetic Lasso tool might not be the best tool to use. To get a good selection, the Magnetic Lasso tool needs a fairly distinctive edge with which to work.

Saving and Loading Selections

After making a selection, you can save it as a Photoshop Elements or TIFF file. If a selection is not saved as a selection, it is lost as soon as the file is closed, even if the file is saved as a Photoshop PSD file.

Saving a Selection

After spending much time creating a selection, as a rule, you'll want to save it. Choose Select, Save Selection. This action opens the dialog that's shown in **Figure 6.80.** If the image already has an existing channel, you can add your new selection to the existing one, or more than likely, you will be saving to a new channel. Choose New and give the channel a descriptive name. In the case of the one in Figure 12.14, I used the one of Michelle that you saw back in Figure 12.9. Three selections were already stored in the

The Alpha Channel

So how do you save a selection? If you invest a lot of time making a selection, it seems reasonable that you would want to save it. The process is simple, but before I tell you how to do it, I must introduce a term that you might have heard before: the alpha channel. Sounds like the name of a science fiction-oriented program channel on your local cable TV. The alpha channel is not a channel at all, but the name assigned by Apple (who created it) for additional storage space in a graphics file format called Tagged Image Format File (TIFF). Why is it called alpha channel? The truth be known. When Apple created the concept of the channel, they weren't sure what it was going to be used for until Adobe latched on to it and made it into the general purpose storage for selections (and what all that has become). Although it is still technically referred to as an alpha channel to differentiate it from the red, green, and blue channels, Adobe and the rest of those working in the graphics industry just call it a channel. How many alpha channels can fit into a Photoshop Elements file? Good question—how big of a file can you live with? For all practical purposes, there's no limit to the number of additional channels that can be included in a TIFF or Photoshop file.

image, but there's always room for a new one. You must save the image as a Photoshop (PSD) or a TIFF file to save the channel information. If you don't, Photoshop Elements gives you a single obscure warning that some features will not be saved in the format that you have chosen.

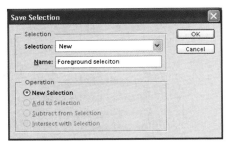

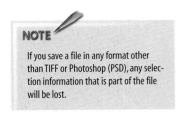

NOTE

If you save a file in any format other than TIFF or Photoshop (PSD), any selection information that is part of the file will be lost.

Figure 6.80
The Save Selection dialog.

Loading a Selection

The next time you open the file, the selection won't be on the image. To get it, you must choose Select, Load Selection, and pick the name of the alpha channel that you or someone else tucked away into the image. This might surprise you, but many stock photography companies offer selections in their photos. Two different companies that offer photographs with selections that immediately come to mind are Photospin (www.photospin.com), which is a great online photo subscription service, and Hemera (www.hemera.com), which offers large collections of photo objects on CDs (lots and lots of CDs).

Magic Wand Tool Magic

The Magic Wand tool is great for making selections of areas containing similar colors. The problem with this tool is not the tool itself, but the fact that many users have no idea how it works and, therefore, are disappointed when the "magic" doesn't work. So, let's figure out how this tool works and then do some cool stuff with it.

The first fact to learn about the Magic Wand tool is—no magic! (Were you surprised?) Until now, all the selection tools we used involved either closed shapes or lassos that surround the subject to be selected. The Magic Wand tool acts a little like dropping a stone into a calm pool of water. The selection, like ripples of water, spreads outward from the starting point. It continues radiating outward, selecting similar (and adjacent) colored pixels until it reaches pixels where the color and shade is so different from the starting point that they can't be included. If you complete the next exercise, the Magic Wand tool will make more sense.

An Exercise in Pane (Window Pane, That Is)

In this exercise, we use the Magic Wand tool (W) and a few other Photoshop Elements features to create a photo composite from two photographs. In this case, I have an excellent exterior photo taken on a bright summer day in a rural Texas town, but I cannot see inside the building. I also have a good photo I took of a stairway in Ybor City, Florida. Our job is to combine the two images into a photo. This newly created photo will be used in a brochure to make people aware of problems with urban decay in the inner city.

1. Download and open the file named **Old_windows.jpg** (**Figure 6.81**) and select the Magic Wand tool (located in the Toolbox).

Figure 6.81
Original photo of darkened windows in Texas.

2. Ensure the Contiguous check box in the Options bar is checked and change the Tolerance setting to 30. Click in the center window pane. The selection instantly expands to select all the black pixels in the pane, as shown in **Figure 6.82.** Because the Contiguous check box was enabled, the selection had to stop at the edge of the window pane.

Figure 6.82
The Magic Wand tool quickly selects all the black pixels in the single window pane.

3. To select the rest of the window panes, choose Select, Similar. Now Photoshop Elements selects all the pixels in the image that are within the Tolerance setting. Because no other black pixels are in the image, all the pixels in the window panes are selected (see **Figure 6.83**).

Figure 6.83
The Select, Similar command quickly selects all the black pixels in this photograph.

4. Download and open the file named **Old_stairs.jpg** (**Figure 6.84**). Select the entire image (Ctrl/Cmd+A). Copy the image to the clipboard (Ctrl/Cmd+C). Close the file without saving any changes.

NOTE

When you use the Paste into Selection command, the original selection disappears and is replaced with a single rectangular selection marquee.

5. With the Old Windows image selected, choose Edit, Paste Into Selection. The photograph of the stairs now appears to be viewable through the window panes, as shown in **Figure 6.85.** With the Move tool, you can move the stairs photograph around.

Figure 6.84
Photo of an old stairway in Florida.

Figure 6.85
Using the Paste Into Selection command, we are able to put stairs into the window.

Tips About Using the Magic Wand Tool

One of the first things you might run into when working with the Magic Wand tool is this: You click in an area and the Magic Wand tool will not produce a uniform selection, but will instead create many little selections. These little selection "islands" are caused when the difference between the color value of the starting point is greater than the color value of the pixels that make up these islands. You can resolve this issue in several ways. You could click all the individual points with the Magic Wand tool until they are all gone. However, that is not the most efficient way to do it, and I am embarrassed to admit how many times I have done just that. Here is the right way to do it: If the colors you are selecting are really different from the rest of the image, you can either choose Select, Similar or try increasing the Tolerance setting and try reselecting the same area. The problem with both of these approaches is that, many times, the selection begins to appear in the part of the image that we do not want selected. If the selection goes too far into the part of the image that you don't want selected (especially at the edge), here's another trick you can try. Did you know that when you use the Similar command, Photoshop Elements uses the current Tolerance setting to determine which pixels can be included in the selection? This means that after you do an initial selection with the Magic Wand tool, you can lower the Tolerance setting to a low value, such as 4 to 8, and when you use Similar, it adds only colors that are much closer to the original starting point. Still, sometimes the selection islands are there because areas of vastly different colors exist. In this case, select a Marquee tool, hold the Shift key (Add To Selection), and drag a selection shape over the islands. That should resolve the issue.

Replacing an Overcast Sky

Taking photographs on an overcast day is always a mixed blessing. Because of the clouds, the illumination is diffused—that's good. But because of the clouds, the horizon on a landscape photograph is uninteresting at best. Using the Magic Wand selection tool you can replace most overcast skies with an artificial one that you create either by using Photoshop Elements or using another photograph of a sky with clouds taken on a clear day.

Here's how it is done using Elements.

1. Download and open the file **Rest_in_peace.psd.** Choose the Magic Wand tool (W) in the Toolbox. Change the Tolerance setting to 70. This high setting ensures that all the areas around the branches will be tightly selected. (If you want, you can load the finished selection that is contained in the file.) Uncheck the Contiguous box in the Options bar. Click the tool on the sky in the upper-right quadrant. The initial selection made by the Magic Wand tool also selected some flowers and other parts of the photo besides the sky (**Figure 6.86**). We'll fix that in the next step.

2. Choose the Rectangle Marquee tool. In the Options bar, click on the Subtract From Selection button. Click and drag a marquee over all the area in the lower part of the photograph that doesn't contain any sky. Now only the sky is selected. Personally, I find the selection marquee distracting, so you might want to turn it off (Ctrl/Cmd+H).

Figure 6.86
The Magic Wand tool selects all of the overcast sky and more.

3. Open the file **Clouds.jpg** (**Figure 6.87**). Select the entire image (Ctrl/Cmd+A) and copy it to the clipboard (Ctrl/Cmd+C). Close the image without saving it.

Figure 6.87
A photo taken of clouds on a sunny day.

4. Now, go back to the original image. From the Edit menu, choose Paste Into Selection (Shift+Ctrl/Cmd+V) and the contents of the clipboard appear in the selection.

5. We're not done yet—this is the cool part. Select the Move tool (V) and click the sky that you just added. You can drag it around the selection. In **Figure 6.88**, I moved it up as far as I could so the clouds matched the existing foreground better. When the replacement sky is where you want it, remove the selection (Ctrl/Cmd+D). It becomes a permanent part of the image.

Figure 6.88
Using the Move tool, you can position the replacement sky inside of the selection.

In this last section, we learned how to use the selection tools to isolate parts of an image so that we can remove or replace them with something else. We learned that although making a selection can be time consuming, it is possible to save the selection as part of the Photoshop Elements file format (*.psd) so that all the work you invested into the selection isn't lost. It might take you some practice to get good at making selections, but the time that you invest in this all-important skill will help you make better compositions and montages with your photographs.

Correcting Distortion in Photos

When you take a photo of any building (your house, university, or anything large), a certain amount of distortion is introduced into the photo. When you stand in front of a large building looking up, the distortion is apparent, as shown in **Figure 6.89.** The top of the building appears to be smaller than the bottom. This distortion, where one end of the image appears either smaller or larger based on its position in relation to the camera lens, is called *keystone distortion*. The distortion in the photo is due to where I was standing in relation to the subject.

Figure 6.89
The distortion created by taking this photograph at an angle is obvious.

Distortion is more common than you might imagine. Most digital cameras have zoom lenses that act as very wide-angle lenses when they are zoomed back to their widest settings. The downside is that while these wide settings of the zoom lens captures more of the scene in every photo, it also introduces distortion called *barrel distortion*. **Figure 6.90** is a photograph I took of buildings in downtown Chicago using a digital camera at the widest setting of its zoom lens. Those buildings weren't leaning inward when I took the photo so the leaning effect must have been caused by barrel distortion.

Figure 6.90
Barrel distortion of the camera lens causes the buildings to appear as if they are leaning inward toward the center of the photo.

Correcting Keystone Distortion

Correcting keystone distortion in a photograph with Photoshop Elements is simple if you know how to do it. The first keystone correction exercise requires the image file **US_Supreme_Court.jpg** which is available from the Peachpit Press Web site. Here is how to do it.

1. Open the file **US_Supreme_Court.jpg.**

2. Make a background copy layer by dragging the background to the Create a New Layer icon (**Figure 6.91**).

3. Turn on the Grid (View, Grid) (**Figure 6.92**).

Drag the background to the Create a New Layer icon

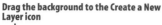

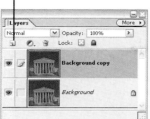

Figure 6.91
The first step is to make a copy of the background.

Figure 6.92
Turning on the Grid provides a visual reference.

4. Select the Zoom tool. While holding down the Alt (Option) key, click on the photo until the image is reduced in size compared to the background as shown in **Figure 6.93.** Now, to be able to see the handles necessary to make the correction, make the image window larger than the photo. This step is critical for all distortion corrections because much of the work that will be done occurs outside the borders of the photo.

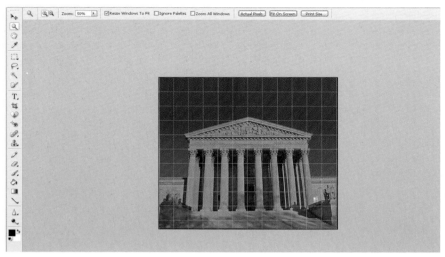

Figure 6.93
Zooming out is an essential next step.

5. With the top layer selected, choose Image, Transform, Distort. Reshape the front of the Supreme Court by grabbing the top corners and dragging it until the photo looks like the one shown in **Figure 6.94.**

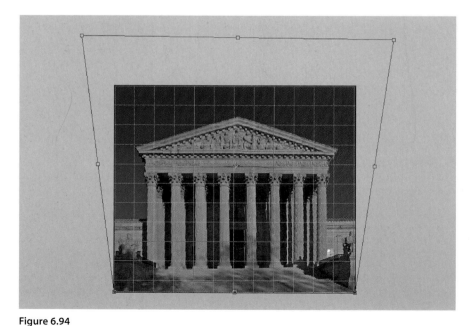

Figure 6.94
After making a background layer, we drag the corners of the image window to make it larger—not the image, just the image window.

6. When the pillars are lined up with the grid and the horizontal lines of the front of the court are also lined up with the horizontal section of the grid, double-click it. After a few moments, the transformation is applied, like the one shown in **Figure 6.95.** By using the Distort transform on the layer, we removed much of the keystoning in this photo.

Figure 6.95
The keystone distortion is removed in six simple steps.

I am just guessing here but the odds are that you will never want to remove keystone distortion from a photo of the Supreme Court. However, you may want to correct a photo of a property that you want to sell. The photo shown in **Figure 6.96** is a close up of a front porch. While there is some minor barrel distortion in this photo, it is the keystone distortion that is pretty obvious in the photo.

Figure 6.96
This close up of a porch shows keystone distortion.

Using the same technique used to correct the keystone distortion in the Supreme Court building, this humble Texas porch looks much better after the keystone distortion is corrected (**Figure 6.97**).

Figure 6.97
Correcting the keystone distortion improves the overall appearance of the property in this photo.

Reducing Barrel Distortion

Unlike the keystone effect, barrel distortion is not easily removed. This is because the distortion is not uniform throughout the photo. The photo of the door to the U.S. Federal bank in St. Louis (they built great-looking doors back in the '20s and '30s) shows the effect of distortion (**Figure 6.98**).

Figure 6.98
This photo of a door shows the subtle effect of barrel distortion.

Notice how the center of the door appears to be very slightly pushed out toward the camera. On the surface this seems like a minor problem. Let's face it, most people don't take photos of doors or care if they are slightly distorted. The problem is that when taking photos of people, barrel distortion makes people appear pushed out in the center as well. The result is they appear rounder or, if you have their face in the center of the photo, their nose actually appears larger. **Figure 6.99** appears to be a normal close-up photo of an individual until the barrel distortion is reduced, making the subject appear like he really looks (**Figure 6.100**).

Figure 6.99
Photo appears normal.

Figure 6.100
When the barrel distortion is reduced, the appearance of the subject is improved.

The reason barrel distortion is difficult to remove is because the distortion is introduced by a circular lens and the sensor is rectangular in its shape. Although, it can be significantly reduced. The following exercise uses a photo I took of a door that was painted on a boarded-up entrance to the St. Louis Opera House. Download the image **Opera_door.jpg.** Here is how to reduce barrel distortion.

1. Open the image **Opera_door.jpg** (**Figure 6.101**).

2. Since the distortion is concentrated on the center of the image, the first step is to create a selection that will limit the filter action to the center of the image. Select the Elliptical Marquee tool in the Toolbox. Place the cursor in the center of the photo and while holding down the Alt (Option)+Shift keys, drag out a circle selection until the edges of the selection touch the top and bottom of the image as shown in **Figure 6.102.**

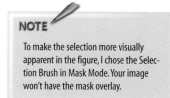

NOTE

To make the selection more visually apparent in the figure, I chose the Selection Brush in Mask Mode. Your image won't have the mask overlay.

Figure 6.101
Barrel distortion has pushed out the center of this photo.

Figure 6.102
Create a circular selection that limits the correction to the center of the image.

3. To reduce the barrel distortion, we will use the Pinch filter. Just select Filter, Distort, Pinch, and make the setting 23%, as shown in **Figure 6.103.** This filter action removes much of the barrel distortion (**Figure 6.104**).

The Pinch filter coupled with a circle selection is effective in reducing the effect of barrel distortion. If you do a lot of work with images that require correction for either keystone or barrel distortion, you should consider obtaining a plug-in filter designed specifically to remove it. The filter is called Lens Doc and is available from Andromeda.com (www.andromeda.com). I have used this filter and find it is the best for removing most forms of lens distortion.

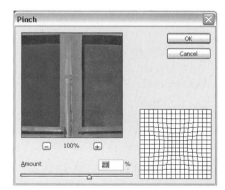

Figure 6.103
The Pinch filter is great for reducing barrel distortion in photos taken with a wide-angle camera lens.

Figure 6.104
The barrel distortion has been significantly reduced.

In the next chapter, we jump into the art form that will make your photography very popular— retouching photographs. This is the neat stuff that makes those of us who are older, look younger (which I greatly appreciate) and also tidies up physical imperfections.

7 Fun with Type, Shapes, and Cookie Cutter Tools

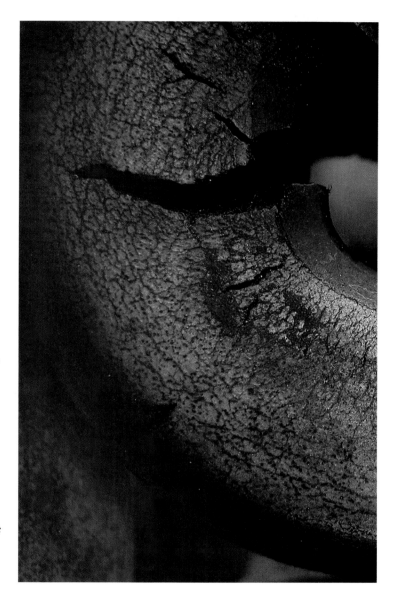

Once your photos are picture-perfect—or nearly so—you can become creative with them. This chapter shows some of the amazing things that you can add to, or do, with the Type, Shape, and new Cookie Cutter tools in Photoshop Elements 3. The Type tool lets you add text to photos for everything from titles, photo credits, and captions. The Shape tools give you the ability to create and add both geometric and custom shapes. The new Cookie Cutter tool lets you quickly change a photo into a shape that you can further modify using Layer styles.

We'll begin by tackling the Type tool, which lets us add text to any image we are working on. Let's start with something simple, like adding some simple text, and work up to more complicated effects.

Before we begin, you need to understand an important concept about working with both text and shapes. Text and shapes are unique in Photoshop Elements because they are vector based, meaning that they are composed of mathematical paths rather than pixels. This is important for two reasons: First, the text and shapes can be resized, twisted, and distorted without any loss of quality. Second, some effects in Elements cannot be applied to a type or shape layer without first converting the layer into pixels—a process called *simplifying a layer.*

Adding Text

The easiest place to start learning how to do tricks with text is simply finding out how to add text and how to edit that text after it's in your photos.

Adding text to a photo has many uses. You can add titles, descriptions, silly stuff, or copyright information. The first example (**Figure 7.1**) is of a youngster who had been left with Daddy to baby-sit while Mommy went to exercise. The expression and the mess make a great picture, but some text explaining the cause of the mess will make it even better.

Figure 7.1
A picture may be worth a thousand words, but adding a few words usually improves the picture.

The Layers Palette

Before we begin the first exercise, it must be noted that I'm a huge believer in setting the Layers palette to be always visible while working. I'll show you how to find and open your Layers palette, if you haven't already found it, before getting to this point in the book. Leave the Layers palette visible in your Palette Bin throughout this chapter because I assume that it's easily within your view through the remaining exercises. By the time you finish this chapter, you might understand why I find this palette the coolest thing since sliced bread.

The Layers palette (**Figure 7.2**) enables you to see text and images that are on separate layers. Think of layers as analogous to the sheets of clear acetate that are used with overhead projectors. If you have drawn an object on one layer (or sheet), you can move it around independently of the objects drawn on the other layers (or sheets). This allows for great flexibility and power while working with your images.

Figure 7.2
The Layers palette lets you see and control the layers in an image.

To open the Layers palette, go to the Window menu and choose Layers to view the Layers palette. If the palette is not docked in the Palette Bin, drag the Layers tab into the Palette Bin to save space on your screen. You can group the Layers (or any) palette into the Palette Bin by dragging its tag into the Palette Bin.

How to Add Text:

1. Open your own image that you would like to use in this exercise or download the image **Messy_baby.jpg** from the Peachpit Press Web page. Press D to set the default foreground and background colors to black and white.

2. Select the Horizontal Type tool (T) in the Toolbox, and the cursor changes into a text bar. The size and font of the type is controlled in the Type Options bar. The example uses the font Impact at a size of 18 points. Click on the image where you want to insert the text and begin to type.

3. When you have finished entering or editing text, click the Commit checkmark icon at the end of the Options bar. Elements will not let you use any other tool until you do so.

4. After inserting the text, a Type layer appears in the Layers palette floating above the background, as shown in **Figure 7.3**. As long as the text remains a Type layer, you can go back and edit it.

NOTE

The icons that appear in the Type Options bar change depending on if you are inserting text or editing existing text.

Figure 7.3
Adding commentary using the Type tool adds to the overall impact of a photo.

That's all that is necessary to place text in a photo. If this is all you want to do, before you save the image, you need to make a decision about the Type layer.

If you think you will want to make any changes to the text at a later date, then use File > Save As and choose Photoshop or TIFF as the format. This way the text remains as an editable Type layer. If you don't think you will ever want to make changes, or if you want to send this as an email (to everyone you know), you need to flatten the layer (Layer > Flatten Image) and save it as a JPEG.

Twisting and Reshaping Text

The text we applied to the baby picture earlier in the chapter used the Horizontal Type tool. There is also a Vertical Type tool that aligns each letter one on top of another. I don't recommend using it, because visually, it is best used with Asian characters. So if you need text to run vertically let's look at a creative alternative.

In this exercise we are going to make a poster and place the name of the tall ship (**Figure 7.4**) running from top to bottom against the blue sky, without using the Vertical Type tool.

1. Download and open the file named **Tall_ship.jpg**.

2. Press D to ensure the default colors are black and white, and then press X to switch the colors—making the foreground color white.

Figure 7.4
In this exercise you will learn to rotate and resize text to fit this photo.

3. Select the Type tool (T) and set the font to Impact at a size of 12 points in the Options bar. Click in the middle of the image and enter the name of the ship— Star of India. Click the Commit checkmark when finished.

4. Select the Move tool (V), and a bounding box with handles appears around the text as shown in closeup in **Figure 7.5**.

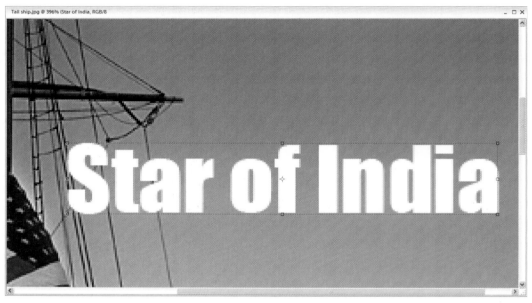

Figure 7.5
The bounding box surrounding the text provides a fast way to rotate and transform text.

5. Position the cursor just outside of a corner of the bounding box until the cursor becomes a double-headed curved arrow (indicating rotation). Holding down the Shift key to constrain the rotation to 45-degree increments, click and rotate the text until it looks like **Figure 7.6**. Release the mouse button *before* releasing the Shift key.

6. Holding down the Shift key again, grab any corner handle and resize the text until it looks like **Figure 7.7**. Click the Commit checkmark in the Options bar to complete the transformation. You can use the Move tool to position the text exactly where you want it in the image.

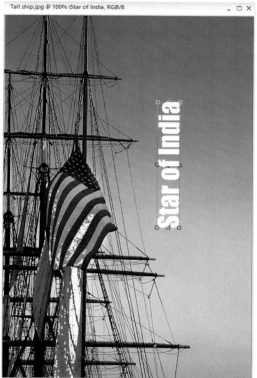

Figure 7.6
Rotate the text 90 degrees to the left using the handles of the bounding box.

Figure 7.7
Resizing using the transform handles is quick and easy.

7. To make the text stand out more from the background, you can add a drop shadow to the text using a Layer Style. Select the Type tool again, and click on the Type layer in the Layers palette to select it, then click on the Style box in the Options bar, which opens a large bunch of choices as shown in **Figure 7.8**. Pick the Style called Low (for low shadow), and it is applied immediately.

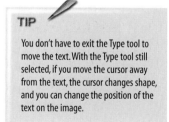

TIP

You don't have to exit the Type tool to move the text. With the Type tool still selected, if you move the cursor away from the text, the cursor changes shape, and you can change the position of the text on the image.

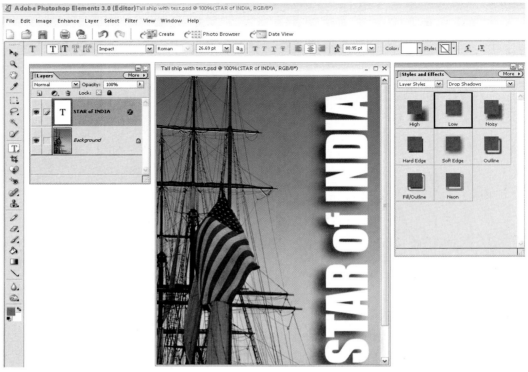

Figure 7.8
Using a Layer Style adds emphasis to the text.

Figure 7.9 is my finished project. As you can see, I added an additional line of text using a smaller font than that used for the ship's name. After rotating the text, I stretched it so its ends were even with the larger text by dragging the bounding box on either end of the text.

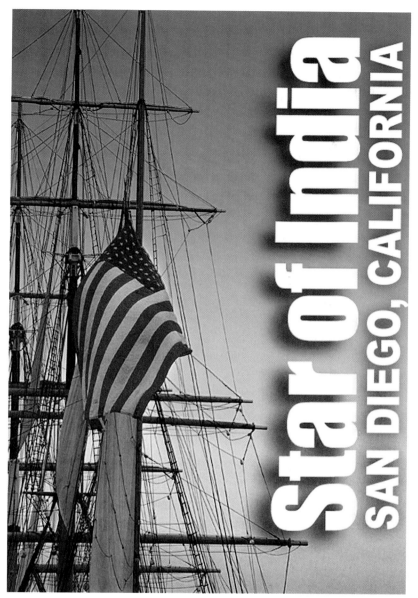

Figure 7.9
This finished poster took less than five minutes to create and position all of the text.

Manipulating Text

Editing text on a Text layer is relatively straightforward. If you want to change the text, simply choose the Type tool, click in the text area where you want to make changes, and then add or delete the necessary text. The Esc key cancels out any changes you make to your text. (In other words, if you change your mind and decide you don't like the changes, the Escape key is your best friend.) The Enter key (Return key for Mac) on the numeric keypad (or Ctrl+Enter) accepts any changes that are made to text.

TIP

If you prefer to click icons instead of using keyboard shortcuts, the universal red bar through the icon (Cancel) rejects changes, and the Commit checkmark icon, found at the top right of the Options bar, accepts changes.

Formatting Text

The basic text formatting options include the following:

- Font Options. Font, style, and size are all controlled in the Options bar. Their operation is pretty self-explanatory. By default, type size is displayed in points (72 pts = 1 inch).

- Leading. This is a new feature in Elements 3. Leading provides the ability to control the spacing between lines. Found in the Options bar, this only works when the text you enter covers several lines.

- Color. The color of the selected type is determined by the current foreground color. You can change that color in several ways:

- Clicking the down arrow next to the Color swatch in the Type Options bar opens the color menu, a palette of pre-set colors (**Figure 7.10**).

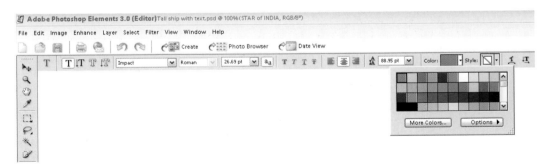

Figure 7.10
The Color menu provides a quick way to select a font color.

- Clicking on the Color swatch in the Options bar or clicking the Foreground Color swatch in the Toolbox opens the Color Picker (**Figure 7.11**). With the Color Picker open, you can visually select a color from the palette by clicking on it or define a color using the data boxes—yeah, that's going to happen.

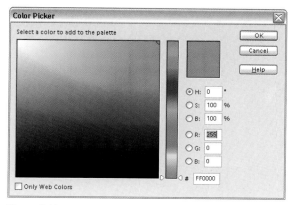

Figure 7.11
The Color Picker allows you to define any color you can imagine.

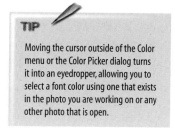

TIP

Moving the cursor outside of the Color menu or the Color Picker dialog turns it into an eyedropper, allowing you to select a font color using one that exists in the photo you are working on or any other photo that is open.

How to Format Text

To change the text in a Type layer, you must first select the text you want to change. This is done by the following:

1. Select the Type tool (T).

2. Either triple-click the text to select all of the type, or click and drag the part of the text that you want to change.

3. Change the font or size, or choose a new color using the Font color in the Type Options bar. Click the Color swatch, and when the Color Picker opens, select a color or position the cursor (which becomes an eyedropper) over the desired color in an open image. Click the selected color to make it the current foreground color. When you have the color you want, click the Commit checkmark to apply the color.

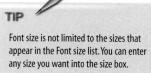

TIP

Font size is not limited to the sizes that appear in the Font size list. You can enter any size you want into the size box.

Quick and Easy Ways to Change Text

To avoid the hassle of first highlighting the text, just click the Type layer in the Layers palette and, with the Type tool active, make the changes on the Options bar. Your changes are applied universally to all the text on that layer only.

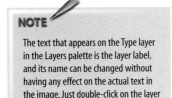

NOTE

The text that appears on the Type layer in the Layers palette is the layer label, and its name can be changed without having any effect on the actual text in the image. Just double-click on the layer and rename it.

Making Text Stand Out from the Background

You may have noticed a small problem with the text we added to the baby photo earlier in Figure 7.3. Part of the dark text was in front of a dark background and therefore wasn't easy to read. Changing the color of the text to white and adding a Drop Shadow layer style is one way to make the text stand out from a similar background (**Figure 7.12**).

Figure 7.12
Changing the color of the type and adding a Shadow layer style make the text stand out from the background.

Cool Effects Using Style Layers

Up until now, we have used Style layers to make drop shadows behind the text. Now let's learn some more about Style layers and see what else can be done with these wonders.

First, Style layers can be selected in the Type Options bar (with the Type tool active) or you can select them from the Style layers palette. Here is how it is done:

1. Enter text on an image using the Type tool and finish by clicking the Commit checkmark icon. I have shown an example in **Figure 7.13**.

2. Open the Styles and Effects palette in the Window menu. Make sure the category selector at the top of the palette is set to Layer Styles and the Library Selector box next to it is set to All (allowing you to see all of the Style layer libraries).

3. Scroll down the palette and pick one of the Wow-Plastic Styles and click it. The text changes immediately (**Figure 7.14**).

Figure 7.13
An example of text in a Type layer.

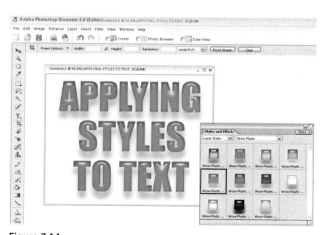

Figure 7.14
Applying one of the many Styles available in Elements 3 dramatically changes the appearance of the text.

Things to Know About Style Layers

Style layers can be used to create a wide variety of effects for both text and shapes (we discuss shapes next). The Photoshop Elements User Guide and the online help provide a lot of detailed information about all their ins and outs. Here are some basic things to know about using them:

- **Undoing a Style**. To undo the last application of a Style, click the Step Backward icon in the menu.

- **Styles are Cumulative**. You can apply multiple styles to text or a shape. When some styles are applied, they replace or modify the effect of similar styles. For example, in **Figure 7.15**, if any other Wow-Plastic styles are applied, the new style completely replaces the existing style. If a drop shadow is applied (Figure 7.15), the text remains unchanged, but the new drop shadow replaces the tinted one.

- **Styles are Adjustable**. Each style can be individually adjusted after it is applied. This is most important when applying drop shadows. The next section shows how to modify the style.

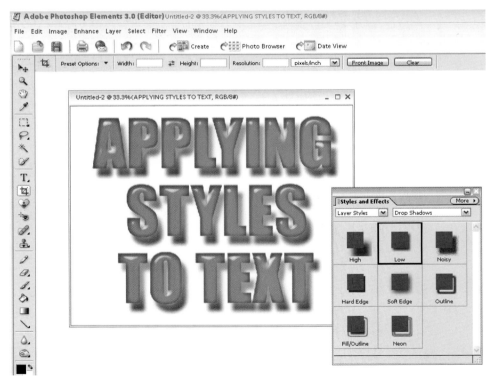

Figure 7.15
Multiple styles can be applied to the same layer.

How to Modify a Style

After a style is applied to a layer, an icon appears on the right side of the layer. Double-clicking the icon opens the Style Settings dialog (**Figure 7.16**). With Drop Shadow styles you can control the direction the light is coming from (Lighting Angle) and how far the shadow appears from the text or shape (Shadow Distance). The other controls maybe grayed out because they are used by the drop shadow.

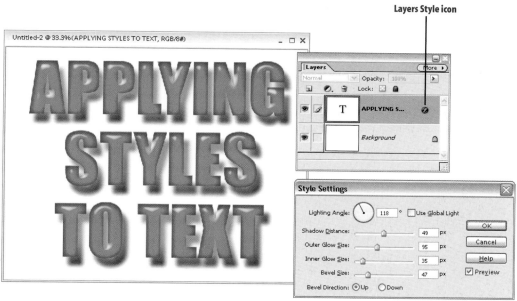

Figure 7.16
The Style Settings dialog controls the appearance of a Style.

Styles are real time-wasters. By that, I mean there is so much you can do with them, you will end up spending a lot of time just playing with them. I have created a small sampling of a few of the styles in **Figure 7.17**.

Using Shapes

A feature in Photoshop Elements that is similar to the Type tool is the Shape tools feature, which is used to create all types of geometric and custom shapes. The control and configuration of these tools are covered in painful detail in both the Elements 3.0 User Guide and in the online help. In this section of the chapter, we will learn how to do some cool things with the tools.

Figure 7.17
The effects you can create using Styles are astounding.

Adding Comic Book Balloons to Photos

Earlier in this chapter, we covered the topic of adding text over a photo. Now, using the Custom Shape tool, we'll learn how to make the subject speak by adding a comic book style balloon to the image. Here is how it's done:

1. Download and open the file **Sleeper_and_puppy.jpg**.

2. Select the Shape tool (U) in the Toolbox. From the Options bar click the Custom Shape tool (**Figure 7.18**), and then click the down arrow next to the Shape option to open the Custom Shape picker.

3. Select the thought balloon near the bottom of the list (Thought 2). Change the color to white. Somewhere near the puppy's head, click and drag a shape like the one shown in **Figure 7.19**. A Shape layer has been added to the Layers palette.

4. Select the Type tool and change the font to Comic Sans MS at a size of 12 points. The leading should be set to Auto, which might create line spacing that is too large to fit into the thought balloon. You can change it to any value from the Options bar. I used 11 points in the example (**Figure 7.20**), which makes the lines closer together and fits better in the balloon. Enter the text and click the Commit checkmark.

Figure 7.18
Selecting a Custom Shape.

Figure 7.19
A thought balloon is easy to create with the Custom Shape tool.

Leading is set here

Figure 7.20
The ability to adjust leading allows more text to be fit into multiple lines.

5. Since the thought balloon is white and the sleeper's shirt is white, we need to make the balloon stand out from the background. Apply the Soft Edge Layer style by clicking the Style button in the Options bar and clicking Soft Edge. Since you will probably always want the thought balloon and the text together, click the cursor in the blank box next to the Type layer, and a small chain icon appears. The two layers are now linked (**Figure 7.21**).

Figure 7.21
Linking the Type and Shape layers groups them together.

Identifying Parts of a Photo with Shapes

Shape tools are great for identifying parts of a photograph. The uses are almost limitless, whether it's showing a specific location on a circuit board for a science project (**Figure 7.22**) or something silly (**Figure 7.24**).

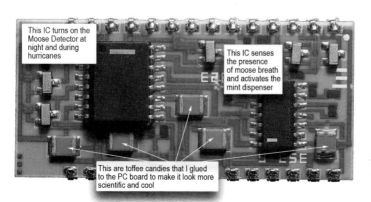

Figure 7.22.
The Shape tools are useful for identifying specific points on an image.

Line Shape tool **Options**

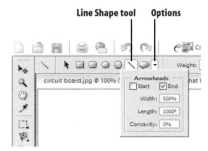

Figure 7.23
The Options button of the Line Shape tool opens the Arrowhead choices.

The rectangles in **Figure 7.22** are made with the Rectangle Shape tool. Making lines with arrowheads is not as obvious. Here is how it's done:

1. Select the Line shape tool in the Shape tool Options bar (**Figure 7.23**).

2. Click the Geometry Options button and by checking or unchecking it, you can determine if lines drawn using the Line Shape tool have arrowheads or not.

Figure 7.24
This is a fun way to make sure viewers see you actually were on vacation.

Simplifying Type and Shape Layers

When you attempt to apply an effect that cannot be applied to a vector layer, Photoshop Elements warns you that the layer must first be converted to a bitmap layer (simplifying the layer) by displaying a warning box like the one shown in **Figure 7.25**. Clicking OK will simplify the layer and apply the effect. Two important things to remember when simplifying a type or shape layer are that it will no longer be editable after it is simplified, and that the text and shapes on a vector layer print out much sharper than possible after the layer has been simplified.

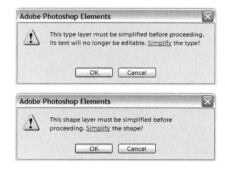

Figure 7.25
These messages appear when you attempt to apply effects to a vector layer. They warn you that the layer must be simplified before the requested effect can be performed.

Alternative Ways to Add Text and Shapes into Photos

When making cover or title pages that really get the viewer's attention, you need to get a little creative, and Elements has the tools to let you do just that.

Making Titles from the Background

Rather than place text over a photo, you can use the Type Mask tool to create a short title from the background of the photo. Here's how it's done:

1. Download and open the file **CHICAGO.jpg**.

2. Select the Horizontal Mask Type tool. In the Options bar select the font Impact, change the size to 48 points, and select the Center text alignment.

3. Click in the lower-center of the photo, and your entire image will turn red. This is a tint overlay showing the part of the image that is selected.

4. Type in CHICAGO (all caps) and it should look something like **Figure 7.26**. Before you click the Commit checkmark, place your cursor outside of the

> **NOTE**
>
> Once you begin moving the selection, don't release the mouse button until it's in the final position. That's because once the mouse button is released, the Mask tool completes its action and the text becomes a selection.

text until the cursor changes to what appears to be an arrowhead with an X. You can now move the selection. Position it so it's centered and slightly above the concrete railing at the bottom of the photo.

Figure 7.26
The Horizontal Mask Type tool places a red overlay over the entire image.

5. Now for the fun part. Open a Levels Adjustment layer (Layer > New Adjustment Layer > Levels). When the New Layer dialog opens, click OK.

6. From the Levels dialog , drag the shadow (left) slider of the Output Levels until it reads 175, and the masked text area will appear (**Figure 7.27**). Click OK, and it's finished.

You could have applied the Levels command (Ctrl+L/Cmd+L) directly to the photo, but by using an Adjustment layer, you can go back and change the Levels settings at a later date.

Figure 7.27
Applying a Levels Adjustment brightens the masked text area.

Variations on an Idea

In addition to the way you just learned to use the Horizontal Mask Type tool, there are other ways to use these features. Using the same technique from the previous exercise (steps 1–4), you can copy the masked area of the photo and paste it into either a blank image or into another photo. In the example shown in **Figure 7.28**, the Simple Emboss style was applied to the layer in the new image.

Figure 7.28
Text created with a Mask Type tool makes great titles and banners.

Combining Type, Shapes, and Photos

The disadvantage of using any type mask is that once the selection is created, it is very difficult to make changes to the shape. To be able to resize and twist the shapes of these photo-filled characters after they are created, we need to use a little-known feature in Photoshop Elements that allows you to fill type or shapes with a photo. Technically, it's called a clipping mask, and it uses Type layers or Shape layers to control what parts of a photo the viewer sees. Rather than spend a paragraph explaining it, let's see how it works. If you want to follow along, download the file **Flowers.jpg**.

1. Open the photo and select the Type tool.

2. Enter the text you want to fill with the flowers. The example I made in **Figure 7.29** was made using the Impact font at a size of 68 points and leading of 62 points.

How Does Group with Previous Work?

After Group with Previous is applied, the Type layer becomes a clipping mask, which makes everything on the top layer transparent, except for the areas where the typed black letters appear. The top layer is still all there—you just can't see parts of it. You can change the size or shape of the text on the Type layer or apply some of the Style layers to it, and it will affect the appearance.

Figure 7.29
Place the text on top of the photo.

3. Make a Background copy layer by clicking and dragging the background in the Layers palette onto the New Layer icon (**Figure 7.30**).

4. Select *Background* in the Layers palette and choose Edit > Fill Layer, then choose Use Background color (white) to clear the original flower background (**Figure 7.31**).

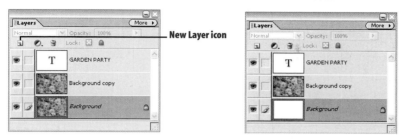

Figure 7.30
Make a copy of the background.

Figure 7.31
Clear the background.

5. Drag the Type layer so it is between the Background and the Background copy layer. The text disappears.

6. Select the Type layer in the Layers palette, and in the Layers menu, select Group with Previous (Ctrl+G/Cmd+G) and see the results (**Figure 7.32**).

Figure 7.32
The Type layer controls what parts of the top layer are visible.

7. Apply the Simple Inner and the Low Drop Shadow styles to the Type layer, and the text takes on a nice, finished appearance. (**Figure 7.33**)

Figure 7.33
Application of Styles really adds dimension to the text.

TIP

Spell Checking in Elements. So when you are adding a lot of text to an image, wouldn't it be great to have a spelling checker? Yes it would. So where is the spelling checker? It's not in this version of Elements—maybe in Elements 4. So how do you check your spelling? Type the text you want to enter in either your favorite word processor or the program you use to send emails and run its checker. Once the spelling is correct, select and copy the text to the clipboard (Ctrl+C/Cmd+C), and then after selecting the Type tool, paste (Ctrl+V/Cmd+V) the text into the image.

A Sample CD Cover

To demonstrate what can be done with Elements, I have used a few of the techniques discussed in the chapter to create a CD insert (**Figure 7.34**). The background is a close-up photo I took of a fencepost (which we have lots of in Texas). The band's name—Twisted Wire—was applied using the mask technique used in the "Chicago" exercise. The album name, *Range War*, was made using regular type to which both the Simple Emboss and the Soft Shadow styles were applied.

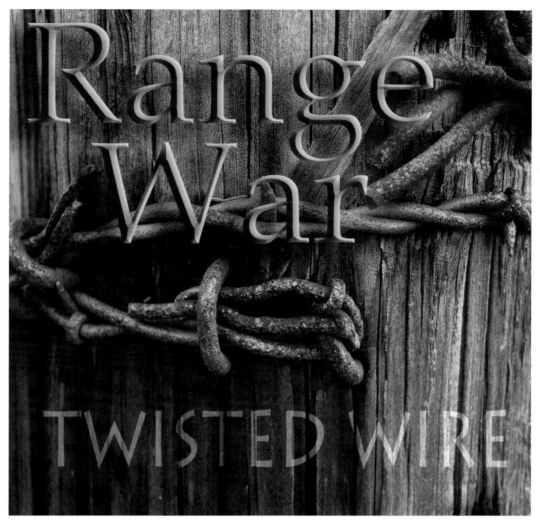

Figure 7.34
The tools in Elements allow you to create professional images like this CD insert.

Warping Text

Warping text is another great time-wasting feature. You can spend way too much time playing with all of the effects possible. Here is how it works:

1. Enter the text using the Type tool.

2. Highlight the text and click the Create Warped Text icon in the Options bar, which opens the Warp Text dialog (**Figure 7.35**).

3. After selecting a Style, use the controls to manipulate the degree and direction of warping.

4. When it appears the way you want it to, click OK, then click the Commit checkmark in the Options bar.

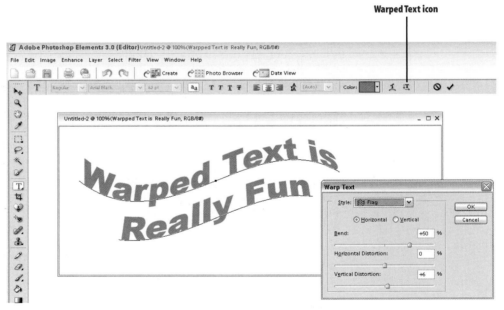

Figure 7.35
The Warp Text dialog.

Here is an exercise to show one of the many uses for warped text. In a world that has elevated my drug of choice, coffee, into a Styrofoam-wrapped concoction, I thought it would be fun to use a photo of a real coffee cup.

1. Download and open the file **Coffee_cup.jpg**

2. Select the Type tool and change the font to Impact at 30 points, the font color to blue, the alignment to centered, and the leading to 30 points.

3. Enter the text Real Coffee Real Cup as shown in **Figure 7.36**.

Figure 7.36
Text on the coffee cup is flat.

4. Click the Warped Text icon and when the Warp Text dialog opens, change the Style to Arc. As you can see (**Figure 7.37**), this style doesn't make the text look like it is painted on the cup.

5. Change the following settings in the Warp Text dialog: Bend to -20%, Horizontal Distortion to 0%, and Vertical Distortion to -14%. Click the OK button and the Commit checkmark in the Options bar. The resulting text should look like that shown in **Figure 7.38**.

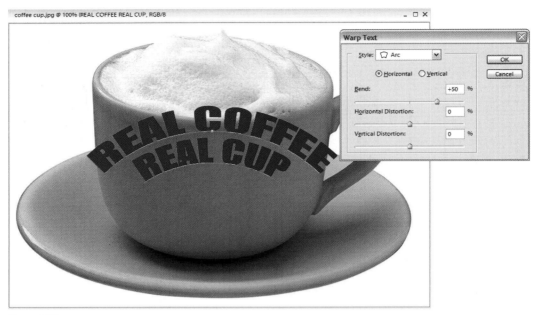

Figure 7.37
The default arc setting doesn't seem to fit the cup.

Figure 7.38
The Warp Text tool adjusts the text to fit the cup.

Using the Cookie Cutter Tool

The Cookie Cutter tool is a new addition to Photoshop Elements 3. It is a great tool that scrapbookers will love that is very easy to use. With it you can reshape the borders of any photograph into a custom shape. The tool uses the shapes from the custom shapes we already saw when we looked at the Shapes tools. The difference between the Cookie Cutter and the Custom Shape tool is that the Cookie Cutter turns the photo into the shape of the custom shape. **Figure 7.39** shows the location of the Cookie Cutter tool and the Options that control how the shape responds when the shape is dragged out.

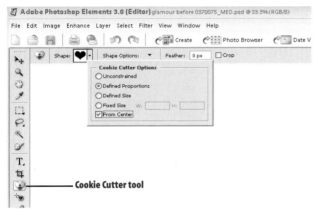

Figure 7.39
The Cookie Cutter tool cuts shapes out of photos like a cookie cutter.

Here is how the Cookie Cutter tool works:

1. Open a photo.

2. Select the Cookie Cutter tool in the Toolbox and choose one of the shapes from the Options bar. Click and drag the shape over the photo. As soon as the mouse button is released, the area outside of the shape is removed (**Figure 7.40**). Click the Commit checkmark to complete the action.

Figure 7.40
The heart shape created with the Cookie Cutter tool produces this lovely effect in seconds.

3. You can apply Styles or any other effect to the shape that is created. In this example, I applied a drop shadow, and the white border around the edge was created using the Style named Heavy. When you are finished, just flatten the Layer (Layer > Flatten Image), and you're finished (**Figure 7.41**).

Summary

This chapter's goal was to provide basic text-handling concepts and to develop skills to increase your confidence when tackling personal projects. We covered many (but not all) of the cool things you can do with Type, Shapes, and even the new Cookie Cutter tool. Somewhere along the way, maybe you even discovered that "Oh wow" factor while working with this program. In the next chapter, you'll learn some retouching tips and tricks that will make your photos look even more professional.

Figure 7.41
This effect took less than three minutes to create with the Cookie Cutter tool.

Cameras can be cruel devices in that they capture images with frightening clarity. Unless you are a member of the camera-toting paparazzi (who appear to enjoy making celebrities look as bad as possible), when most of us take a photograph of someone, we want to capture an expression reflective of the individual's personality. We want to capture a moment in time, in a photograph. The camera has no such agenda. It faithfully captures every wrinkle, mole, scar, and blemish on the subject. It can also, with an uncanny ability, discover double chins where none before existed, bulging tummies, the shiny noses and faces, yellowed teeth, and bloodshot eyes in a teetotaler. What makes the camera so mean? It isn't mean; it can only faithfully record what it sees. We, as humans, on the other hand, tend to tune out these physical aberrations when we are with the subject, however it is difficult to overlook them later when looking at the photograph you took.

Why do I mention this? Because this chapter is devoted to using Photoshop Elements to make your photos of people and other subjects look better, and not necessarily look the way the camera records them. If you are a photojournalist (paparazzi are not photojournalists), quit reading now because this chapter is devoted the one subject you are opposed to—changing reality.

Preparing for Retouching

You will learn as you go through this chapter that in most situations, retouching a photo requires working at high zoom levels. For example, the first exercise in this chapter requires zooming in very close to remove the chocolate from the subject's face. It is difficult to see the effect changes on the entire image when working at that high of a magnification. Fortunately, Elements has provided an excellent solution called View New Window.

Figure 8.1
Open a New Window from the View menu.

Viewing Zoomed Images in a Separate Window

1. Open the image that you will be working on.

2. Choose View, New Window for (*file name*) (**Figure 8.1**).

3. A second window with the image opens (**Figure 8.2**). Any changes made to the original image instantly appear in the new window. Using the Zoom tool (Z) you can zoom in and out of the original, while the zoom setting of the new window remains unaffected. Even though both windows are showing the same image, you can change the zoom settings on each one independently.

TIP

Using the New Window feature, you can open up multiple new windows on a single image. The only limitations on how many images can be open are the physical size of your screen and the amount of memory you have available.

Original image at 200% zoom   **New window showing entire image**

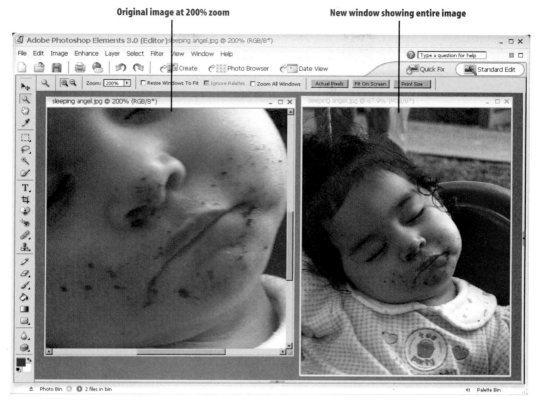

Figure 8.2
The new window allows you to see "the whole picture" while working on an area at high magnification.

Using Pressure-Sensitive Tablets

One of the greatest tools you can buy to improve your work with Photoshop Elements is a pressure-sensitive tablet. These tablets (also called digitizing or digitizer tablets, or Wacom tablets), provide you with an input device that is in the shape of a pen. If you have never worked with a pressure-sensitive tablet, you will be surprised how easy it is to work on images with a pen rather than a mouse.

Not only is the shape of the stylus (the pen) something we are accustomed to, but the digitizer tablet is an absolute pointing device in comparison to a mouse (which is a relative positioning device). See the sidebar, "Relative Vs. Absolute Positioning" for more information. To demonstrate the difference, in **Figure 8.3** I signed my name with a mouse and with my Wacom tablet. You should be able to tell which is which without me even telling you. (OK, the red was written with the mouse.)

My first experience with a digitizer pad (yet another name for the tablet) was over ten years ago. They were large, very expensive, and had more than their share of software conflicts with other applications. There were quite a few tablet vendors back then, but few would disagree that today Wacom has become the industry-standard in this area. Recently, I have seen some new vendors offering pressure-sensitive tablets, and while I haven't tried them all, I have yet to use a tablet with better feel and operation than my Wacom.

In the early days of pressure-sensitive tablets, purchasing one could cost several thousand dollars. Today, I have seen Wacom's Graphire tablets selling for under $100. **Figure 8.4** is a photo of the 6 by 8 Graphire 3 tablet that I use with my laptop computer.

Figure 8.3
Which one was written with a pressure-sensitive pen and which with a mouse?

NOTE

During a conference, I was approached by a person after my workshop who declared that he could write with a mouse very well. I told him he needed to date more.

Relative Vs. Absolute Positioning

A mouse is a relative positioning device. That means that as you move the mouse, it sends information to the computer about how far in any particular direction it is being moved. If there is an obstacle on the desk, you simply pick up the mouse, move it back toward you, and move it again. The cursor on the screen is unaware that the actual position of the mouse was changed when you picked it up and moved it.

An absolute positioning device, like a digitizer tablet, tells the computer where on the digitizer pad that the pen is located. To move the screen cursor from the left to the right side of the screen requires that you move the stylus from the left to the right side of the pad.

If you have used a mouse for any amount of time you will be surprised how accustomed you have become to relative positioning. This is especially true if you are using a large tablet. Suddenly, a movement on the screen that was a short mouse move becomes a very long reach on a large tablet. Fortunately, Wacom allows you to customize the stylus settings so that the mouse movements can be mimicked by the pad or only a small area of the pad is used for positioning, thereby preventing you from developing the digitizer pad equivalent of tennis elbow.

Figure 8.4
The Graphire 3 pressure-sensitive tablet is an excellent choice for working with Photoshop Elements 3.

What Does Pressure-Sensitive Mean?

Pressure-sensitive means that when you press the stylus on the pad, it literally detects the full range of pressure from the pen on the tablet. When used with a pressure-sensitive tool, such as Photoshop Elements' Clone Stamp tool, Liquify filter, or the Brush tool, you discover a new dimension of control. Press hard, and the parameters of the tool changes. In exercises in the other chapters of this book, I have had the reader stop to change a brush size or opacity setting before proceeding. With a pressure-sensitive brush, these parameters can be changed by increasing or decreasing the pressure on the tablet surface. It feels more natural because that's how brushes work in the real world.

NOTE

While using pressure information to control tools in Elements is important, the truth is that even if they weren't pressure-sensitive, the feel of the pen and the absolute position is a tremendous help when retouching or making selections.

Dave's Favorite Tablet Questions

When I teach a workshop, I typically get questions from users who have never owned a tablet before. Here are my favorites because they're good questions:

- **If I use a tablet, will I have to give up my mouse?** No. In the early days of tablets, this was an issue, but today your mouse and your tablet can both be active at the same time.

- **Since the tablet ships with a mouse, do I have to use it?** No. Don't tell the Wacom people, but I don't use the mouse that came with my Graphire tablet. I use my favorite wireless optical mouse.

- **Will the tablet work with all of Elements tools?** Yes and no. Yes, it works with everything in Elements 3. Not all of the Elements tools use the pressure information. For example, what affect would you expect increasing pressure would do to the Type tool?

- **Does the pressure-sensitive tablet work with other software applications, or does it only work with Elements?** All software applications can receive positioning information from a tablet, and many applications can use pressure-sensitive input from a digitizer tablet.

- **Will it work on my Mac?** Yes, it works great under OS X.

- **Does it use batteries?** No, it gets its power from the cosmic energy of the universe (kidding). It draws its power through the USB connection to the attached computer.

Using Elements with Your Pressure-Sensitive Pen

To get the most out of your pressure-sensitive tablet you need to tell Elements how you want a particular tool to respond when you press either harder or softer. One of the greatest improvements of Elements 3 with regards to its operation with pressure-sensitive pens is how Adobe has streamlined the settings. Bravo Adobe.

Many programs that support pressure-sensitive tablets offer a daunting list of tool parameters that are changed based on the pressure information that is received. It is often so complicated that few ever use it. An example is the Tablet options for the Brush tools (**Figure 8.5**). They are basic and, more importantly, essential for retouching and making selections.

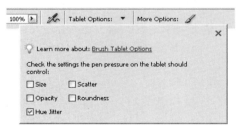

Figure 8.5
The tablet controls for the Brush tools in Elements.

In addition to the tablet support for the individual tools, you can customize your pressure-sensitive tablet using the software control panel provided by your tablet manufacturer (**Figure 8.6**).

From this panel you can customize stylus button settings, control how the stylus acts (like a mouse or a pen), define what part of the tablet is active (important with large tablets), vary brush tool properties, and many, many more items.

As we go through the retouching exercises, I will point out settings for those that have pressure-sensitive tablets. It is not necessary to have a Wacom tablet to do any of the exercises in this chapter; it's just more fun if you do.

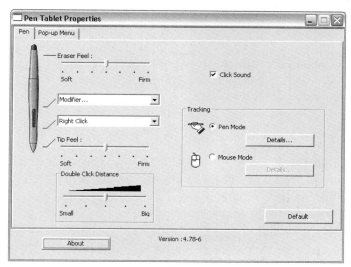

Figure 8.6
This control panel for the Wacom Graphire 3 is representative of some of the many features that can be customized.

Basic Photo Fix-Ups

We begin with some common and not-too-difficult photo fix-ups that I run into all of the time—cleaning up photos of children. I take a lot of photos of kids because they make great subjects and I've yet to encounter a five-year old who shields their face with their hands saying, "Don't take my picture! I'm not photogenic." Another good thing about these little darlings is that they are not self-conscious about their appearance. The little girl in **Figure 8.7** is not self-conscious, in fact she's not even awake.

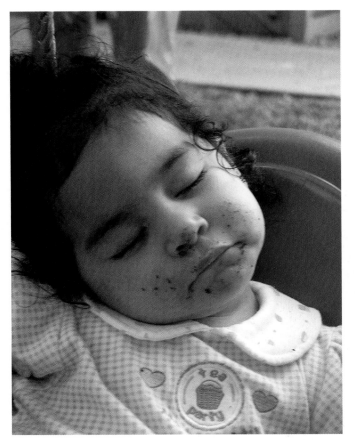

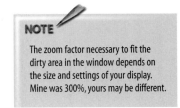

NOTE

The zoom factor necessary to fit the dirty area in the window depends on the size and settings of your display. Mine was 300%, yours may be different.

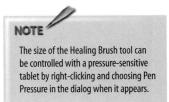

NOTE

The size of the Healing Brush tool can be controlled with a pressure-sensitive tablet by right-clicking and choosing Pen Pressure in the dialog when it appears.

Figure 8.7
Beautiful sleeping girl with a messy face.

Cleaning Up Photos

The chocolate she ate (much of which remains on the face) probably did her in. For my money, I would leave the snack on her face, it's just that cute. In fact, this is exactly the kind of photo you want to preserve to show at her wedding twenty years hence. Still, she might be even cuter without the distraction of the mess on her face.

In learning how to clean up a photo, we will be using both the Healing Brush and the Spot Healing Brush.

To do the following exercise, you will need to download the image **Sleeping_angel.jpg** from the Peachpit Press Web site. Let's clean this little girl up.

1. Open the file **Sleeping_angel.jpg** (**Figure 8.7**). The first step is to zoom in on the messy area. Select the Zoom tool (Z) from the Toolbox and drag a rectangle around the messy area. Your display should look like the one shown in **Figure 8.8**.

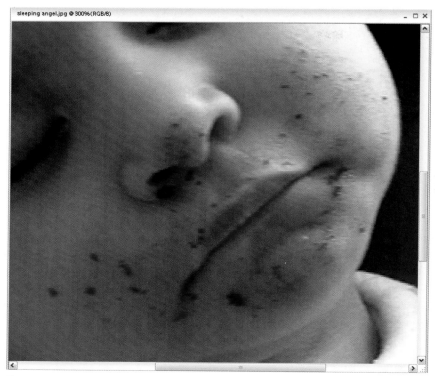

Figure 8.8
First step: zoom in on the area to be worked on.

2. Create a new window of the photo so that you can see how the changes being made affect the appearance of the whole photo. Choose View, New Window for the sleeping angel picture. A new window of our darling appears. Move it to another part of the screen, away from the area in which we are working (**Figure 8.9**).

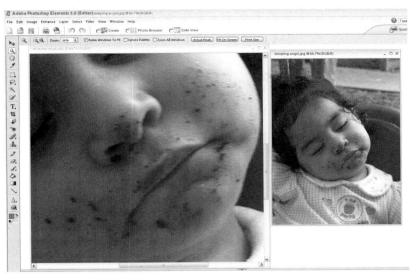

Figure 8.9
Next, make a new window to see how the changes affect the photo.

3. Select the original image. Choose the Spot Healing Brush 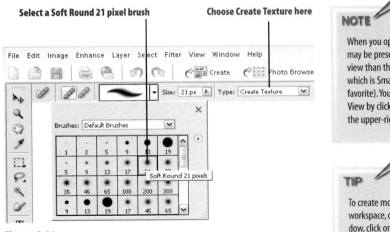. Select the Soft Round 21 pixel preset and change the Type setting in the Options bar to Create Texture. For more information on Spot Healing Brush settings see the side bar, "The Healing Brushes."

Figure 8.11
Select and change the settings of the Spot Healing Brush.

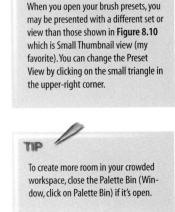

NOTE

When you open your brush presets, you may be presented with a different set or view than those shown in **Figure 8.10** which is Small Thumbnail view (my favorite). You can change the Preset View by clicking on the small triangle in the upper-right corner.

TIP

To create more room in your crowded workspace, close the Palette Bin (Window, click on Palette Bin) if it's open.

4. Beginning with her cheek, on the left side of the photo, click once on the first spot. A selection surrounds the spot momentarily and then the dark spot disappears like magic. Continue clicking on the dark spots until that side of the cheek is clear (**Figure 8.11**). The skin color remains uneven, but we will take care of that soon.

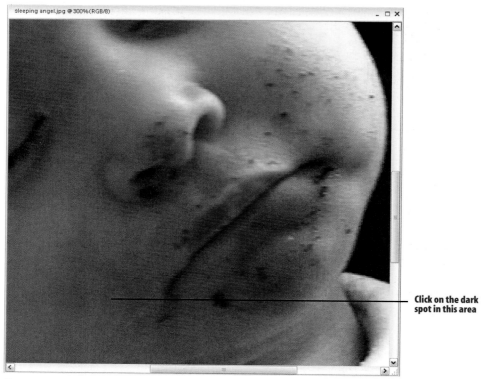

Click on the dark spot in this area

Figure 8.11
The Spot Healing Brush quickly eliminates the dark spots of chocolate.

There is one big glob of chocolate on her nose. If you attempt to use the Spot Healing Brush it will turn the area into a dark smudge because the nearby pixels that would be used in the healing calculation are too dark. This is a job for the Healing Brush.

5. Choose the Healing Brush from the Toolbox. Change the settings so they match those shown in the Options bar (**Figure 8.12**). Alt/Option-click on the area of the cheek indicated in the figure. With the Healing Brush over the dark spot, click the brush one time. Repeat on either side of the dark area until it looks like the one shown in Figure 8.12.

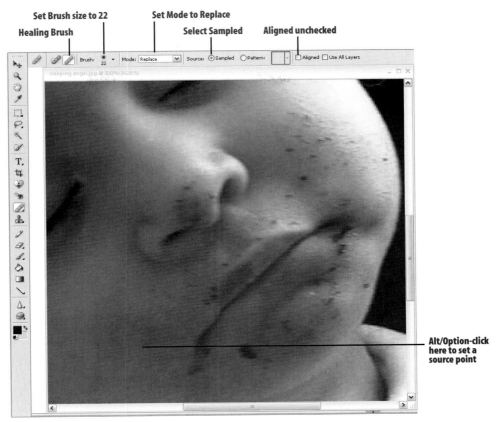

Set Brush size to 22

Healing Brush

Set Mode to Replace

Select Sampled   **Aligned unchecked**

Alt/Option-click here to set a source point

Figure 8.12
Select a source point to use for removing the dark spot on the nose.

6. Return to the Spot Healing Brush and using the same settings as before, clean up the rest of her face (**Figure 8.13**). The skin still has a mottled appearance, but we'll correct that in the next step.

7. Use the Healing Brush to clean up the appearance of skin where we removed the mess. You will achieve the best results by using a large brush size. This is because the Healing Brush will blend all the different shades together. Use a Brush size of 50. Alt/Option-click on the spots indicated (**Figure 8.14**), and apply the brush to the areas with the similar shading. For example, use the brighter-colored skin to clean up the brighter areas. The little girl is all cleaned up (**Figure 8.15**). Now let's see a different way to solve another blemish problem.

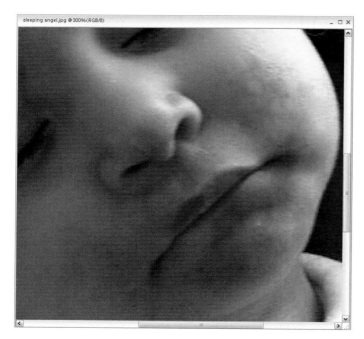

Figure 8.13
The mess is gone but the skin has a ruddy appearance.

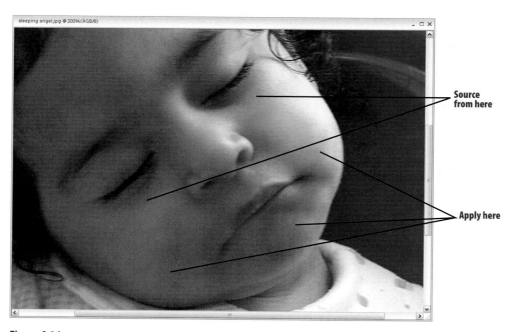

Figure 8.14
Apply pixels from smooth skin using the Healing Brush tool.

Figure 8.15
The mess is gone and she never woke up.

The Healing Brushes

The Healing Brush first appeared in Photoshop as a godsend for removing scars, blemishes, and all manner of debris. There are two different Healing Brushes in Elements—Spot Healing and Healing. While they are similar in how they work, the results they achieve are quite different. The Healing Brush is used to fix larger areas of imperfections, while the Spot Healing Brush is designed to quickly remove isolated imperfections.

The Healing Brush acts like a smart Clone Stamp tool. You must select a source point for the pixels you want to replace and then paint them over the area that your want to "heal." Unlike the Clone Stamp tool (which just applies the pixels) the Healing Brush blends the new pixels with the existing ones seamlessly.

The Spot Healing Brush doesn't require selection of source pixels to operate. Depending on the Type setting, the Spot Healing Brush either uses the pixels around the edge of the selection to find an image area to use as a patch for the selected area (Proximity Match), or uses all the pixels in the selection to create a texture in which to fix the area (Create Texture).

Dealing with Blemishes and Flash Glare

A messy face is cute, acute acne is not. In the next exercise, you will be removing facial blemishes and getting rid of the glare that was caused by the flash on my camera. To do this exercise, you will need to download **Man_in_tux.jpg** from the Peachpit Press Web site. You will have the opportunity to use some of the techniques you learned in the previous exercise, as well as some new ones.

1. Open the file **Man_in_tux.jpg**. Zoom in until his face fills the image window. (**Figure 8.16**).

Figure 8.16
Zooming in close is the first step of any retouching job.

2. Open a New Window and select the Spot Healing Brush. Use the Spot Healing Brush to remove the blemishes. Use a small brush and ensure the Type setting in the Options bar is Create Texture. It took me about 20 minutes to clean up this photo. You can either work on this photo, or use the cleaned up version I have included (**Man_in_tux_cleaned_up.jpg**) (**Figure 8.17**) for the next steps.

I recommend using a brush size that is just large enough to cover the defect you are trying to remove. The temptation is to use a large brush to cover a larger area, but it often produces an unacceptable effect. The downside of using a small brush size is that it takes a lot longer to clean up a photo, but the results are usually very good.

Figure 8.17
It takes some time, but the Spot Healing Brush can perform miracles.

3. To get rid of the flash glare, we will cover it with paint—no kidding. Select the Eyedropper tool (I) in the Toolbox. In the Options bar, make the Sample Size: 5 by 5 Average. Click on the forehead (**Figure 8.18**) to change the Foreground color to one that matches the skin color.

4. Select the Brush tool in the Toolbox. Change the Size to 65 px (pixels), Mode: Darken, Opacity: 65%. Paint the flash glare over the eyes. (**Figure 8.19**)

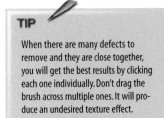

TIP

When there are many defects to remove and they are close together, you will get the best results by clicking each one individually. Don't drag the brush across multiple ones. It will produce an undesired texture effect.

Sample Size

Eyedropper

Click Here

Sampled Color

Figure 8.18
Use the Eyedropper tool to select a cover-up color that matches the skin color.

Figure 8.19
Paint the flash glare above the eyes with the matching sample color.

5. Paint the rest of the areas that have flash glare (upper forehead and nose). You will need to use a smaller brush to get the glare on his ear (**Figure 8.20**)

Figure 8.20
The blemishes and flash glare are gone.

6. The areas under the eyebrows are dark—raccoon eyes. Select the Dodge tool from the Toolbox. Change the Options bar setting to a Brush size of 65 px, Range: Midtones, and the Exposure of 15%. Paint the areas under the eyes to reduce (not completely remove) the shadows (**Figure 8.21**).

7. Now that you have lightened up the eye areas, you need to add a little edge to them. Select the Burn tool in the Toolbox. Change the Options bar settings to a Brush size of 90 px, Range: Shadows, Exposure: 10%. Paint over the eyes again. The Burn tool darkens only the darker colors (Shadows). This increases the contrast and brightens up the area around the eye.

8. The last step is to blur the background using the Layer mask technique described in Chapter 6.

Figure 8.21
Use the Dodge tool to reduce shading around the eyes.

Figure 8.22
The original and the finished retouched photo.

Body Sculpturing

When people give me a photograph asking me if I can make it look better, they often ask if I can get rid of some pounds. The best answer you can give is a classic smile and say, "I'll see what I can do." Photoshop Elements is a powerful photo editor, but if someone weighs 400 pounds, there's not much you can do to make them look three hundred pounds lighter. Often, the problem isn't extra poundage but terrible camera angle. The photo of the speaker in **Figure 8.23** was taken at a terrible angle, making the speaker look plump.

Figure 8.23
Poor camera angle can produce an unflattering photo.

The most powerful tool in Elements for changing the shape of people or things, is the Liquify filter. The following exercise demonstrates how you can use this tool to reshape people. This exercise uses the file named **Speaker.jpg** which is available for download on the Peachpit Press Web page.

1. Open the file **Speaker.jpg**. Choose Filter, Distort, Liquify which opens another dialog that almost occupies the entire screen (**Figure 8.24**).

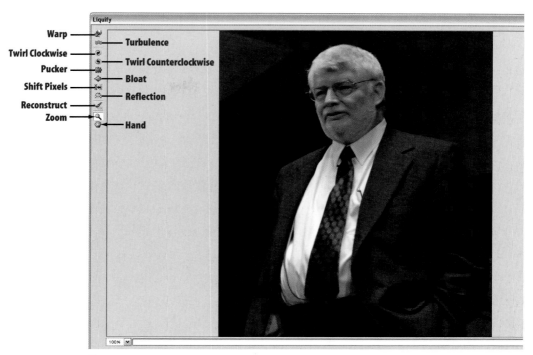

Figure 8.24
The Liquify filter can distort and reshape almost anything and in the process do a great job of rearranging body shapes.

2. When the file appears in the Liquify workspace, use the Zoom and Hand tools to make the photo fit the screen. Select the Warp tool on the left side of the dialog. Change the Brush size in the Tool Options to 300 pixels. Click and drag the cursor as shown in **Figure 8.25**. As you drag the tool the shape of the subject changes. You can use Ctrl/Cmd+Z to undo the last action—but only the last action. To completely reset the image to what it was when the Liquify Filter was opened, you must click the Revert button.

3. When you have finished moving the pixels around, click OK, and the Liquify Filter changes are applied (**Figure 8.26**).

There is much more you can do with the Liquify Filter other than make minor alterations to body shapes. You can do major alterations (**Figure 8.27**) that are just plain silly.

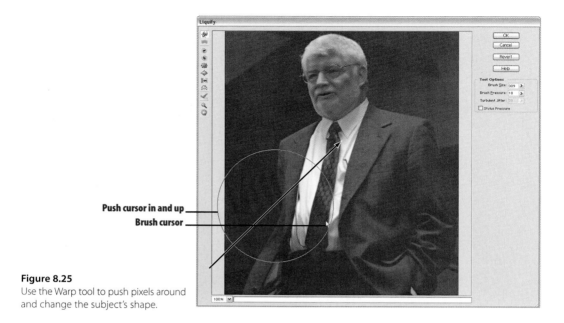

Figure 8.25
Use the Warp tool to push pixels around and change the subject's shape.

Figure 8.26
Using the Liquify Filter allows you to reshape people without making it obvious that you have been altering their appearance.

Figure 8.27
You can really do some wild and crazy distortions with the Liquify Filter.

Making a Brighter Smile

If you see any commercials on TV, you are aware of the latest obsession our country is having with the possession of white teeth. While naturally healthy teeth will have a slightly yellowish-crème color, everyone wants their teeth to be bright enough to require others in the room to wear sunglasses. Because of the heightened interest in white teeth, I thought it appropriate to show you how to make the teeth of people in your photos whiter than they are in real life. While you can use any photo to do this exercise, I have provided the one used in the exercise (**Father_and_son.jpg**), on the Peachpit Press Web site.

1. Open the file **Father_and_son.jpg** (**Figure 8.28**). The teeth on the dad have a healthy, slightly yellow tint. With everyone bleaching their teeth white these days, naturally-colored teeth seem out of step.

2. To brighten the dad's teeth, select the Dodge tool in the Toolbox. Change the settings to a 30 px Brush, Range: Midtones, and an Exposure value of 25%. Apply the brush to his teeth. (**Figure 8.29**)

NOTE

Be careful not to make his teeth appear too white or you will draw attention to them. The goal is to make them appear white enough to look "healthy" but not so bright that they detract from the subject of the photo.

Figure 8.28
Original photo is great except that Dad could stand to have brighter teeth.

Figure 8.29
Use the Dodge tool to make teeth just a little bit brighter. The flash that reflected off of the glasses was removed using the Spot Healing tool.

9 Scan and Repair Photographs

There is no time like the present when it comes to preserving photographs or any other media. That's because they're not getting any younger. By that I mean that they are aging, and the older they get the less information can be recovered from the image. Once the photograph has been scanned and stored in the computer, you have stopped the aging process and, as you will learn in this chapter, you can reverse most of the damage done by time and mishandling.

Scanning Photos

Even with a digital camera, you can still use a scanner to capture existing photographs, memorabilia, and important documents like diplomas. Scanning can be accomplished in one of two ways:

- Press the button located on the front of the scanner that launches the scanning software installed onto your computer when you set up your scanner. Most scanning software will offer you the choice of sending the image to Photoshop Elements, printing it, or saving it as a file.

- Start the scanner directly from Elements by choosing File > Import, and a list of installed imaging devices (cameras and scanners) appears (**Figure 9.1**). Click the scanner in the list and your scanner's user interface (UI) appears (**Figure 9.2**).

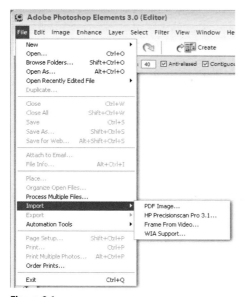

Figure 9.1
You begin the scanning process from this list of input devices.

NOTE

Windows users may see devices listed with the letters WIA preceding their names. See the sidebar "The Disadvantages of WIA" for more information.

NOTE

The scanner control that appears on your system is determined by the make and model, so it may appear different than the one shown in **Figure 9.2**.

The Disadvantages of WIA

If your digital camera or scanner is connected to a computer using Windows XP each time you attach your camera to the computer, you will be asked what you want the computer to use to talk with your camera. One of those choices will be to move pictures from the camera into the computer using the Windows Imaging Acquisition (WIA) interface. WIA provides a very simple way to move pictures directly from your digital camera (or scanner) to the computer. There is, however, a disadvantage to using the WIA interface. It is a generic, no-frills control interface, and therefore not as full-featured as the controls found on the software that comes with your scanner or camera. This is especially true of the WIA interface for your scanner. Many of the features in your scanner that allow you to get the best possible scan are usually not available using the WIA interface.

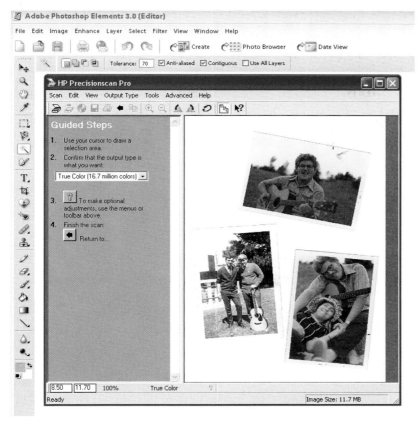

Figure 9.2
The scanner controls appear inside of the Elements workspace.

Basic Scanning in Elements 3

Here are the four basic steps to follow to scan an image:

1. Preview the image.

2. Select the image.

3. Verify the color mode.

4. Scan the image.

Preview the Image You're Scanning

Most scanner software produces a preview image as soon as the scanner is started. In some cases, the preview scan will not occur immediately because the software is waiting for the lamp in the scanner to warm up, which assures the color accuracy of the scan. In rare cases the scanner may be waiting for you to initiate the preview scan.

Preview images are not high quality. They are low-resolution representations of the scanned image used as a guide for selecting the part of the image to be scanned.

NOTE

Your scanner may attempt to automatically select the image area for you, and most of the time it will do a good job. If it doesn't you can always adjust the selection manually.

TIP

Even if the image will be used on a Web page, don't use the 256-Color setting, as many features in Elements are not available when working on a 256-color image. You can always change it to 256-color when you have finished working on the image.

TIP

Scanning printed material can create moiré patterns, and some scanners offer a feature that eliminates, or at the least greatly reduces, these patterns. Called **de-screening**, it typically must be selected from a toolbar in the scanning software user interface (UI). After selecting it, the scanner will rescan the preview. The speed of the Preview mode is much slower than normal preview.

Select the Area to be Scanned (cropping)

Unless instructed otherwise by making a selection, the scanner will scan the entire length of the scanner. You must select the part of the photo you want to scan by clicking over one corner of the image in the preview screen and dragging a selection area over the part of the photo to be scanned (**Figure 9.3**). After you have created a selection you can fine-tune it by moving the selection bars with your mouse. For selecting really small photos, see the section "Selecting Small Images" later in this chapter.

Verify the Color Mode

The scanner may ask the user to select the Color Input Mode with choices like Line Art, Halftone, Grayscale, 256-Color, RGB Color, plus all of the possible naming variations of these modes used by different scanner manufacturers. **Figure 9.4** is one example of the choices you may see. The scanner software attempts to determine what kind of image you are scanning and set the color mode for you. Since it isn't always correct, you should make sure it is either set to its highest color setting—even if it is a black-and-white document—or Grayscale.

Figure 9.4
Make sure your color mode is set to its highest color setting or Grayscale.

Selection determines area to be scanned

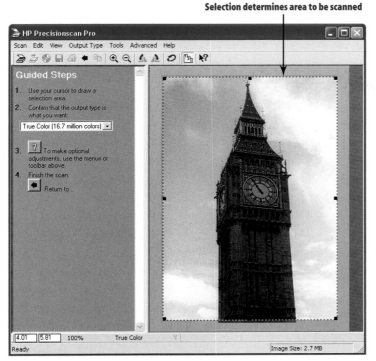

Figure 9.3
Click and drag a selection over the part of the photo to be scanned.

Scanning the Image

The final step is to scan the image, after which the scanner usert interface (UI) closes. The scanned image then appears in an image window within Elements (**Figure 9.5**).

Cool Things You Can Do Using Your Scanner and Photoshop Elements

The previous section covered the basics of scanning in a photo; now we'll look at some other feats your scanner can perform that you may not know about, and learn about a cool new scanning feature in Photoshop Elements 3.0.

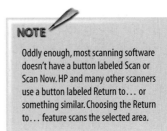

NOTE

Oddly enough, most scanning software doesn't have a button labeled Scan or Scan Now. HP and many other scanners use a button labeled Return to... or something similar. Choosing the Return to... feature scans the selected area.

Figure 9.5
The scanned image appears in an image window in Elements.

Accurately Select Small Images or Areas

When you are selecting a single item out of many on a sheet of paper, a very small original, or when the selection of the area to be scanned is critical, here is how to make an accurate selection.

1. On the preview, click and drag a rectangle of the area that you want to scan. After you have made a rough selection (**Figure 9.6**), you can move the selection bars by clicking and dragging them to the desired position.

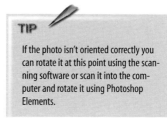

TIP

If the photo isn't oriented correctly you can rotate it at this point using the scanning software or scan it into the computer and rotate it using Photoshop Elements.

2. After you have made the first selection, locate the button or command that allows you to zoom in on the selected area. On the HP Precisionscan Pro dialog (**Figure 9.7**) it is the magnifying glass button. When enabled, the scanner will scan the image again, and the selected area will fill the preview window. Now that the preview scan fills the screen area, you can make any critical adjustments to the selection bars and also see if you need to clean your scanner copy glass.

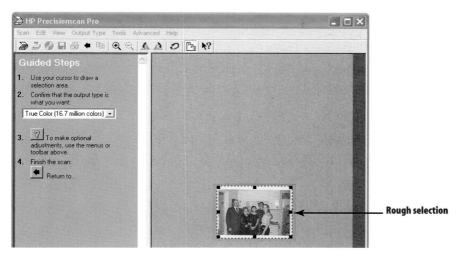

Figure 9.6
Begin by making a rough selection.

Return to... button
starts the scan   Zoom button

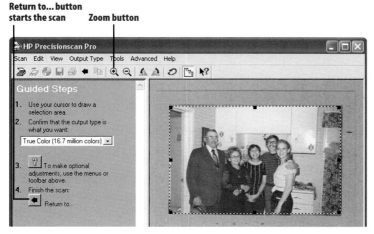

Figure 9.7
Zooming in fills the preview window with the scanned image.

Enlarge Photos with Your Scanner

One of the great features of a scanner that is rarely used is its ability to change the size of an image. The size of an image can be enlarged in Photoshop Elements through a process called *resampling*. No matter how good Elements is, when you increase the size of a photo through resampling, the image is visibly degraded—it loses sharpness and detail. If the same photo is scaled by the scanner when it is scanned, it can be made several times larger without the accompanying loss of detail.

The scanning software assumes you want to scan the image at 100%—the final size is the same as the original. Every manufacturer's scanning software controls the size of the resulting scan in a different location. In most HP scanners it is found in the Tools menu and is called Resize.

NOTE

If the original photo is of poor quality, the enlarged image will also be poor quality, and as a result of being larger, the defects will be more apparent.

Scanning Multiple Images

If you have ever scanned a lot of photos on a flatbed scanner, it can be quite a process. Each photo must be accurately placed on the scanner glass, previewed, scanned, removed from the scanner glass, and then the process is repeated.

With Elements 3, you can now place as many photos as will fit on the scanner glass, scan them all at once, and then let Elements sort them out for you. Here is how it works:

1. Place the photos on the scanner glass in any order or orientation and choose File > Import, and select your scanner, which then makes a preview scan.

2. Create a selection that includes all of the photos, as shown in **Figure 9.8,** and scan the image.

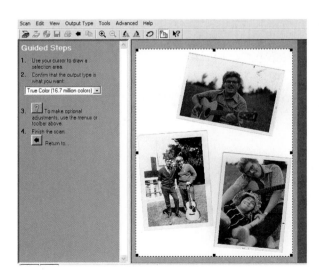

Figure 9.8
Select all the photos on the scanner.

3. Choose Image > Divide Scanned Photos (**Figure 9.9**). Elements begins to straighten and separate each photo and place them in their own image window, as shown in **Figure 9.10**. That's all there is to it. All that remains is to name and save each image.

TIP

The Divide Scanned Photos command can also be used to straighten and crop a single image on the scanner, which can be a real time-saver.

Figure 9.9
The Divide Scanned Photos command.

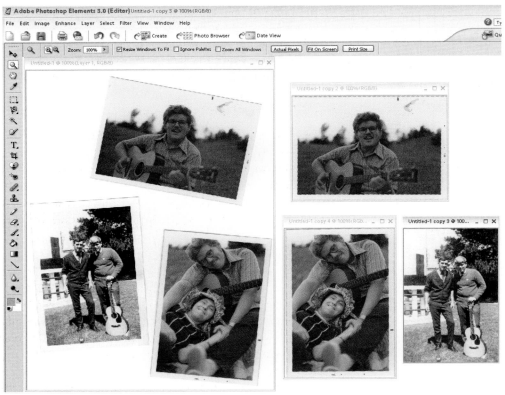

Figure 9.10
Elements automatically separated, cropped, and placed each photo in its own image window.

Preparing to Restore Photos

If you are scanning an image for the purpose of restoring it, you will need to make a few adjustments to the normal scanning routine we have been learning.

> **TIP**
> If the photo or image that you are scanning is old and fragile, you should exercise caution when handling and preparing it for scanning.

Scanning Photos for Repair

If you are scanning a photo or other document to repair it, follow these scanning guidelines. They differ from normal scanning in several ways.

Enlarge the Original

Make it a general rule to scan images that are to be repaired, or otherwise restored, at twice the original size. By doubling the size of the original, you are forcing the scanner

General Print Handling Procedures and Precautions

Here are some points to consider when handling prints, slides, and negatives:

- Always hold prints or negatives by their edges. Do not touch the surface if you're not wearing cotton gloves; even clean fingers can leave natural secretions that can damage a photo over time. You can purchase cotton gloves specially made for handling photos at your local camera store.

- Don't mark the back of your photo permanently in any way. The chemicals in some markers (especially a Sharpie) will eventually find their way to the other side of the photograph and ruin it. If you must make a temporary identification, write brief information gently with only a very soft 2B or 4B pencil.

- Never repair a photograph by applying adhesive tape to it. I saw the Dead Sea scrolls last year, and after talking to one of the archivists, I discovered that one of the major restoration tasks they have been doing for the past five years was removing the Scotch tape that the original curators used to piece it together. If you have a photo that is in several pieces, keep all of the pieces in a clean, chemically inert polyester bag or sleeves.

to capture the maximum amount of detail in the original photo and giving yourself more material to work with. There are some exceptions to this rule: When the original is really small, you should consider using an even larger resize factor (like 300%–500%). Also, if the original image is so huge that it covers the entire scanner glass, then 100% will probably be sufficient.

When you have completed the restoration, resize the image to return it to its correct size, which produces a natural softening that is the result of making it smaller. This can sometimes make a harsh image look better. If it softens it too much, use an application of the Unsharp Mask Filter (Filter > Sharpen >Unsharp Mask) at a low setting.

Use the Highest Quality Scan Setting

In short, you want to get the maximum amount of image detail from the scanned image as is possible, with little to no concern about how big the final file will be. For photos and memorabilia that you want to preserve, scan the original as RGB (24-bit) color. Black-and-white photos in most cases should be scanned as grayscale, the exception being if they have been hand-colored, or have a colored stain on them. Preserving the color in such cases allows isolation of the stain using color-sensitive selection tools.

Store Using a Lossless File Format

Do not save the original as a JPEG file. For restoration work, you should not save the images you are working on using any file format that uses lossy file compression. This includes Wavelet, JPEG, and JPEG 2000. Lossy file compression degrades the image. Probably the most popular graphic format to use is TIFF (Tagged Image File Format), and you can choose one of several compression options that are lossless, meaning they do not degrade the image. Be careful not to choose the JPEG compression option, which is now available as a choice for TIFF.

Repairing Tears and Creases

One of more common problems with old photos is that they usually have not received museum-quality care and storage. Unprotected, important images can easily become bent, folded, and otherwise damaged. Physically, there isn't anything that can be done for the original (with the exception of work done by a restoration specialist), but it's relatively easy to repair an electronic version and then to print it.

The damage caused by folding a photograph depends on its age and the material it is printed on. Photos taken in the past decade are printed on a flexible Mylar that can stand almost any degree of contortion, while photos printed around the turn of the 20th century were printed on stiff material, and in most cases even a slight bend produces a hard, raised crease from which the image surface may flake off, like the example shown in **Figure 9.11**.

Figure 9.11
Creases and tears are a common form of damage found in old photos.

The Power of the Healing and Spot Healing Brushes

Before Elements 3, the repair of the crease would have required the Clone Stamp tool, and it would have taken some effort to make the repair and not leave any sign of the previous damage. Now Elements has added two new tools, the Healing Brush and the Spot Healing Brush, which make the repair of image defects much easier.

How the Healing Brush Works

The **Healing Brush**, inherited from Photoshop CS and located in the Toolbox, is a brush that is similar in operation to the Clone Stamp tool in that it takes samples from one part of an image and paints them onto another. Selection of the source pixels is accomplished by Alt-clicking (Option for Mac) on a source area.

What makes the Healing Brush different from the Clone Stamp tool is what happens after the pixels are applied. The Healing Brush blends the texture and color from the sample area with the pixels where the brush is applied. You can actually see the blending happening after applying the brush.

The **Spot Healing Brush** is completely new. Instead of using pixels from another part of the image, the Spot Healing Brush produces a selection, evaluates the surrounding pixels, and then blends them before removing the selection.

Removing a Crease or Tear

I have scanned a photo that was taken over 100 years ago on which you can practice using the Healing and Spot Healing Brushes. Here is the step-by-step procedure:

1. Download the photo **Bearded_man.jpg** from the Peachpit Web site and open it.

2. Select the Healing Brush tool (J). Right-click (Option-click for Mac) opening a separate Brush Settings dialog. Change the brush setting to a 30 px brush with a Hardness of 0% (**Figure 9.12**). We are using a brush wide enough to cover the entire width of the crease. In the Options bar ensure Source is Sampled and Aligned is checked.

3. Place the Healing Brush tool on the spot shown in **Figure 9.13** and Alt-click (Option for Mac) the brush to establish the source point. Next, click (don't drag) the brush one time at the point on the crease indicated in Figure 9.13. The crease underneath the brush, where you applied the Healing Brush, disappears.

Healing Brush   Set to 30   Set to Zero   Sampled   Aligned

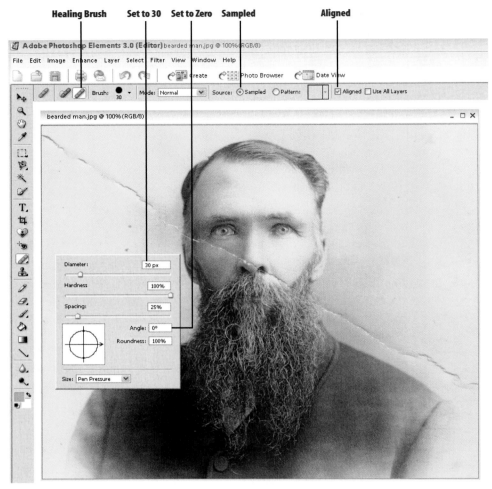

Figure 9.12
Select a brush size that is wider than the crease being repaired.

4. Hold down the Shift key and click at a point at the top of the crease shown in **Figure 9.14**. The entire crease disappears. What happened? The Healing Brush tool painted a straight line from the first click made in the previous step to the second click just made.

5. Use the Zoom tool (Z) to zoom in close enough so the left side of the subject's face fills the display (**Figure 9.15**). When working on areas that have detailed information, I don't recommend using the automatic Shift key feature because it will produce a

visibly brighter area. When restoring the damage on the cheek, try picking a source point below the damage. When working on the nose, and on the hair, a point above the damage appears to work best. We're done with the Healing Brush.

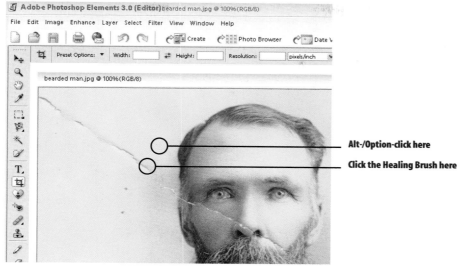

Figure 9.13
Select a clean point near the crease as source pixels before clicking the Healing Brush tool on the crease.

Figure 9.14
Smaller brush sizes produce better results.

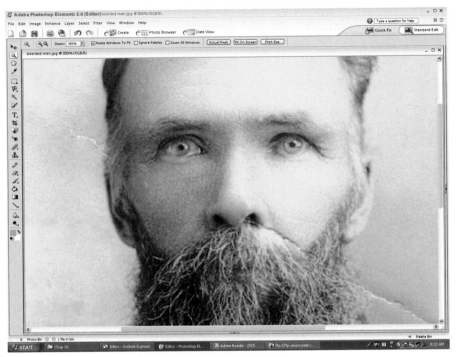

Figure 9.15
The Healing Brush is also used to repair the cheek and nose areas of the photo.

6. There isn't a good source area for the dark area in the nostril (ugh) so we'll switch to the Spot Healing Brush (which doesn't require a source point). In the Options bar set the brush size to 6 pixels and click (don't drag) on the damaged area. This brush works best when used with small brush sizes and on isolated areas of damage or debris.

7. Use the Spot Healing brush to remove the remaining parts of the crease near the head and some of the dark spots on the background. Be careful not to apply the tool to areas that are too close to adjacent areas that are either much darker or much brighter than the area you are fixing. The Spot Healing Brush uses those pixels when calculating the blend, and if their shading differs greatly from the area you're working on, a noticeable smudge will result.

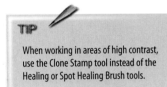

TIP

When working in areas of high contrast, use the Clone Stamp tool instead of the Healing or Spot Healing Brush tools.

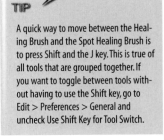

TIP

A quick way to move between the Healing Brush and the Spot Healing Brush is to press Shift and the J key. This is true of all tools that are grouped together. If you want to toggle between tools without having to use the Shift key, go to Edit > Preferences > General and uncheck Use Shift Key for Tool Switch.

8. Return to Actual Pixels (Alt+Ctrl+0/Option+Cmd+0) to see how the restoration appears (**Figure 9.16**).

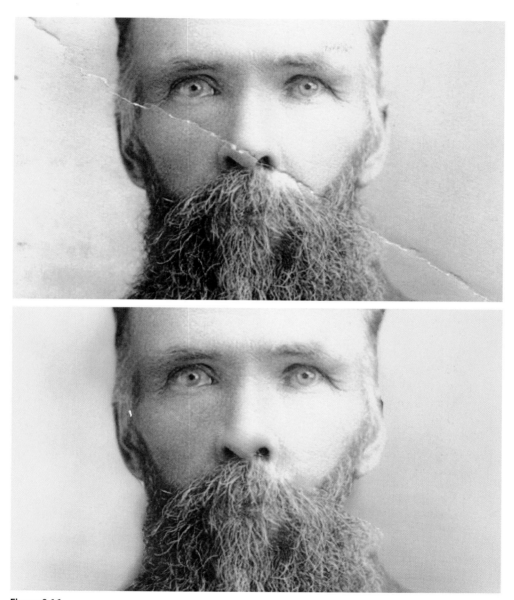

Figure 9.16
The damage to the photograph has been removed, and the digital image is immune to further aging.

Fixing Other Photo Problems

While fixing antique photos is fun, a more common problem is working with color photos taken in the last 40 years. Even if not exposed to daylight, the dyes in the photos are changing color. In the next exercise, we'll color-correct an image and learn a different way to remove damage and debris. This exercise uses the file, **Guitar_man.jpg**, which is available from the Peachpit Web site.

1. Open the file **Guitar_man.jpg** (**Figure 9.17**). The photo was taken in the early '70s, so there are several things that need attention. The colors are shifting with age (moving toward magenta), and something is splattered on the photo. We'll tackle the splatter first.

Figure 9.17
There is junk splattered on the photo, and the colors are shifting with age.

2. Select the Rectangular Marquee tool (M) in the Toolbox. In the Options bar change the Feather value to 3 pixels. Click in the image and drag a rectangle selection over a section of the background that is relatively free from defects (**Figure 9.18**). Size and location are not critical.

Figure 9.18
Create a selection over a clean area of the background.

3. Select the Move tool (V). Hold down the Alt key (Option for Mac). Click the cursor inside the selection and drag it across the photo until it is on top of the debris (**Figure 9.19**), and then let go of the mouse button. The selection becomes a floating selection containing a copy of the pixels that it originally surrounded. When the mouse button is released the pixels in the selection replace the pixels below it.

Figure 9.19
Dragging a floating selection partially covers the debris on the photo.

4. With the Alt key still held down, drag the selection up until it covers the remainder of the debris and release the mouse button again (**Figure 9.20**). As long as the Alt key (Option for Mac) is held down when you move the selection, a copy of the originally selected pixels move with it.

5. When you are rid of the debris in the sky, Ctrl+D/Cmd+D removes the floating selection.

Figure 9.20
Continue to drag the floating selection until all of the debris has been covered up.

6. Correcting the color shift in photos like these is quite simple. Click Enhance > Auto Color Correction (Shift+Ctrl+B/Shift+Cmd+B). The color shift is almost completely removed (**Figure 9.21**).

Figure 9.21
The Auto Color Correction removes the color shift caused by aging.

7. Final cleanup: Use the Spot Healing Brush to remove the debris around the head. Apply Smart Auto Fix (Ctrl+M/Cmd+M) to balance out the darker areas. At this point the image will appear a little noisy so apply the Reduce Noise filter (Filter > Noise > Reduce Noise) at the default settings. You're done (**Figure 9.22**).

NOTE

One of the reasons Auto Color Correction works so well with old color photos like this is because the photo's white border serves as a good reference point for Elements' color correction feature.

Figure 9.22
After performing some final cleanup tasks, the photo is once again ready for prime time.

Summary

We have covered some of the basics of scanning and photo restoration in this chapter. It is so much fun to restore old photos and not-so-old photos to see what things used to look like. In the next chapter, we'll really kick out the stops and learn how to do all kinds of wild and crazy things with Elements.

10 Creating Stunning Panoramas

Before I began using Photoshop Elements, I had limited experience creating panoramas. This was because making them without using a program specifically designed to create them was a major effort. After I began using Photoshop Elements' Photomerge feature, I was hooked. One of the challenges for me in writing this chapter was to remember that not everyone makes panoramas or photo montages. So I promise not to get too carried away—maybe. But after you read this chapter, you might get inspired!

The Power of the Panorama

Panoramas are not a new thing. Soon after the invention of photography in 1839, the desire to show the broad expanse of both cities and landscapes—or large groups of people—prompted photographers to begin creating panoramas. Say the word *panorama* and most people envision a wide, full-color photograph of some majestic landscape, such as the Grand Canyon, or a tropical paradise. But panoramas have most often been used to document people, places, and events. Pictures of high school graduation classes are often captured using specialized (and expensive) panorama cameras, which were the only way to produce a panorama before digital photo editing came along. Today, any camera can take the picture elements required to build a panorama—with a little help from Photoshop Elements.

Taking Pictures for a Panorama

Of all the features and projects that can be accomplished by using Photoshop Elements, making a good panorama is unique in that it requires preparation on the photographic side. Taking photos to be used in a panorama isn't *that* hard—it just takes some getting used to.

What You Need to Take Panorama Photos

Probably the most important item that you need to take panoramas is a tripod. It keeps the camera on an even plane as you rotate it. That said, some of my best panoramic shots were taken without using a tripod; the resulting panoramas came out because of my using a tripod substitute, or just by dumb luck.

The second thing necessary for creating a great panorama is having the sun or other light source behind or above you, rather than at one end of the scene or the other. If the sun isn't where you need it to be—it rarely is—you can usually lock the automatic exposure (AE) settings by pressing the shutter button down halfway. The goal is to prevent the individual photos used to make the panorama from having different levels of brightness that result in light and dark lines of demarcation in the final image, as shown in **Figure 10.1**. This panorama was created from three photos. The center photo was lighter than the other two. When Photomerge merged the photos, it attempted to blend the edges, resulting in the unique area of light in the middle.

Following are a couple of rules and general guidelines that might help you take good panorama photos.

Figure 10.1
If the separate photos have different overall brightness, it can produce dark and light panels in the panorama.

Don't Get Too Close

When taking panoramic pictures, you want to get as far away from the subject as is reasonable. The closer you are to the subject, the wider the setting on your zoom lens; this produces greater barrel distortion on each photo. If there's too much distortion, even Photomerge cannot prevent weird-looking gaps between each panel, like the image shown in **Figure 10.2**. So get a good distance away from your subject when possible.

Figure 10.2
Using photos too close to the subject often results in a panorama that looks like it was made by Picasso.

Controlling Overlap

Panoramas are made by stitching several photos together using the Photomerge Panorama command. To make a panorama that appears seamless, it is necessary for there to be some amount of overlap between each photo—just enough to get the job done. With too much overlap, the panorama file becomes huge and the program often has trouble stitching the photos together. How much overlap is enough? For this program 30 percent overlap is about right.

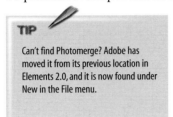

TIP

Can't find Photomerge? Adobe has moved it from its previous location in Elements 2.0, and it is now found under New in the File menu.

So how do you measure a 30 percent overlap? Here is a trick that I use. When I take the initial photograph, I note some point of reference in the LCD frame of my digital camera. As I rotate the camera (more on that in a moment), I try to make sure that the reference point remains in the right or left third of the frame (depending on which way I turn it).

If you aren't using a tripod, when you turn the camera, make every effort to have the camera lens rotate around an imaginary axis. When I first started taking panoramic photos, I held the camera and turned my body. By doing that, I changed the angle of the camera in reference to the scenery that I was photographing. It is less important when the subject is a great distance away, but it becomes important when the subject matter is close.

We cover additional tips later in this chapter. Now it's time to make a simple panorama.

Creating a Simple Panorama

For the first panorama, let's make a simple one from two photos. If you downloaded the files for this chapter, we will be using **Left_gate.jpg** and **Right_gate.jpg**.

1. Choose File > New > Photomerge Panorama. The dialog that appears enables you to select the photos used in the panorama (see **Figure 10.3**) using the Browse button. If any photos are already open in Photoshop Elements, they appear on this list. Photomerge uses the order of the files in the dialog to assemble the panorama. Click OK.

2. Photomerge works on the image for a few moments. How long this takes is a function of the size and number of the photos and the horsepower of your system. If Photomerge can't figure out how to assemble the photos, a message is displayed telling you to manually align the photos (**Figure 10.4**). If this happens, just click and drag the thumbnails into the workspace and put the photos in the correct order. Use the Navigator on the right side to zoom in and fill the screen with the panorama (**Figure 10.5**). After you have the photos in the right order, go to the next step, but don't click the OK button yet.

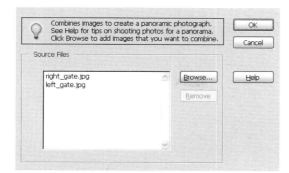

Figure 10.3
The images to be included in the panorama are selected from the Photomerge dialog.

Figure 10.4
If Photomerge cannot automatically determine the correct order of the photos, it asks you to put them in the right order.

Figure 10.5
Use the Photomerge control dialog to edit the panorama.

3. Now look carefully at the bottom of the gate under the letters "A" and "S" (**Figure 10.6**), and you can see that the pieces don't exactly match up. Why? The camera was handheld and the orientation of the camera changed slightly between photos. Here is how to fix it. Click the Perspective button on the right, which slightly distorts one of the photos to make all of the edges fit (**Figure 10.7**). Now click OK and Photomerge will grind away for a few minutes before producing the panorama.

4. To finish up, flatten the panorama (select Layers, Flatten Image), and select the Crop tool (C) to remove parts of the image that are not required.

Figure 10.6
Using the default setting causes there to be mismatch at the edge.

Figure 10.7
Photomerge seamlessly (almost) made the two halves of the plane into a single image.

Figure 10.8
A simple panorama made by using Photomerge and two photographs.

Creating a Panorama from Three Photos

Since aligning edges is something that will always be part of making panoramas, the next exercise uses three photos, and will let you see more features. If you want to try your hand at this, the files have been made available for download on the Peachpit Web page:

1. From the Create Photomerge dialog select **Town_left.jpg**, **Town_middle.jpg**, and **Town_right.jpg**. Use the Browse button to locate the three files and click OK. The photos may or may not stitch together in the correct order. If not, click and drag them into the correct order.

2. When the stitched image appears in the Photomerge dialog, it is apparent there are two potential problems (**Figure 10.9**) with the image. The first problem is misalignment. Just like the first exercise, clicking the Perspective button corrects the misalignment (**Figure 10.10**) but not the shading.

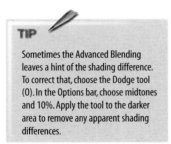

TIP

Sometimes the Advanced Blending leaves a hint of the shading difference. To correct that, choose the Dodge tool (O). In the Options bar, choose midtones and 10%. Apply the tool to the darker area to remove any apparent shading differences.

3. Even though these photos were taken in diffused light (overcast), there is a noticeable shading difference, as shown in Figure 10.9. To correct this, select the Advanced Blending option. A preview of the blended image appears (**Figure 10.11**). Click Exit Preview and then click OK. After a few moments, Elements creates the initial panorama. The effect of the Advanced Blending is shown in **Figure 10.12**.

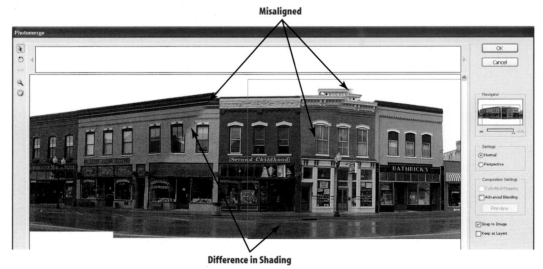

Figure 10.9

This panorama, made by using three photos, has two challenges to overcome.

Figure 10.10
The Perspective feature corrects the misalignment.

Figure 10.11
Using the Perspective and Advanced Blending corrected the initial problems of this panorama.

Figure 10.12
Before Advanced Blending was applied. After the Blending was applied.

4. Several things need to be done next. First, from the Layer menu, choose Flatten Image. Next, crop the image using the Crop tool (C). What you crop is purely subjective. I chose to crop the building on the far right (**Figure 10.13**) because its architecture didn't blend well with the other buildings, but to each their own.

Figure 10.13
After you flatten and crop, the panorama looks pretty good.

Adding Some Life to a Dull Sky

The photos that made up the panorama in Figure 10.13 were taken under almost ideal conditions. It was an overcast sky (diffused light), it had rained earlier that morning so the street was wet, and since it was still early on a Saturday morning, no cars were parked on the street. In case you were wondering, the photos were taken in Stillwater, MN.

> **NOTE**
>
> Wet pavement is always better. If you doubt that, watch new car commercials; the cars are always parked on wet pavement.

The problem with this ideal lighting is that the sky is almost pure white. Let's fix that. If you didn't keep (or make) the panorama, I left a copy of mine you can download. For this exercise, you will need **Stillwater_pano.jpg.**

1. Locate and open the image **Stillwater_pano.jpg**.

2. Select the Magic Wand tool (W) from the Toolbox. In the Options bar change the Tolerance to 20 and ensure the Contiguous check box is not checked. Click anywhere in the sky, and the selected area will be surrounded with the marquee (marching ants). In selecting the white sky, the white parts of the building were also selected, so we need to remove those selections by using the Selection Brush tool (A) in the Toolbox.

3. The most important area is the white top portion of the building on the right side of the panorama. Select the Zoom tool (Z), and zoom in on it until that part of the building fills the screen. Then, select the Selection Brush tool, which turns the screen pink (**Figure 10.14**). If your screen doesn't change colors, change the Mode setting in the Options bar from Selection to Mask.

4. Right-click to open the brushes palette (Option-click for Mac), and choose the 19 px brush with a hard edge. Paint the white areas of the top portion of the building near the edge. Leave the areas in the lower part of the building untouched.

5. Change the View to Fit to Screen (Ctrl+0/Cmd+0) and select the Rectangular Marquee tool (M). Holding down the Alt (Option for Mac) key, click and drag a rectangle over any remaining areas on the building that remain selected. You may have to make small rectangles in several spots.

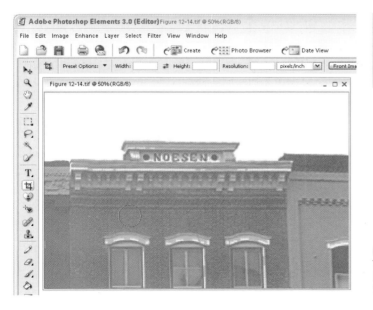

The Unique Way Photomerge Stitches Photos

When you looked at Figure 10.1 you may have wondered why the brighter center photo made a triangle of light when it was stitched together, rather than a bright rectangle in the center. This is because Photomerge stitches photos together along a diagonal line rather than the vertical line that naturally exists between the photos. While I don't know for sure, it seems that it is done this way to reduce the appearance of any hints of lines by spreading them across the diagonal. You also see the same effect in Figure 10.12.

TIP

It is faster if you click on the areas to be de-selected rather than clicking and dragging the Selection brush.

Figure 10.14
The red mask overlay of the Selection Brush tool indicates the areas of an image that are and are not selected.

6. Click on the Foreground Color swatch at the bottom of the Toolbox, and when the Color Picker opens (**Figure 10.15**), pick a blue fit for a sky and click OK.

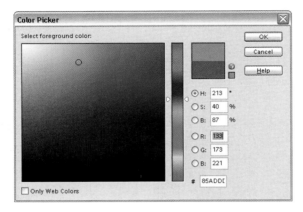

Figure 10.15
Use the Color Picker to select a realistic blue for the sky.

7. Select the Gradient tool (G) from the Toolbox, and in the Options bar click the down arrow to open the Gradient picker (**Figure 10.16**), then choose Foreground to Transparent.

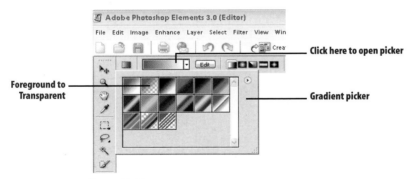

Figure 10.16
The Gradient picker.

8. At the top and middle of the panorama, click and drag a line straight down and release the mouse button when you are halfway down the upper windows. This produces the graduated sky shown in **Figure 10.17**.

Figure 10.17
The graduated-blue-to-transparent gradient makes a realistic replacement sky for an overcast day.

9. To make the sky look even more realistic, click Filter, Render, Clouds. Remove the selection, and you're done (**Figure 10.18**). The overcast sky has been replaced with a realistic substitute.

Figure 10.18
The finished panorama.

Panorama Examples

I wanted to show you some of the projects that I have created with the newest version of Photomerge in Elements 3.0.

Figure 10.19 was created from three handheld photos I took one evening as I was driving home and stopped the car long enough to take about five sets of photos. This was the best.

Figure 10.19
This panorama was made from three handheld photos.

The Kansas field in **Figure 10.20** was also made from three photos, but I replaced the original overcast sky with a sunset I had taken the previous evening. Replacing the sky is done like the previous exercise except, instead of using a gradient fill, you select and copy an existing sky to the Clipboard and use the Edit > Paste into Selection option.

Figure 10.20
This panorama was made from three photos, and the sky was from another sunset.

Figure 10.21
One of my longest panoramas, this one was made from seven photos.

Really Wide Panoramas

Of course, some panoramas are very wide and narrow. I shot this one of a pier in La Jolla, California (**Figure 10.21**). It was made from seven photographs taken using a tripod. When a panorama gets this wide, the perspective becomes distorted, making either of the panorama's ends very small.

Vertical Panoramas

Not all panoramas are wide. Photomerge has the ability to make vertical as well as horizontal panoramas. There are a lot of things in this world that are taller than they are wide—Michael Jordan comes to mind. The panorama in **Figure 10.22** was made from three photographs. In Photomerge, all that was necessary to arrange them into a vertical format was to drag each image on top of the other. The challenge faced when using vertical panoramas is that they can be difficult to lay out in a publication like this book.

Multiple Panels Overlaid

The challenge I had with the waterfall on Bull Creek panorama (**Figure 10.23**) was that diffused light from the overcast sky had made the falls dark. The solution was to take two sets of panoramic photos. I shot the first set using the sky as the light source. The second set of photos I took by using the spot setting on my camera, so that the exposure would be adjusted correctly for the waterfall portion, even though the sky would be overexposed (washed out). I created two separate panoramas from the photos, and

Figure 10.22
Not all panoramas have to be horizontal.

then merged the two panoramas using layers in Elements. **Figure 10.23** shows the final result.

Figure 10.23
This photo was made from two sets of photos taken at two different exposure settings.

How Big Can You Make Them?

When it comes to making panoramas, this is the most frequently asked question. There isn't a really good answer to that. Because I like to make panoramas that print flat, I limit my photos to take in no more than 180 degrees.

How to Print Panoramas

Because I like to print the panoramas that I make, I make sure that the width is 20 inches or less. The trick with printing panoramas is to have a printer that can print either on panorama-sized paper, or a printer that accepts roll paper. This typically means that the preferred printer accepts paper from the rear. Since every HP printer I have ever worked with feeds paper from the front, with few exceptions, they cannot be used to print panoramas.

TIP

If your panorama is larger than the paper you are printing on, you should resize the image using your photo-editing software. Do not let the printer software do it because the quality of the resized image will not be as good.

Pick the Right Paper

Epson offers panorama paper in a single, fixed size, but if you use this paper you must make sure that your panorama fits the paper you are using. If you are using roll paper then theoretically you can make your panoramas any size you want. However, when you want to frame your panorama, you will discover that panorama frames are not common and custom frames are expensive.

11

Sharing Your Photos

Once you have sorted, organized and fixed all of your photos, the next logical step is to share these photographic masterpieces with others. Back in the days of film, the only way to share your favorite photos was to make multiple prints and mail them to others, or gather your friends together in your home and have them watch a slide show. The latter event was often considered torture for the viewers. With Photoshop Elements 3, you have many more choices. In this chapter, you will learn how to make a wide variety of cool creations both printed and electronic. We'll begin by learning how to use Elements and your printer to create stunning photographs that look as good, or even better, than what you would get from your local one-hour photo service.

Making Great Photos on Your Printer

Printing from Elements, as with any other program, is easy. Just select the Print command and your photo prints comes out of your photo printer. But, regardless of how good you make your photographs look on the computer, if you cannot get good-quality prints from your printer, it can be frustrating. If you ever printed something using Adobe Photoshop, you were faced with a bewildering selection of features, options, and what-have-yous to pick from. You'll be relieved to learn that Elements has really streamlined the printing process.

In this section, we learn about how to make all kinds of cool picture packages with the click of a button. Also, we learn much about how to make great photos on almost any inkjet printer. Finally, we explore some of the options available to you for making hard copies of your masterpieces.

Basic Photo Printing

Basic printing using Elements has changed a little in version 3.0 It is now a two-step process:

- Preview Size and Orientation. This ensures the photo is the right size and orientation.

- Print. This controls printer selection and provides access to printer properties.

While printing with Elements is really simple, I have included the following step-by-step exercises so that you can see how the different parts of the print dialogs interact with one another. To do this exercise you will need to download the photo **Jonathan_and_Grace.jpg** from the Peachpit Press Web site.

1. Select Print from the File menu (Ctrl/Cmd+P), and when the Print Preview dialog opens (**Figure 11.1**) you can see that the photo appears very small in the Preview window. The size of the image that appears in the Preview window reflects the paper size setting of the selected printer. For example, in Figure 11.1, the selected printer is currently set to use letter-sized paper.

NOTE

You can't change the printer paper size from this dialog. See the section "When the Photo Doesn't Fit" for details on changing paper size.

2. The settings on the right (Print Size and Scaled Print Size) control the size of the printed image and both functionally do the same thing. The Print Size contains a short list of standard print sizes in addition to Fit On Page and Custom. The Custom setting appears if you manually enter in a new size using the Scaled

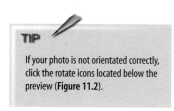

TIP

If your photo is not orientated correctly, click the rotate icons located below the preview (**Figure 11.2**).

Print Size. Change the Print Size to 4" x 6" and the size of the preview changes. Also notice that the Scaled Print Size dialog now indicates that the printed image will be enlarged 35% (or 135.44%).

3. Change the Print Size to 5" x 7". Notice that a warning now appears (**Figure 11.3**) letting you know that if you enlarge the photo to this size, its resolution will drop below 220 dpi meaning it will result in a poorer quality photo.

NOTE

There is nothing magic about the 220 dpi threshold. As a general rule, when working with a good quality full-color (24-bit RGB) image, you won't see a noticeable loss of image quality when printing at a lower resolution.

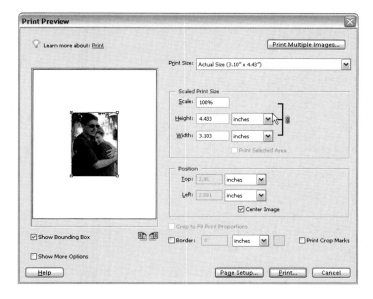

Figure 11.1
Check and make sure that photo orientation and size are correct before pressing the Print button.

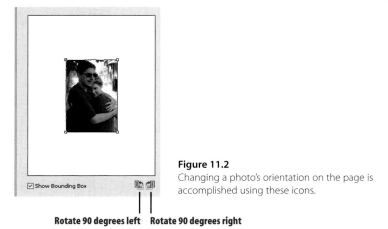

Figure 11.2
Changing a photo's orientation on the page is accomplished using these icons.

Rotate 90 degrees left   **Rotate 90 degrees right**

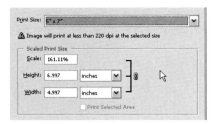

Figure 11.3
A warning appears
when the resolution
of the enlarged
photo gets too low.

When the Photo Doesn't Fit

If the photo in the Preview area doesn't fit, there are several possible reasons: the paper size is too small or the image is too large. If the paper size selected by the printer is too small, do the following:

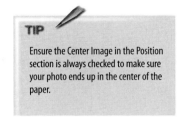

TIP

Ensure the Center Image in the Position section is always checked to make sure your photo ends up in the center of the paper.

1. Click the Page Setup button opening the Page Setup dialog (**Figure 11.4**).

Figure 11.4
Choose Page Setup to change Paper Size.

Image Size Vs. Resolution

How can an image that is 4 by 3 inches at the same time be 18 by 13 inches? The answer is resolution. At a resolution of 300 dots-per-inch (dpi), the image will print out at approximately 4 by 3 inches. If the resolution is changed to 72 dpi the same photo would print at 18 by 13 inches. The quality of the larger image would be much poorer due to the lower resolution. While everyone has a different opinion about what is minimum resolution for a good print, I find that 150 dpi produces a good quality print.

2. Select a larger Paper Size setting. If the paper size you want isn't on the list, it may be because the currently selected printer doesn't support it. You can't tell which printer is currently selected from this dialog either.

If the paper size is the correct size, the image itself may be too large—see the sidebar "Image Size Vs. Resolution." You can make Elements resize the image by choosing one of the preset sizes back in the Print Preview.

What happens when the image appears to be the size of a postage stamp (**Figure 11.5**)? This is usually caused by the resolution of the image being set too high. You can change the size of the photo in the Print Preview but I recommend that you exit Print Preview and change the size in Elements Editor using Image, Resize, Image Size.

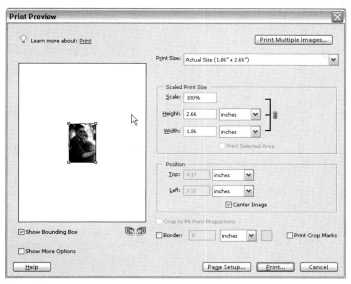

Figure 11.5
When the resolution is too high the image preview reveals a very tiny photo.

Where is the Printer?

Seeing which printer is selected and how that printer is set up from within Elements requires the navigation of a couple of dialogs—from the Print Preview (File, Print, Print button) or the Page Setup (File, Page Setup, Printer).

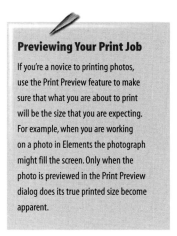

Previewing Your Print Job

If you're a novice to printing photos, use the Print Preview feature to make sure that what you are about to print will be the size that you are expecting. For example, when you are working on a photo in Elements the photograph might fill the screen. Only when the photo is previewed in the Print Preview dialog does its true printed size become apparent.

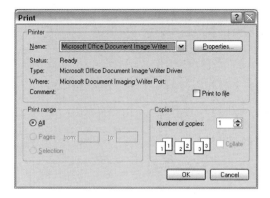

Figure 11.6
Two different ways (Page Setup and Print) to choose and configure a printer.

Setting Up Your Printer

Once you have selected the printer, the next step is to set up your printer. This is done by clicking the Properties button. The Printer Properties dialog appears (two samples are shown in **Figures 11.7** and **11.8**). Each dialog is unique to its manufacturer, but they all have certain items in common. The following items must be checked before you start printing your first job of the day:

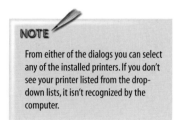

NOTE

From either of the dialogs you can select any of the installed printers. If you don't see your printer listed from the drop-down lists, it isn't recognized by the computer.

- Type of paper. With inkjet printers, this setting is critical. Many users are disappointed with the photographs they print because the printer is set up to print to plain paper when photo paper is installed.

- Paper size. Generally, it should be set to letter size in the United States.

- Orientation. Is the photo in landscape or portrait orientation? Does the setting of the printer match the orientation of what you are printing?

Speeding Up Your Print Jobs

Printing a photo can take a lot of time. This section discusses some ways in which you can speed up the job while maintaining excellent results.

Flatten Your Picture

If you are about to print a photograph that contains layers, you can print out a photo quicker if you flatten the image before you print it. First, you need to save the photo as a PSD file to preserve the layers, but then save a copy and flatten the photo by using the Flatten Image command (found in the Layers menu).

Figure 11.7
The dialog that appears for the printer properties is designed and provided by the printer manufacturer and, therefore, is unique.

Figure 11.8
The Properties dialog for an Epson Photo Stylus printer contains more choices for you to make when compared to the dialog shown in Figure 11.7.

Resolution—More Is Slower

Every printer manufacturer that sells printers that will be used for graphics or printing out photos heavily advertises the resolution of its printers. I am using an Epson Stylus Photo 960 to proof my pages for this book. It advertises that it can print at a resolution of 2,880 dpi. That is an incredible resolution, so it stands to reason that a photo printed at that resolution would be razor sharp with fantastic detail, right? Actually, that's not true. The first stumbling block to this printing miracle is your eyes. That is more than most anyone's eyes can resolve. Ignoring that minor problem, when you print at the highest resolution that the printer can spit out, it consumes large amounts of ink and takes up to four times as long to print.

Getting the Best Quality Prints from Your Printer

The three most important things that affect the quality of the photographs that you print are the resolution settings, the paper quality, and the ink quality.

Optimum Resolution Settings

So what resolution setting should you use to get the best possible photographic prints? For a majority of your printings, the default automatic photo setting should work great. If you go into one of the advanced settings pages (**Figure 11.9**), you might be surprised to discover that most photo printers normally print quality photographs at a resolution of 720 dpi. The reason has to do with the human eyes' limitation that we mentioned previously. If a photograph has a wide palette of colors, it's almost impossible to tell the difference between a photo printed at 720 dpi and one printed at 2,880 dpi.

Figure 11.9
For all the advertising for monstrously high resolutions, most photo printers print beautifully at their default setting of 720 dpi.

So when should you use the higher resolutions? If the photograph you are printing is 5 by 7 or larger, you might benefit from printing at 1,440 dpi. But don't take my word for it—run a little test and print your favorite photograph at the top three resolutions of your printer. See how long it takes to print each one and write on the back of each photo what resolution it was printed at. After you do that, put the photos in a file folder or a big manila envelope, and the next time you are tempted to print at a higher resolution, pull out those prints to remind yourself of the difference (or lack thereof).

Your Photo Is Only as Good as the Paper

Like it or not, the best photo printer in the world produces pretty crummy photos when it prints them on copier paper. Another general fact of life: Your printer will do better on its own brand of specialty paper than it will with the generic stuff you bought at the local super center. This has nothing to do with the superiority of the printer manufacturer's paper and, even though I recommend their paper, I still have to buy my own just like you. It has to do with the settings of the printer software being fine-tuned to get the best-looking result using its own paper. Look at the list of papers (media) that are listed for my Epson Stylus Photo 960 printer (**Figure 11.10**). Two types of paper are listed: A large variety of Epson papers and others. So when I have important samples of my photographs I need to produce on my Epson printer, I use their premium photo stock and get great results.

Figure 11.10
For the best possible photos from your printer, you should always use the specialty paper provided by the printer's manufacturer.

Now, if you are printing cute sticker buttons for your kids' birthday paper, making invites for a bash, or punching out the dreaded annual holiday newsletter, get the best deal on paper you can and go for it.

Ink Quality, Refills, and Other Fun Stuff

Because the cost of ink refills is getting to be almost as expensive as the printers, it becomes tempting to get generic ink cartridges or refill kits. I cannot address the non-photo ink refills because I haven't done any testing with them, but I have done some serious testing of the generic photo-printer inks, and they don't compare to the real thing. The colors are not the same; they are never as vivid as the original—period.

Working with PIM and Exif 2.2

Sometimes when you save an image, you might get a message that tells you the PIM data isn't being preserved. So, just what is this, and do you need it? The acronym PIM stands for PRINT Image Matching and it is endorsed primarily by Epson and some other camera manufacturers. The idea behind this standard is that PIM-enabled digital cameras and printers are designed to share PIM data that allows them to produce the best possible prints.

Another attempt at establishing a common language for digital cameras and printers is the Exif 2.2 (called Exif Print). It uses the information (Exif tags) in photos from digital cameras that support Exif 2.2. The Exif Print-supported printer reads this information and, in theory, produces optimum quality photos. The advantage of Exif 2.2 is that it uses the existing Exif data format, which your digital camera already uses whereas the PIM is proprietary. The idea that the printer can read color management information from the camera will become an industry standard, but it is still a work-in-progress at the time of this writing.

Anytime you notice that the colors of your inkjet printer aren't quite right, you need to run the test pattern and see if any of the printer's ink nozzles are blocked. If just one of the printhead nozzles are not working, a few of the colors in your photo can radically change. Clean the nozzles. This is especially true if you haven't printed on the printer in over a week. The printhead nozzles tend to dry up a bit.

Printing Multiple Copies of a Picture

One of the coolest features in Photoshop Elements is the capability to print many different-sized copies of a single image with a single click of a button. I'm talking about the Print Multiple Photos option (Windows) or the Picture Package feature located in the File Menu under Print Layouts (Mac).

In Windows, the Print Multiple Photos feature is started either by selecting it in the File menu, or by clicking the Print Multiple Photo button in the Print Preview dialog which then launches the Print Photo dialog (**Figure 11.11**) in Photo Organizer.

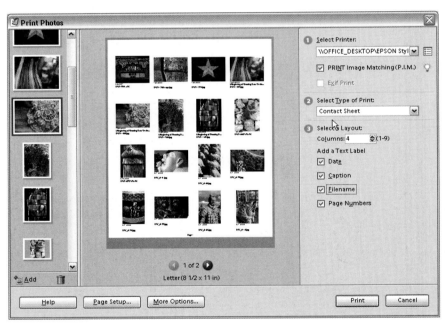

Figure 11.11
The Print Photo dialog.

From the Mac, you select the Picture Package feature from the File menu. Regardless of the platform and the program, they both work essentially the same way. The Mac version doesn't print directly to the printer. Instead, the application takes the image(s) and the layout you selected, and creates an Elements document that you can print or save and print at a later time. The Windows version can print to a file (select Microsoft Office Document Imaging as your printer choice).

Making a Contact Sheet

Contact sheets are invaluable summaries of the photos that you have. Here is how to make a contact sheet on the Windows platform. The Picture Package command on the Mac works in a similar fashion, except that the operation is simpler since it doesn't involve the additional program.

1. From Elements Photo Organizer choose Print, opening the Print Photo dialog (**Figure 11.12**).

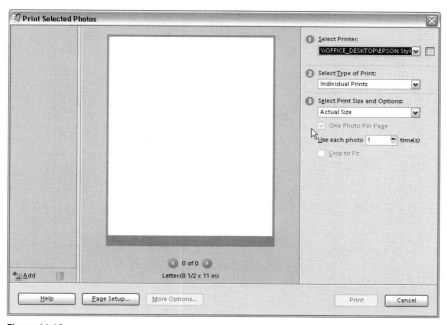

Figure 11.12
The Print Dialog in Photo Organizer is the starting point for multiple operations.

2. To select the photos to be included in the contact sheet, click the Add icon in the lower-left corner of the dialog, which opens another dialog (**Figure 11.13**).

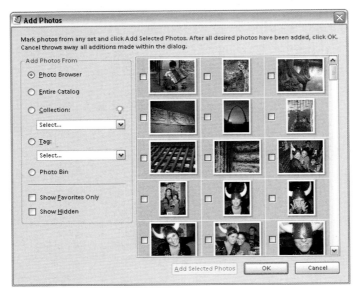

Figure 11.13
The Add Photos dialog, from which you select the photos to be included in the contact sheet

3. The choices of sources in this dialog is mind-boggling. Select the source from the Add Photos From section. Check the photos you want to include and then click the Add Selected Photos button. Click the OK button to return to the Print Selected Photos dialog (**Figure 11.14**).

4. Check the Select Printer setting to ensure it is set to the correct printer, also making sure you choose Microsoft Office Imaging Document if you want to make a file rather than choosing to print the image. The icon is to the right of the printer selection in the Printer Properties box. Clicking on the icon opens the printer properties for the selected printer.

5. Select Contact Sheet from the Select Type of Print. Then choose the number of columns you want to use for the contact sheet.

6. Check what information you want included under the thumbnails when the contact sheet is printed. Once it's all selected, click the Print button. **Figure 11.15** shows a completed contact sheet.

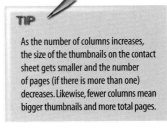

TIP

As the number of columns increases, the size of the thumbnails on the contact sheet gets smaller and the number of pages (if there is more than one) decreases. Likewise, fewer columns mean bigger thumbnails and more total pages.

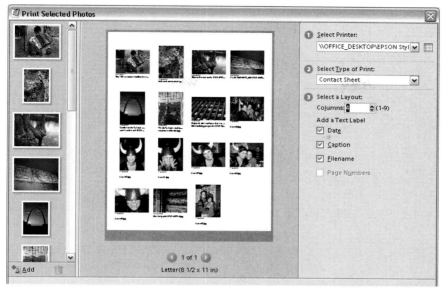

Figure 11.14
From here you can define how your contact sheet appears when it is created.

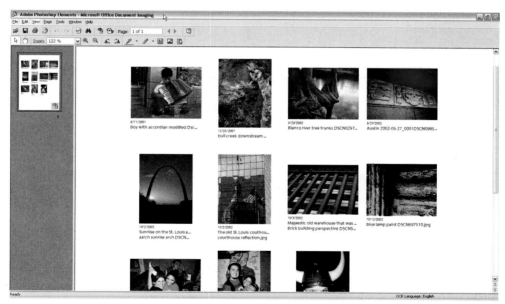

Figure 11.15
The completed contact sheet.

Creating a Picture Package

Picture Package lets you create a limitless combination of photos and styles on a single page. For those of you who like to share prints of favorite photos with friends, the Picture Package allows you to place multiple copies of the same photo (or even different photos) all on the same page in much the same manner as the smaller sets of school photos are printed on single sheets of letter-sized photo paper.

Creating a Picture Package is done in nearly the same way as the previous contact sheet.

1. From Elements Photo Organizer, choose Print, opening the Print Photo dialog.

2. To select the photos to be included in the Picture Package (even if it is only one), click the Add icon in the lower-left corner of the dialog box, which opens the Add Photo dialog.

3. Select the source containing the photo(s) you want to include in your Picture Package from the Add Photos From section. Check the photos you want to include, and then click the Add Selected Photos button. Then, click the OK button to return to the Print Selected Photos dialog.

4. Check Select Printer to ensure it is set to the correct printer. Make sure you choose Microsoft Office Imaging Document if you want to make a file rather than printing the image.

5. Select Picture Package from the Select Type of Print.

6. If you are making multiple copies of a single photo, make sure that you check the One Photo Per Page check box. Then, choose the layout you want to use and the preview reflects how it will appear when printed (**Figure 11.16**).

7. Wait—there's more. Adobe felt that you needed even more goodies on your Picture Package, so they added the option to add one of 24 frames like the one shown in **Figure 11.17**. Most of these jewels are too frilly for this Texan, but I am sure they will be appreciated by most users.

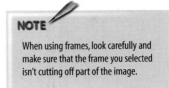

NOTE

When using frames, look carefully and make sure that the frame you selected isn't cutting off part of the image.

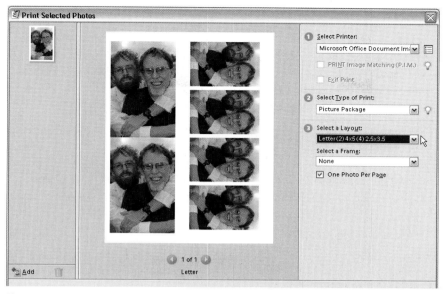

Figure 11.16
This represents only one of the more than 14 layout combinations.

Figure 11.17
This is only one of the 24 different frames that are available to include with your Picture Package.

Really Getting Creative with Creations

Photoshop Elements (Windows) lets you go far beyond just printing photos or attaching them to emails to send to friends. You can use your photos and video clips to create a great variety of photo albums, cards, postcards, wall calendars, web photo galleries, and slide shows. The slide shows can be saved on CDs in a format called VCD, that lets them be played on a DVD player as well as another computer. Regardless of which one you make, they are all called creations.

If the idea of making something as complicated as a slide show or photo album makes your heart skip a beat, fear not. Most of the creations in Elements use a Wizard that walks you through from start to finish. It is a step-by-step process in which you select one of the many templates, arrange your photos (hardest part), and when you are happy with it, you publish your creation.

Starting the Creation Process

From either the Elements Editor or the Photo Browser, you start the process by clicking the Create button ⟨🖼 Create⟩ in the menu bar, opening the Creation Setup dialog (**Figure 11.19**). This is the locus point—all creations begin here.

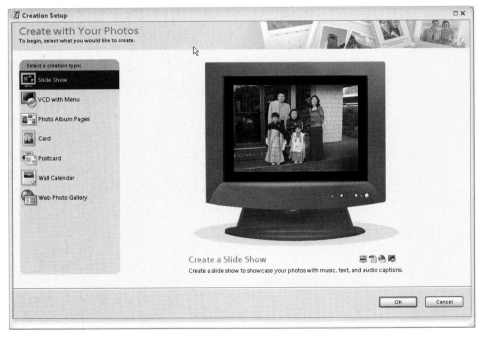

Figure 11.19
The Creation Setup dialog is the starting point for any creation that you want to make.

From here you select what you want to create in the left side of the dialog. As you select each item, a description of the creation appears in the lower-right corner of the dialog, as well as some tin icons that indicate how the selected creation can be shared (**Figure 11.20**).

Can be viewed on a computer   **Can be shared over email**

Can be saved and viewed as a PDF file   **Can be burned to a CD and viewed on most DVD players**

Figure 11.20
These icons tell you how the selected creation can be shared

Create a Slide Show

Gone are the days when a slide show involved a slide projector and a box containing several hundred slides. Now you can easily make a slide show of your vacation, or an important event like a graduation or wedding. You can select the slides, organize them, add text and titles, and then save them in one of several formats to share with friends and loved ones. Here is how to make your very own slide show. If you want to make the same slide show, you will need to download the sample files that were used in Chapter 5 which can be found on the Peachpit Press Web site.

1. From the Creation Setup, select Slide Show and click the OK button in the lower-right corner.

2. Your first choice is whether to make a simple slide show or to get fancy and make one with music, text, and a lot more frills (**Figure 11.21**). The simple slide show can be saved and played as a PDF (which means it can be attached to an email if the slide show isn't huge) while the Custom slide show can only be saved in a format that can be played on a CD/DVD player or another computer. In this example, we'll see how to make the Custom slide show.

Figure 11.21
Select the type of slide show you want to create.

3. When the Slide Show editor opens, you need to add photos to the slide show. Click on the Add icon and select the source for your photos (**Figure 11.22**). For this example, pick Photos from Folder and select the folder containing the downloaded files. Select the photos you want to use and click OK.

Figure 11.22
Select a folder containing photos that will be used in the slide show.

4. Once the slides are loaded, the slides appear in the Slide Show Editor (**Figure 11.23**). At anytime during this process, you can see a full screen preview of the slide show by clicking Full Screen Preview in the upper-right corner.

Figure 11.23
The slides are loaded and we're ready to make a slide show.

5. Let's add a title slide. Click the Add Blank Slide. It appears to the right of the first slide. Click on the blank slide in the thumbnail row at the bottom and drag it to the far left to make it the first slide. You can rearrange any slide in the show this way. Click the Add Text button, and when the Add Text dialog opens (**Figure 11.24**), add a title. I added the very original title: My Slide Show. Feel free to use it.

Figure 11.24
Add title page and a brilliant title.

6. Add some music. Adobe has provided a nice collection of music to go with your slide shows. Click on the music note icon. Choose Add Audio from Organizer and choose from the list of the recorded music that comes with Elements that appears. Pick something from the music selection, then click OK. You can also load your own favorite music instead of using the music provided by Adobe. Once the music is loaded, you can click the Fit Slides to Audio, and the transition time of each slide will be set so that the slides fit the length of the selected music.

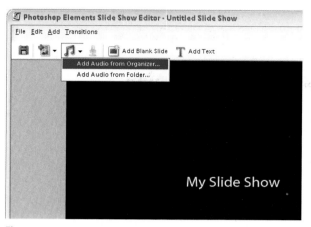

Figure 11.25
Adding music can really make your slide show special.

7. When you are finished with your slide show, you can save it in Organizer (File, Save). When the dialog opens (**Figure 11.26**), give the slide show a name. The file that you save is in a unique format that can only be opened by the Slide Show Editor.

Figure 11.26
Saving the file in Organizer.

8. To save it in a format that can be shared with others, you must save it as a Windows Meta Video (WMV) file or burn it as a Video CD. You can select either one from the File menu. The WMV files can be played by the Windows Media player and the Video CD can be played on most DVD players.

9. The second choice in the Creation list is VCD with Menu. This Creation allows you to put all of the slide shows that you made into a single Video CD with a menu. Now that you know how to make a slide show, let's see what other creation is possible.

Create a Photo Album

With this Creation Wizard, you can lay out your favorite photos using a variety of templates and design styles and then print a photo album on your photo printer.

1. From the Creation Setup, select Photo Album Pages and click the OK button in the lower-right corner to start the Wizard (**Figure 11.27**). The hardest part of using this wizard is that there is such a large number of choices that is it difficult to settle on one to use.

2. The next step is to add photos (**Figure 11.28**)

Figure 11.27
The Creation Wizard for setting up the Photo Album Pages

3. In the next step, you can add titles to the photos. The first photo is used as the title page. The photo's caption (if present) is replaced by the title text you add in this step. If you select Title but leave the title text blank, no text appears on the title page. A title page isn't mandatory, but a collection is improved by a brief descriptive title page.

TIP

Deselect Title if you want the photo's caption to appear on the title page.

4. The last three steps are self-explanatory. You save the photo album pages by giving them a name and choosing what format (PDF, email or Print) you want to save your pages in.

The Wizard for the Card, Postcard, and Wall Calendar is easy to use and so we won't cover it here. For details about these features, you can check the on-line users' guide or the users' manual.

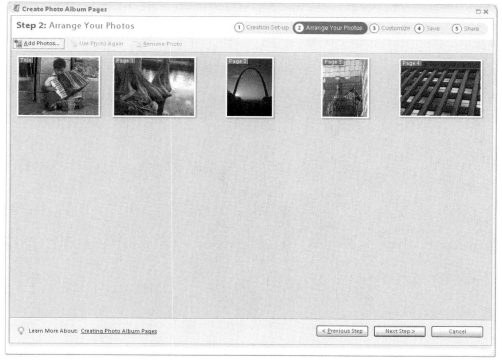

Figure 11.28
Add and sort the photos you want in your Photo Album pages.

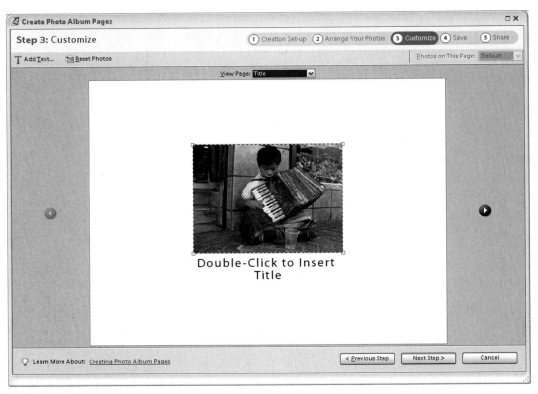

Figure 11.29
The addition of titles rounds out the photos on the pages.

Making a Web Photo Gallery

Sending photos to people as email is cool, but not nearly as cool as having your own Web page. If you are thinking, "I don't know the first thing about Web pages," then this next feature was made with you in mind. I have a confession to make at this point. I know next to nothing about Web pages myself, and yet I maintain a Web site with my latest photos (www.davehuss.com). So how do I do it? I use the Web Photo Gallery in this program.

Here is a summary of how this works.

- I pick the photos that I want to make into a Web page.

- I select a template that seems appropriate for the photos from the Web Photo Gallery Creation Wizard. When finished, I have a set of files.

- I copy the files to my Web site.

- Anyone accessing the Web site runs the Web page.

Running the Web Photo Gallery

The Web Photo Gallery Wizard does everything necessary to create a Web photo gallery that, when loaded to a server, works as a Web site that features a home page with thumbnail images and gallery pages with full-size images.

Getting A Web Site

So how do you get a Web site? If you have a cable modem, you often have Web space already available to you at no extra charge. In my case, I purchased the domain name davehuss.com and I also rent space on a Web hosting site. It doesn't cost much, I pay less than $40 per year for the whole thing. I still don't know anything about HTML or making Web pages, but with the help of Web Photo Gallery I am able to maintain a Web page.

1. From the Creation Setup select Web Photo Gallery and click the OK button in the lower-right corner (**Figure 11.30**).

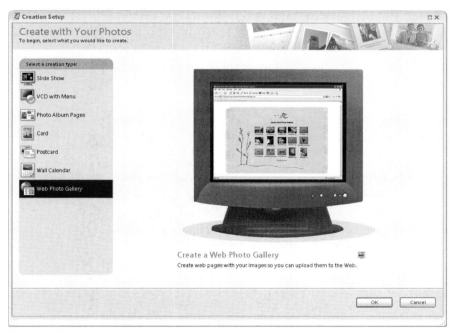

Figure 11.30
The Web Photo Gallery creation wizard starts here.

2. The next step involves adding the photos that you want to appear in the Web page. As with the other Creation Wizards, you add photos by clicking the Add icon and choosing the photos you want to appear in the Web page. This page can also be one of the most difficult. Adobe has included 35 Gallery Styles (**Figure 11.31**), making the choice of which one to use not an easy one.

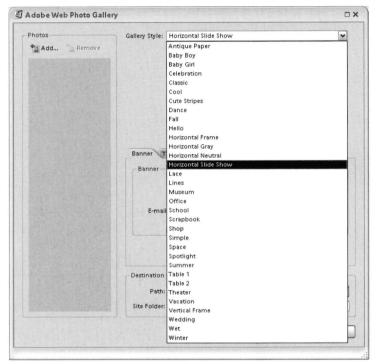

Figure 11.31
The next step involves the difficult decision of which gallery style to choose.

3. After adding your photos, you need to open the Banner tab and add Title, Subtitle, and so on (**Figure 11.32**). You also need to add a destination for where the Web files made by Web Photo Gallery will be stored. All of the other settings can be left at their default settings if you want.

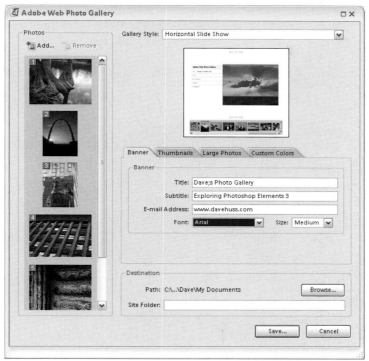

Figure 11.32
Make the necessary changes in the Banner and Destination value boxes.

4. When you are finished, click Save, and the Web pages will be built. When it is finished, the Web page you just created is launched (**Figure 11.33**). The next step is to run the Web Gallery again and make all the changes that you decide to make after you see the completed pages. Don't kid yourself, after you see the page, you'll start wondering what it would look like if you used a different font, thumbnail size, different gallery, and many other variables. Thus begins a long cycle of trying something different, rebuilding the Web page, and then trying another combination. There is just something that is addictive about it—in a fun way.

Figure 11.33
This finished Web page took only five minutes.

A Working with RAW Format

One of the exciting new features of Photoshop Elements 3 is the ability to import and work with RAW format images using the Camera RAW plug-in. While RAW is the image format of choice for professionals, many digital photographers either can't or don't use it. It was for this reason that I chose to make this section an appendix rather than a chapter in the mainstream of the book. If you aren't familiar with the RAW format, the first part of this appendix begins by explaining what the RAW format is, and the advantages of using it.

What Is RAW Format?

Many new mid-range to high-end digital cameras have the ability to save images in a unique format called RAW. The word RAW isn't an acronym as you might think, but literally means raw, as in "unprocessed." It refers to a format containing the unprocessed data from the digital camera's sensor. The format name RAW is always written using all capital letters.

A RAW file contains the original image information, as it comes off the sensor before in-camera processing is applied. With RAW format files, you do the processing on your computer with Photoshop Elements 3 or special software provided by the camera manufacturer. RAW files have unique file extensions depending on who makes that camera. For example, a RAW format file from a Nikon camera has an NEF extension; Canon uses CRW; Olympus, ORF; Fuji, RAF; and Minolta MRW, to name only a few.

Can Elements 3 Read RAW Files from My Camera?

Because new digital cameras are being introduced all the time, the ability to read and process RAW files from newer or improved models requires that the Camera RAW plug-in be frequently updated. If you go to www.adobe.com and search for RAW file support, you will find a list of the digital cameras that are currently supported. If your camera has a RAW format support but Elements 3 doesn't support it, be patient. Continue to use the software provided by your manufacturer and keep checking the Adobe Web site for the next Camera RAW plug-in update.

Does Your Camera Offer RAW Format?

The only way to tell if your camera offers RAW format is to read the manual. On every camera I have worked with, the choice of RAW format is part of the Quality settings. Quality settings are where you choose which JPEG setting to use, and they are selected either on the LCD menu or by clicking a button. The RAW format option is typically found on many mid-price to high-end consumer digital cameras and always on digital-SLR (Single Lens Reflex) cameras.

How Regular and RAW Images Are Processed

A lot happens inside your digital camera from the moment you press the shutter button until the image is tucked away into your camera's media card. The digital data from the camera's image sensor is sent to the camera's internal processor, at which time the white balance (WB), exposure, and other settings are applied. Next, the image is converted to a standard graphic format—typically JPEG, although some cameras can also save photos as TIFF files. Last, the processed files are stored on the media card.

If an image is saved using RAW file format, the camera does not apply any processing of the sensor data except to include time/date, camera settings, and more before

NOTE

In case you hadn't noticed the name, Camera RAW plug-in is a play on words. When you don't emphasize the ending "a" in camera, the name of the plug-in is Cam-er-RAW. Get it? While it's cute, it is generally accepted that if you have to explain the joke, it doesn't work.

saving it. When you attempt to open a RAW format file in Photoshop Elements 3, the program detects it as a RAW format file and opens the Camera RAW plug-in dialog (**Figure A.1**) to process the image, convert it, and open it in the workspace.

Figure A.1
The RAW file import dialog.

Why Use RAW?

RAW format files are often compared with film that has been exposed but not yet developed. The degree of control that is possible when opening a RAW format file is very impressive. Camera settings such as white balance, exposure, sharpening, and tone can be adjusted or changed when the image is opened. **Figure A.2** shows a RAW file that was opened with no changes applied alongside the same image that was corrected using the Camera RAW plug-in when it was opened.

Original **Corrected using Camera RAW plug-in**

Figure A.2
Many color cast and exposure problems can be resolved using the Camera RAW plug-in feature of Elements.

The only image problems that cannot be resolved using the Camera RAW plug-in controls are images that are out of focus and photos in which parts of the image have gone either completely white or black.

Another advantage to saving images as RAW files is that the image can be saved as a 16-bit image. See the sidebar "Why 16-Bit Is Bigger than 24-Bit" for further details. Photoshop Elements 3 offers limited support for 16-bit images, but the features that are supported are the essential ones like Auto Levels, Auto Contrast, Shadows/Highlights, Levels, and many more. The advantage of saving an image as a 16-bit/channel is helpful for the following types of images:

- An image that needs to be resized (made larger).

- A prized photo that you want to make into a spectacular one.

- An image with limited tonal range to which either Auto Contrast or Auto Levels needs to be applied.

- A noisy image that requires some extensive work to clean up.

Resizing, correcting, or removing noise from a 16-bit image will produce superior results than can be expected from applying the same actions to an 8-bit image. This is because a 16-bit image has more color (tonal) information in it for Photoshop Elements 3 to work with, and thus, you generally get superior results.

Disadvantages of RAW

Along with all the advantages of the RAW format come some drawbacks. It takes much longer to open RAW files and process them than it does with JPEGs due to their larger size. Workflow is another factor when working with RAW files. While a JPEG image can be attached to an email or viewed by almost any Windows or Mac application, a RAW format file must be converted before it can be used with any application.

As noted above, RAW files are larger than JPEGs. For example, a 512 MB CompactFlash (CF) card on my camera can hold either 51 RAW images or 179 images if saved as high-quality JPEG images. With the cost of memory cards decreasing every day, that shouldn't be a major concern, but it is still a factor when going out to take photos. It should also be noted that using RAW on cameras that are not digital SLRs can increase the time between shots because the larger file takes longer to write to the memory card. This is why professional digital cameras have large buffers that allow photographers to continue to take more photos while the previous images are still being written to the memory card.

The Camera RAW Plug-in Dialog

Before working with a RAW file, here is a quick look at the essential parts of the Camera RAW plug-in dialog (**Figure A.3**).

Why 16-Bit Is Bigger than 24-Bit

Referring to an image as 16-bit can be confusing. After all, the color depth of an image we typically work with is described as being 24-bit—therefore, describing an image as being 16-bit sounds like it would contain less color information, when in it in fact has twice as much. The term 16-bit describes the number of bits per color channel, while 24-bit refers to the total number of bits in all three color channels. So a 16-bit image actually has a color depth of 48-bits (16 x 3 color channels). So why not call them 48-bit images? Therein lies a mystery. Several years ago, scanners began offering the ability to send unprocessed (raw) data to the computer in 16-bit-per-channel format. They described the files as having a color depth of 48-bit. When digital cameras began to offer the same ability, the images were described as being 16-bit (per channel). For reasons unknown to this cowboy, the 16-bit handle stuck and continues to gain in popularity.

TIP

A CF memory card that claims it writes faster than normal CF cards offers no advantage on cameras that are not digital SLRs. This is because the write-accelerated memory usually operates from five to ten times faster than the non-SLR camera can write.

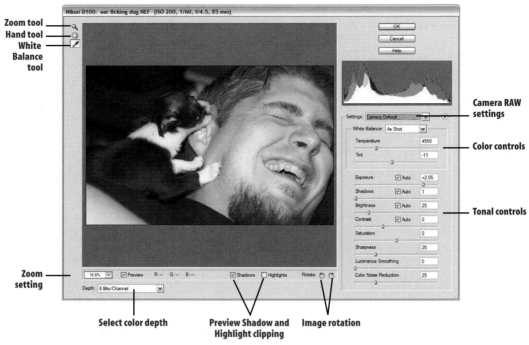

Zoom tool

Hand tool

White Balance tool

Camera RAW settings

Color controls

Tonal controls

Zoom setting

Select color depth

Preview Shadow and Highlight clipping

Image rotation

Figure A.3
The Camera RAW plug-in dialog.

What Is Color Temperature and White Balance?

These are terms that you hear a lot when working with digital cameras. Quite simply, color temperature is a measure of the color produced by light. You know that on a bright, sunny day, subjects tend to have a bluish color cast, and yet, as the sun begins to set, everything appears to take on an orange tint. The color temperature ranges from cool colors to warm colors and is measured in degrees Kelvin. Ironically, the higher the color temperature, the cooler the colors produced—the opposite of what we would expect.

White balance (WB) is a setting that establishes neutral colors, which is the key to accurate color reproduction. In camera film, the chemical composition of the film determines what colors are produced when it is properly exposed. Most film that people use to shoot pictures is balanced for daylight. A digital camera doesn't have a preset balance and must try to automatically calculate the correct WB (called automatic white balance, or AWB). While cameras are improving all of the time, oftentimes the digital camera gets fooled, and the result is an unwanted color cast, which should be removed using either the Camera RAW plug-in or the Editor in Photoshop Elements. When you open a RAW image, Elements attempts to read the WB setting that was included in the RAW file by the camera. If the WB setting in the dialog is set to As Shot, it uses the camera's white balance settings that are part of the image. Elements can't read the white balance settings with some digital cameras, either because the camera is a new model or the manufacturer used a non-standard format for the WB information. In such cases, Elements reads the image data and automatically calculates the white balance the best it can.

The controls for the Camera RAW plug-in are organized by their functions. Some of them are self-explanatory while others could use some explanation.

In the upper-left corner are the standard Zoom and Hand tools, while the tool below these two standard icons (the one that looks like the Eyedropper tool) is the White Balance tool. The color and tonal control give you an enormous amount of control over the color temperature, contrast, and other aspects of the image when the RAW file is processed. For more information, see the sidebar "What Is Color Temperature and White Balance?"

When either the Shadows or Highlights check box at the bottom of the dialog is enabled, the preview window shows areas of the image that have turned pure black (shadow) or pure white (highlight), which is discussed further below in the exercise.

The Settings area is where you can save your current settings in order to apply them to other RAW files when you open them. In the next section, we'll open and process a RAW file, as well as learn how to use it.

Correcting RAW Files in Elements 3

If you are new to working with RAW files, you may feel that there are so many adjustments that you don't know where to begin. I recommend the following order of events:

- Rotate—if required
- White balance correction
- Adjust exposure
- Tweak shadow and contrast
- Other adjustments—only as needed

To really get a feel for the power of working with RAW files, I have provided a RAW file to use for this exercise. **Ear_licking_dog.NEF** (NEF is the extension for a Nikon RAW file) is available for download on the Peachpit Press Web site. Because of the large size of the RAW format, the files are compressed and must first be uncompressed before you can use them.

1. With Elements in the Standard Edit mode, open the file **Ear_licking_dog.NEF**. Photoshop Elements automatically detects that this is a RAW file and opens the Camera RAW plug-in dialog (**Figure A.3**). By default, the Auto check boxes are selected when the Camera Raw dialog opens. The photo was taken using a flash relatively close to the subject so it is slightly overexposed and has a bluish cast.

NOTE

Adjustments to a photo made by controls using the Auto setting aren't necessarily the best settings. This is because Elements can't make decisions based on seeing the photo as a picture, but rather by making changes based strictly on its analysis of pixel values.

2. Correct the white balance by selecting the White Balance tool and then click on the white fur of the dog. Notice how the Temperature slider changes each time you click on a different white area of the dog's fur (**Figure A.4**). With the white balance corrected, the image remains slightly blue because the light of the flash makes colors appear cooler. See the sidebar "Accurate Vs. Desired Color" for more details. If you want a warmer image, choose the Flash preset in the White Balance menu.

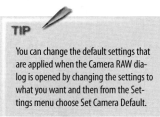

TIP

You can change the default settings that are applied when the Camera RAW dialog is opened by changing the settings to what you want and then from the Settings menu choose Set Camera Default.

3. Before making any adjustments to exposure, click the Shadows and Highlights buttons at the bottom of the screen. Areas of the image that are too bright (blowouts) appear as red. Areas that are too dark appear blue in the preview. In this case it is only a tiny reflection in the victim's ear and the puppy's paw, which are not critical. Had there been large areas of either red or blue, you could adjust the Exposure slider until the highlighted areas disappear (**Figure A.5**). See the sidebar "What's Too Dark or Too Light?" for more details.

NOTE

If there are no neutral colors in the image to select for Automatic White Balance, you can adjust the White Balance setting manually using either one of the White Balance presets or dragging the Temperature and Tint sliders.

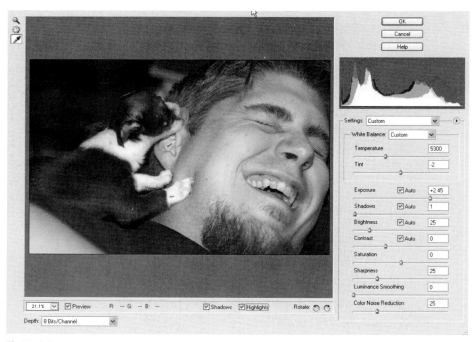

Figure A.4
Auto White Balance corrects color temperature.

Tiny areas of pure white (blowouts)

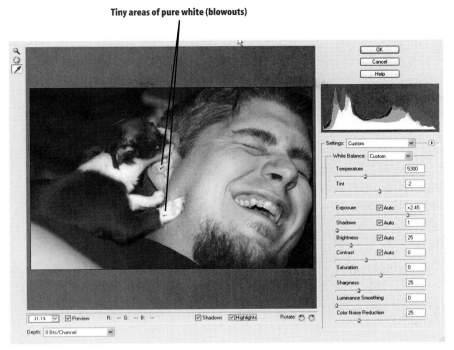

Figure A.5
Areas that have become pure white are indicated in the preview.

4. At this point you have made the most important corrections. If your photo seems a little flat, try adjusting the Shadows slider. There are many more controls that can be adjusted. If you will be working on the image using Elements, you shouldn't apply noise reduction or sharpening in the Camera RAW plug-in dialog.

Saving Your RAW Photos

Once you are satisfied with the color and tonal correction, you have several options when it comes to saving the images. Here are some basic facts about saving images from the Camera RAW plug-in:

- When the file is opened, the file extension and bits-per-channel information are displayed in the title bar (**Figure A.6**).

What's Too Dark or Too Light?

While it is great to use the Shadows and Highlights feature to visibly see areas in the photo that are either too white or too dark, you should be aware that it isn't necessary to adjust the exposure to prevent both of them. This is because the program can't tell the difference between part of the image that is blown out (gone to pure white) and contains detail that must be preserved and blowouts that are acceptable. For example, there are occasions when there will be small areas of pure white (like the reflection of a light in someone's glasses) or solid black (like dark areas of the dog's black fur) when the exposure is properly adjusted.

- You cannot save the files in the original RAW format you started with.

- Changes that you make when opening a RAW file aren't applied as permanent changes to the RAW file; instead, changes are maintained in a separate file and can be applied when the file is opened at a later time. This maintains the integrity of the original RAW file.

- You can save images as either 8-bit/channel or 16-bit/channel images. Saving as a 16-bit image creates much larger files with increased color information, but eventually you will need to convert them to 8-bit/channel to use the image in most applications. In most cases, you should save as 8-bit/channel images.

Accurate Vs. Desired Color

A question that often arises when you are correcting colors in an image is, should you make the colors accurate or make them look as you want them to look? As a rule, only ad agencies need to be concerned with accurate colors. I encourage you to make the colors look like you want them to appear. For example, in the exercise with the ear-licking dog, the goal isn't to make the colors as they were at the moment the flash fired, but to make them appear warmer so the photo has even more appeal to the viewer.

Figure A.6
The type and channel bit depth are displayed when the file is opened.

Speeding Up RAW File Processing

If it were necessary to individually correct and adjust each photo, most people wouldn't use the RAW format because it would be just too time-consuming. Many photos require similar corrections, so Adobe has provided several different ways to apply the same corrections to multiple images.

NOTE

To convert a 16-bit/channel image to an 8-bit/channel image in Elements Editor, choose Image, Mode, Convert to 8 bits/channel.

Opening Without a Dialog

If you want to apply the last conversion settings when opening an image without opening the Camera RAW plug-in dialog, here is how it's done:

1. Open the File Browser (File, Browse Folders). Locate the RAW file you want to open.

2. Holding down the Shift key, double-click on the thumbnail. The photo will open using the last conversion settings.

NOTE

It may take a little longer than usual for a RAW image to open because of the additional processing that must be applied.

Applying the Same Settings to Multiple RAW Images

When you have a series of photos that were taken under similar lighting conditions, you can make the correction to one image and then simultaneously apply the same correction to many more RAW images. Here's how it's done:

1. In the File Browser, select the RAW images you want to update.

2. From the File Browser menu bar, choose File, Apply Camera Raw Settings (Windows) or Automate (**Figure A.7**), Apply Camera Raw Settings (Mac).

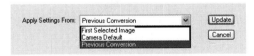

Figure A.7
The choices available are dependent on whether one or multiple files are selected.

3. Select one of the following choices from the Apply Settings From menu:

   - **Selected Image.** Applies the current settings within the camera RAW file.

   - **First Selected Image.** Available when more than one image is selected. It applies the current settings from the first selected image in the File Browser.

- **Camera Default**. Applies the default camera RAW settings using the settings from the camera that created the image.

- **Previous Conversion**. Applies the last conversion.

When you have selected one, click Update.

Working with RAW files takes a little extra effort. For myself, if I am shooting photos at a birthday party or a watermelon-seed-spitting contest (no kidding), using JPEG will work great. For the once-in-a-lifetime photos like weddings, vacations, and such (the watermelon-seed contest in Luling, Texas is an annual event), I always shoot RAW. If your camera supports the RAW format, you owe it to yourself to experiment with it. Don't expect stellar results the first time you work with it (and if you do get fantastic results, I don't want to know about it). After a while you will come to like it.

Adobe Digital Negative

Just as we were going to press with this book, Adobe announced a new way of handling RAW format files. It is called the Digital Negative specification and it describes a uniform way of storing the RAW data created by any digital camera. The specification offers something that is currently missing from the RAW format—a common standard. Similar to existing camera-specific RAW formats, a Digital Negative (DNG) is composed of two parts: the actual image data and the metadata that describes it. The format of the image data is very similar to the existing format used by digital cameras today. The key to the power of the Digital Negative format is in its metadata which contains all the information needed to convert the RAW file into a standard graphics format.

There are many ways in which you might see the Digital Negative manifest in your digital photography experience. In the future, digital cameras will begin to support the format directly, either as their default RAW format or as an optional choice. Alternatively, manufacturers may include conversion utilities to convert their proprietary RAW formats into a Digital Negative file. But both of those are future events—what can you do now?

Adobe has released the Adobe Digital Negative Converter, which converts the raw format from more than 60 different digital cameras, the same cameras supported by the current Adobe Camera Raw plug-in found in both Photoshop CS and Photoshop Elements 3 —into DNG files. This converter is available at no charge from the Adobe website. It allows you to take advantage of the archival benefits of Digital Negatives or to convert your camera-specific RAW files for use in a raw converter that supports Digital Negatives. Additionally, the current Adobe Camera Raw plug-in of Elements is already Digital Negative-compatible, By converting your camera-specific raw files to Digital Negatives, you can archive your RAW images without fear that at some later date your camera manufacturer's conversion software will no longer recognize its older RAW format (which has happened already). By archiving your RAW images to a DNG format you will always be able to open and use them a few years or a few decades from now.

Index

Peachpit
Essential books for the creative community

New Photoshop Elements 3 Books and DVDs From Peachpit

Learn Elements From the Experts

Enjoy the newest version of Elements with books and DVDs that teach the program the way you want to learn it: quickly, step-by-step, and with plenty of help from the experts.

Adobe Photoshop Elements 3: Classroom in a Book
By Adobe Creative Team
ISBN: 0-321-27080-0 • $35.00

Photoshop Elements 3 for Beginners DVD
By Scott Kelby
ISBN: 0-321-31629-0 • $39.99

The Photoshop Elements 3 for Digital Photographers DVD
By Scott Kelby
ISBN: 0-321-321340-0

Photoshop Elements 3 for Windows and Macintosh: Visual QuickStart Guide
By Craig Hoeschen
ISBN: 0-321-27078-9 • $19.99

Adobe Photoshop Elements 3 Idea Kit
By Lisa Matthews
ISBN: 0-321-27079-7 • $19.99

Adobe Photoshop Elements 3: Visual QuickProject Guide
By Katherine Ulrich
ISBN: 0-321-27081-9 • $12.99

Managing Your Photos in Photoshop Elements 3
By Michael Slater
ISBN: 0-321-24696-9 • $19.99

Photoshop Elements 3 Down and Dirty Tricks
By Scott Kelby
ISBN: 0-321-27835-6 • $39.99

Adobe Photoshop Elements One-Click Wow! Third Edition
By Jack Davis
ISBN: 0-321-30468-3 • $29.99

Peachpit Press   Adobe Press